ALBANY

A R C H I T E C T U R E

ALBANY
ARCHITECTURE

EDITED BY

DIANA S. WAITE

PHOTOGRAPHS BY

GARY GOLD AND MARK McCARTY

CONTRIBUTORS

MATTHEW BENDER IV

CORNELIA BROOKE GILDER

DUNCAN E. HAY

PAUL R. HUEY

MICHAEL F. LYNCH

JOHN I. MESICK

ANTHONY OPALKA

LORRAINE E. WEISS

MOUNT IDA PRESS

PUBLISHED IN ASSOCIATION WITH THE PRESERVATION LEAGUE OF NEW YORK STATE

ALBANY, NEW YORK

A GUIDE TO THE CITY

To Louise McAllister Merritt Mitchell,
who had the vision and determination to
open our eyes to the quality of Albany's
architecture and lead us to appreciate
and preserve it for the future.

Printed in the United States of America.
Second printing 1997

Mount Ida Press
152 Washington Avenue
Albany, New York 12210
Telephone 518-426-5935
Fax 518-426-4116

ISBN 0-9625368-1-4

Design: The Market Street Group
Printing: Thomson-Shore, Inc.
Cover illustration: New York State Dept. of
Economic Development

Contents

Foreword

John I Mesick

*A city is a place where a small boy, as he walks through it, can see
something that will tell him what he wants to do his whole life.*—Louis I. Kahn

More than half a century separates present-day Albany from my earliest
recollections of it. As a small boy approaching the city at night, crossing the former
Dunn Memorial Bridge, I recall my delight in glimpsing the flapping wings and
galloping hooves of the red neon Pegasus flying above downtown. Socony-Vacuum's
icon enlivened the city's skyline from atop 112 State Street. Later, during World War
II, we would never miss a chance when crossing the bridge to spot the submarine
anchored at the old Albany Yacht Club.

Rather more prosaic childhood memories rush in, of Albany sites no longer extant.
After a train ride on the Boston and Albany from Van Hoesen station a dozen miles
to the southeast in the countryside, we would arrive at Union Station with its cool,
reverberate interior ringed by iron galleries, then ride a trolley up State Street hill to
the optometrist on Lark Street. Afterwards, ice cream at Stittigs and perhaps a visit
to Great-aunt Ida. Her tall, dark Italianate brownstone at 226 State Street had a
lofty front parlor overlooking West Capitol Park through long French windows.
There were gilded pier mirrors, hanging gasoliers, and white marble fireplaces.
Downstairs in the low basement was the kitchen with its great cast-iron coal range
set between brick piers; we sometimes remained for supper, served in the basement
dining room at the front of the house.

The memory of shopping on North Pearl Street evokes the spacious, perfumed
main floors of Myer's and Whitney's department stores, where I was engaged by
the mystery of the pneumatic cashier's system. At Lodge's what happened to our
money was less mysterious, but much more fascinating, as the individual cash boxes
took flight to the cashier's perch up in the rear mezzanine. Then the guessing game
began: which of the returning boxes would fly to your clerk via the maze of moving
cables and spinning sheaves? At the Albany Savings Bank the white marble splendor
of the glass-domed interior was memorable, but to an eight-year-old a model tank
with moving tracks in a war-bond display, mounted in a showcase on the exterior,
left a more indelible impression. At the other end of North Pearl, in the Grand
Theater, I saw my first movie with my second-grade class—Disney's *Bambi*.

Later, at the age of ten or eleven, I recall a more instructive trip with my grandfather on a visit to the state Education Building. To this day I can recall the thrill of
entering through the great Corinthian colonnade, turning right, grandly ascending
the easy flight of stairs to the State Library rotunda, seeing splendid murals by Will

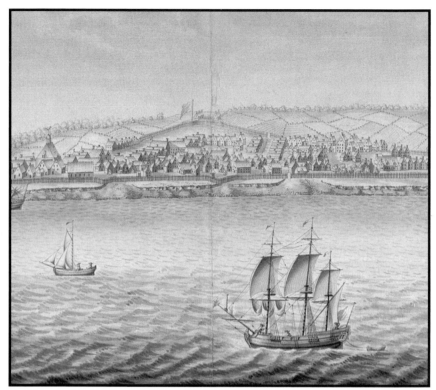

Fig. 1   Prospect of the City of Albany in
the Province of New York in America, 1763,
attributed to Thomas Davies.

Low and massive Doric columns (not yet encumbered by card catalog files),
proceeding through the glassy screen into the main reading room, the smell of
furniture polish mingling with the cork of the floors and the hushed voices of readers
approaching fearsome librarians as supplicants before deities in that high, vaulted
hall that remains for me as remarkable as any cathedral. Then we went on to the
Albany Institute; only two recollections remain with me from this visit: the mummies,
of course, (especially the unwrapped one) and, for some obscure reason, De Witt
Clinton's chair with a writing arm. Afterwards, my first fast-food experience when I
was treated to a hamburger at the White Tower located next door to the Institute.
Finally, on a visit to Mr. Lockrow's bookshop on Spring Street, I was offered my first
architectural book, Mariana Van Rensselaer's 1888 *Henry Hobson Richardson and
His Works* for three dollars and fifty cents. I turned it down—too Victorian—little
realizing that nearly forty years hence I'd have a hand in restoring Richardson's
principal rooms in the Capitol.

Perhaps it's not surprising for an architect summoning boyhood memories to find himself recalling buildings, objects, and spaces that undoubtedly played a large role in forming career ambitions. Yet, while the city remains, the scenes of nearly all these recollections have disappeared over the course of five decades. Most have been demolished. Some have been renovated beyond recognition. The mummies, of course, continue to spellbind school children at the Albany Institute. The splendid interiors of the old State Library barely survive intact. Now, with their fate in limbo, they evoke ancient Rome even more potently—not the Rome of Augustus or Hadrian, but Rome after the Vandals had ravaged the temples.

Why this concern with recollections at the opening of an architectural guide? First of all, buildings are significant carriers of cultural memory. Buildings survive the builder. They might be likened to seashells washed ashore—reminders of remoter lives and other times. A city over time takes on an almost geological aspect, with successive generations leaving behind a "layering" of buildings, parks and streets. In this accretion of forms and spaces may be "read" evidence of commercial activity, industrial development, governmental growth, social attitudes, and an evolving building technology. This guide has been prepared to enable both native and visitor to better "read" the city and its individual buildings and, thereby, render the experience of Albany more memorable. Certainly future generations will also consult these pages as architectural benchmarks of the city in the 1990s.

While this is the first architectural guide devoted to Albany, guides have been describing this place for more than 350 years. One need only spend a few hours perusing these volumes in the library to gain a good notion of architecture evolving here. At the outset the demands of commerce and defense did not allow architectural display. Dutch building was Old-World vernacular adapted to New-World conditions. Immediate need and familiar usage generated building form. Later, in an increasingly Anglicized world, Dutch ways were viewed as anomalies to be remarked upon. They had become the first "stratum" in the deep "layering" of Albany's architectural history. More than a century elapsed after initial settlement before writers commented on the uniqueness of Albany's buildings. After a visit in 1749, the Swedish clergyman-botanist Peter Kalm recorded one of the earliest surviving descriptions of Albany architecture:

The houses in this town are very neat, and partly built of stones covered with shingles of white pine. Some are slated with tile from Holland, because the clay of this neighborhood is not considered fit for tiles. Most of the houses are built in the old Frankish way, with the gable-end towards the street, except for a few, which were recently built in the modern style. A great number of houses are built [with]. . .the gable-end towards the street being of bricks and all the other walls of boards. The outside of the houses is never covered with lime or mortar, nor have I seen it practiced in any North American towns which I have visited; and the walls do not seem to be damaged by the weather. The eaves on the roofs reach almost to the middle of the street. This preserves the walls from being damaged by the rain, but it is extremely disagreeable in rainy weather for the people in the streets, there being hardly any means of avoiding the water from the eaves. The front doors are generally in the middle of the houses, and on both sides are porches with seats, on which during fair weather the people spend almost the whole day, especially on those porches which are in the shade. The people seem to move with the sun and the shade, always keeping in the latter. When the sun is too hot the people disappear.

By the close of the 18th century, travelers took a dim view of the Dutch architectural heritage. As always it was the latest construction which made the greatest impression. To Lt. John Enys, a British veteran of the Revolution passing through Albany in 1787 on a tour of the United States, "the old part looks dreadfully Ill as they only present the Gable end of the house to the street." Nine years later, Issac Weld, Jr., a European on a tour of the United States and Canada, commented on "old" and "new" Albany: "In the old part of town streets are very narrow, and the houses are frightful, they are all built in the old Dutch style, with the gable end towards the street. . .but in that part which has been lately erected, the streets are commodious and many of the houses are handsome."

At the close of the 18th century it was the English building style of the brothers Adam that drew favorable response. The city's first architect, Philip Hooker, would

Fig. 2 State Street, Albany, 1805, drawn by James Eights from memory in the 1840s.

soon enrich his town with numerous dwellings and public buildings in this style. Yet, near the close of his career in the mid-1830s, new classical Greek architecture in Albany drew the public's acclaim. During Hooker's lifetime, Albany was transformed from a provincial settlement to a splendid city as the capital of the nation's most prominent state. First, river traffic increased with the advent of steamboats; then commerce and industry mushroomed with the opening of the Champlain and Erie canals. These developments were soon followed by the confluence of several railroad lines at Albany. While the city's population had doubled in the last decade of the 18th century, during the course of the next century it would increase more than a dozen fold.

Fig. 3   City of Albany, Capital of the State of
New York, c. 1820, by Jacques-Gerard Milbert.

In the early 19th century, as tens of thousands of westward-bound settlers passed through Albany, the first guidebooks were published for the traveler's benefit. *The Tourist or Pocket Manual for Travellers on The Hudson River, The Western Canal and Stage Road, to Niagara* by Robert Vandewater, printed in 1831, declared Albany "the oldest settlement in the United States" and singled out the principal public buildings for brief description. In 1844 Wilson's *Albany City Guide: Being A General Description of the Public Buildings, Literary, Charitable and Benevolent Institutions, &c., with Numerous Useful Tables and Statistics, Relating to the City* illustrated the major buildings with woodcuts. These views made it readily apparent that Dutch Albany had been replaced by classical Albany. With the Capitol, the new State Hall, the City Hall, and the Albany Academy clustered about Capitol Park at the head of State Street forming a veritable "acropolis," Wilson observed that "almost every vestige of ancient Dutch architecture has disappeared and given way to the modern style of building."

A few years later, during the California gold rush, the printer-historian Joel Munsell published *The Albany Annual Register for 1849*. In the preface he signaled his passionate interest in Albany's past:

> At a time when the subject of gold is so peculiarly the engrossing theme of public and private speculation, it may be hazardous to introduce any thing which does not glitter, with the expectation of arresting attention. We have ventured, however, to the present the avails of some mining operations in a field but little noticed; but which, it is believed, with a reasonable amount of patient toil, may be made to yield abundantly of a similar material.

In the course of ensuing decades, Munsell produced two multi-volume works devoted to his "mining" of the city's history: *Annals of Albany* and *Collections on the History of Albany from Its Discovery to the Present Time*. His research led him to produce also a twenty-five-cent guide to an Albany then no longer extant. In *Men and Things in Albany Two Centuries Ago*, none of the buildings shown in the engravings survived even to his day. Hereafter, nearly every succeeding guide to the city prefaced

Fig. 4   View of State Street, Albany, New York, 1848, by John Wilson.

contemporary descriptions with reference to former times and lost buildings. The prevailing faith in progress became tempered, as the 19th century waned, by the recognition that the nation's oldest city possessed little physical evidence of its antiquity.

By the end of the century, articles on early Albany buildings were appearing in national magazines. A young Albany architect, Marcus Reynolds, published "The Colonial Buildings of Rensselaerswyck" in an 1895 issue of the *Architectural Record*. His article dealt in large part with the Van Rensselaer Manor House of 1765, which together with its extensive grounds had recently fallen prey to industrial expansion along the riverfront in the northern end of the city. When constructed, the house had been one of the most splendid dwellings in British America. In 1897 Cuyler Reynolds, brother of Marcus, wrote an article for the *Cosmopolitan* magazine entitled "Relics of Rensselaerswyck" in which he described the dismantling of the manor house.

Perhaps, this dispersion of Albany's greatest 18th-century building precipitated a change of attitude towards the continued depletion of architectural heritage. After lamenting the loss of old Albany for several generations, prominent citizens undertook numerous efforts to resurrect the early architecture of the city. Their endeavors affected the style of new buildings, as well as the preservation of old ones. Dutch and Flemish gables reappeared on the streets as new buildings were erected: State Street mansions, firehouses, the Pruyn Library at North Pearl Street and Clinton Avenue, several commercial buildings on State Street and Broadway, the Hudson River Day Line ticket office, and, most notably, the combined buildings of the Delaware and Hudson Railroad and the Albany Evening Journal of 1914-18, which transformed an entire section of the city. Georgian- and Federal-style features also made their appearance on new buildings of all types. Schuyler Mansion was acquired by the state in 1914, restored and opened as a museum in 1917. The State Bank of Albany incorporated Philip Hooker's facade of 1804 in the construction of its new sixteen-story building on State Street in 1927. The city purchased and restored Hooker's 1817 Albany Academy in the mid-1930s.

Unfortunately, during the middle decades of this century Albany experienced its architectural nadir. First came stagnation, occasioned by the Great Depression, World War II and the migration of families and business to the suburbs. These trends engendered municipal lethargy. Then an attendant indifference to the city's architectural heritage allowed further desolation to occur under federal urban renewal and interstate highway programs. Finally, ninety acres in the historic core were cleared to make way for the Empire State Plaza.

In the wake of this wholesale demolition, however, a strong public reaction set in. As the sentiment to preserve Albany's buildings became more widespread, the city government responded by establishing a Historic Sites Commission in 1964. Several streets were designated as historic districts. All exterior changes to buildings in these areas came under the review of the commission. These protected areas were extended over the intervening years to encompass many of the city's historic neighborhoods. In 1974 Historic Albany Foundation was established as a preservation organization to coalesce citizen concern for rescuing the city's historic structures and open spaces. For the first time in Albany's history, progress was no longer equated with demolition and new construction. An almost curatorial zeal, focused on the existing city, took root. Techniques in planning, financing and construction— once the concern of developers bent on rebuilding the city—became new challenges for preservationists as they sought to conserve older structures for continued usefulness and enhancement. Old rowhouses—not only grand townhouses on State Street, but modest frame dwellings on Jefferson Street—were infused with new life. The attrition of historic architecture was slowed. The present-day city became the beneficiary of these endeavors as old urban fabric was knit with new.

This guide has been prepared to increase your knowledge and enjoyment of Albany's architecture. Take it in hand, and like a small child with wonder and joy discover the city anew. Everywhere you will find evidence of marvelous things erected before your time. As you read this book and look about Albany, several realizations will take hold. In architecture, as in so much else, it's nearly a truism that we reject outright what our fathers have done, ignore the work of our grandfathers, and treasure only what remains from our great-grandfather's time or before. Our generation lays but brief claim to the city, and the builders amongst us are optimists leaving the fate of their handiwork to those who come after them. We hope succeeding generations will strive to preserve what they inherit and in their turn will build with vision and clarity of purpose sufficient to gain the gratitude of posterity.

Preface

The publication of a book on Albany architecture is long overdue. The quality of the city's public and private buildings has deserved a thoroughly researched, well written and photographed book. *Albany Architecture: A Guide to the City* is published to provide an accurate and interesting guide for both the scholar and the casual reader.

The genesis of this book was the founding, in 1974, of Historic Albany Foundation, a city-wide preservation organization dedicated to saving the city's buildings and educating the public about their value and architectural importance. The time was right for capturing the public's attention and support, for Albany had an abundance of historic buildings intact and was ready to appreciate their value. The person responsible for articulating the opportunity before the city in 1974 was a young professional preservationist, Louise McAllister Merritt. She recognized the city's long-ignored building resources and saw their potential if they were properly restored. The vehicle for achieving her vision, and later that of many others, was Historic Albany Foundation.

During the next decade, Albany responded. From Mayor Erastus Corning II to the banking community, the neighborhood associations around the Empire State Plaza (led by the Center Square Association), the city's Community Development office and the public—all supported and many participated in Historic Albany programs. Their success can be seen in the tours in this book that deal with Albany east of Washington Park, and a resulting preservation ripple effect has helped newer neighborhood associations in the western sections of the city appreciate their 20th-century buildings.

The work of producing *Albany Architecture* began early in 1988, when members of Historic Albany's Education committee—Matthew Bender IV, George F. Carpinello, Dennis McFadden and John Polnak—met with the Foundation's staff (director Ned Pratt, Sandra Gally, Lorraine E. Weiss and Douglas Sinclair) and two guests, Donald Cornell, then co-owner of the Boulevard Bookstore, and Diana S. Waite of Mount Ida Press. The group discussed the need for a guidebook that was broad in scope and suggested that it be published in 1994, to coincide with the twentieth anniversary of the founding of Historic Albany.

More advisors were soon brought in to share their expertise—Norman S. Rice, director emeritus of the Albany Institute of History and Art; Christine M. Miles, the director of the Institute; Martin Sullivan, then director of the State Museum; and

Historic Albany trustees Carolyn Anderson, Josephine Auchincloss and Kristine Herrick. This group, working with the Foundation's director, Lynn Dunning-Vaughn, selected Gary Gold and Mark McCarty as the photographers and Diana Waite as the project coordinator. Douglas Sinclair agreed to draft the text for the downtown tour. A grant from the Architecture, Planning and Design Program of the New York State Council on the Arts made it possible to begin work on this initial chapter.

In the early phase of the book, William M. E. Clarkson of Buffalo provided advice and encouragement, and a bevy of Albany enthusiasts made financial contributions: Gordon and Lucy Ambach, Jeffrey P. Bender, Dennis and Mary Buchan, Charles and Charlotte Buchanan, John and Sally Carter, Gail Catlin, Henry and Agathe Crouter, Thomas and Nancy Dolin, Steven and Lucia Fischer, John and Sandra Gillespie, John and Jane Hanna, Charles and Nancy Liddle, William and Beverly McCarthy, Robert and Dorothy Meyer, Ian Porter, Ten Eyck and Barbara Powell, Thomas and Anne Older, James and Ann Sidford, Jack and Alice Sallada, William and Stevi Swire, David and Candace Weir and Michael and Margery Whiteman.

With the initial chapter underway and the Preservation League of New York State assuming stewardship for the project, we brought on board seven writers who agreed during the summer of 1992 to research and write the remaining sections of the book—Cornelia Brooke Gilder, Duncan E. Hay, Paul R. Huey, Michael F. Lynch, John I Mesick, Anthony Opalka and Lorraine E. Weiss. The Albany Institute of History and Art offered to exhibit photographs from the book during the popular Festival of Trees in November, 1993, thereby accelerating the publication date.

Over the past year the writers and publishers called upon numerous individuals and the staffs of many institutions for assistance with research and personal recollections. Through his vast and intimate knowledge of Albany and his unflagging enthusiasm for the project, Norman Rice contributed immeasurably and untiringly. Frederick D. Cawley, vice president of the Preservation League, deserves special mention for his design and editorial advice. The chapter on early Albany could not have been written without the pioneering work of Roderic H. Blackburn on colonial Albany architecture; Stefan Bielinski of the Colonial Albany Social History Project at the New York State Museum and Charles T. Gehring and Janny Venema of the New Netherland Project at the New York State Library also made important contributions. The plaques placed on buildings by Historic Albany and the texts of the Foundation's early walking tours were welcome touchstones in the writers' progress through the city.

Among the institutions and their staffs to whom we owe special gratitude are Christine Miles, Tammis Kane Groft, Wesley G. Balla and Marcia Moss at the Albany Institute of History and Art and the staff of the McKinney Library at the Institute; Albany County Clerk's Office; Tracy Grimm, Ginny Farinacci, Garry Bourdeau and

Helen Chmielewski at the Albany County Hall of Records; Albany County Surrogate's Office; Warren Amiel, Albany Fire Department; Albany Public Library and the Pruyn Room; Richard Nicholson, Albany City Planning Office; Robert Dillon, Albany Department of Public Works; Elizabeth Spencer-Ralph, Albany Urban Cultural Park; Minna Zinnershine, Blackman and De Stefano Real Estate; Wanda Styka, Chesterwood; Leonard Sippel, College of Saint Rose; Jane De Somma, First Church of Christian Science; Ethel Weaver, Madison Avenue Presbyterian Church; James Corsaro and Billie Aul, Manuscripts and Special Collections division of the New York State Library; Peter Dunning, New York State Office of General Services; Saint Andrew's Episcopal Church; Saint Teresa of Avila Church; Saint Vincent de Paul Church; Schuyler Mansion State Historic Site; and the library, archives and public relations staffs at SUNY Albany. Tony Opalka provided research for tour 8.

Special thanks are also due to John Auwaerter, William and Mary Barnet, Brooks R. Barvoets, Evelyn Battin, Phoebe Powell Bender, Elizabeth Blatner, Samuel Bloom, Barbara S. Brenner, Prentiss Carnell III, Elizabeth Chandler, James Cohen, Elaine Conway, Cathy and Joseph Culver, Carroll Devitt, Mary Arthur Doolittle, G. Steven Draper, Steven Einhorn, William G. Foulks, John A. Gallery, Glenn Gibbs, Louisa and Mellie Gilder, Grace Green, James Gwynn, John J. Kelliher, Florence Harris, Bruce Hungershafer, Jay Jakovic, Meyer A. Jeneroff, E. J. Johnson, Violet Keleshian, Andrea Lazarski, Nancy Liddle, Grace Vander Veer McDonough, Benjamin Mendel, Louise Merritt Mitchell, John I Mesick, Lewis Muhlfelder, Susan Mumford, John Myers, Lee Kaplan Myers, Richard Nagengast, Paul Nobes, Anne Older, Marion Pitts, Elinor Posner, Warren and Anne Roberts, Christine Robinson, Caroline Peltz Schultze, Peter Shaver, Betty Sonneborn, Delores Souzzo, Ida Spier, Mary Ellen Stewart, Peter G. Ten Eyck, Mary Raddant Tomlan, Timothy Truscott, Janet Walker, Lawrence Wilson, Charles Wing, Joseph Woollett, David Youmans and Samuel Youmans. We are grateful to Patricia Hughes, Carol Marino and J. David Waite for typing the manuscript.

The following institutions and individuals granted permission to reproduce illustrations from their collections. Collection of the Albany Institute of History and Art, pages 8, 11, 12, 32 bottom, 36 top, 55. Collection of the Albany Institute of History and Art, Bequest of Ledyard Cogswell, Jr., 36 bottom. Albany Institute of History and Art, McKinney Library, 52. Albany Institute of History and Art, McKinney Library Photograph Collection, 10, 29. Stefan Bielinski, 30 top, 35, 37. Roderic Blackburn, 32 top. Kenneth Hay, 83. Paul R. Huey, 25, 41. Peter G. Ten Eyck, 46. New York State Office of Parks, Recreation and Historic Preservation: Crailo State Historic Site, 30 bottom; Bureau of Historic Sites, Archeology Unit, 25; Bureau of Historic Sites, Restoration Unit, 38, 40, 49; Bureau of Historic Sites, Research Unit, 48. Frank Lloyd Wright Foundation, © 1987 FLW Fdn., 171 top. The quotation on page 7 appeared in the *Architectural Forum*, Vol. 137 (July-August, 1972), 46. The quotations by Huybertie Pruyn were published in *An Albany Girlhood* (Albany: Washington Park Press, 1990). The glossary is excerpted from *What Style Is It?* © 1983, National Trust for Historic Preservation in the United States.

We extend special thanks to Douglas Bucher, Frederick Cawley, Patricia Gioia, Norman Rice, John G. Waite and Richard Wheeler, who graciously read the manuscript, inspected buildings and offered many corrections and suggestions.

Matthew Bender IV
Diana S. Waite

Highlights of
Albany Architecture

Matthew Bender IV

If Albany can be your host for only a few hours or a day, you might like to sample some of the major public buildings and get the flavor of a few of the distinctive neighborhoods in the heart of the city.

Begin at the New York State Capitol, which dominates the brow of State Street hill. It is one of the last state capitols to be constructed in the midst of an urban setting. Inside, guides will let you in on the marriage of politics and architecture that produced this monumental granite chateau. Begin at tour 1, entry 2, page 68. Tours are given daily. Allow sixty to ninety minutes.

Step out from the Capitol on the State Street side, and walk west one-half block to Swan Street. You will be on the fringes of the Center Square and Hudson-Park neighborhoods, twenty-two blocks of residential buildings dating mostly from the mid- to late 19th century, Albany's most prosperous years. Here you will find elegant homes designed for the city's most prominent citizens by its most famous architects and builders, including Albert Fuller, Marcus T. Reynolds, James Eaton and Marcus Ryder. Begin at tour 4, entry 1, page 126, and end on Swan Street at the entrance to the Empire State Plaza. Allow sixty minutes.

Refreshments and lunch are available at restaurants on Lark Street, cafeterias on the concourse level of the Empire State Plaza and, from May to October, from street vendors at West Capitol Park.

To continue in the afternoon, select from the following walking tours on Capitol Hill or drive through some 20th-century neighborhoods. Two of the three tours will comfortably fill the time.

Walking tour 1. Walk south along the Empire State Plaza, a futuristic complex of office buildings, cultural centers and art-filled public spaces. (In inclement weather, use the concourse under the Plaza, accessible through the Legislative Office Building on the corner of State and Swan streets.) If the day is clear, stop at the Corning Tower, and take the elevator to the observation deck on the forty-second floor to enjoy a panoramic view of Albany, the Hudson River, the foothills of the Berkshires, the Green Mountains and the northern Catskills. Continue walking south to the Cultural Education Center, home of the New York State Museum, which features life-size permanent exhibits focused on the diverse characters and activities of the state's regions, as well as travelling shows. Allow sixty to ninety minutes.

Walking tour 2. Walk to the east front of the Capitol and the equestrian statue of the great Civil-War hero Gen. Philip H. Sheridan (see tour 1, entry 1, page 68).

Continue along tour 1 (omitting the Empire State Plaza). Conclude with a visit to the Albany Institute of History and Art, whose galleries are filled with paintings and decorative arts from the Upper Hudson region. Allow ninety minutes to two hours.

Driving tour. Tour 7 will lead you through early streetcar neighborhoods and 20th-century residential developments. Start at the corner of Madison Avenue (U. S. Route 20) and South Lake Avenue. Head south on South Lake, and begin at entry 9, page 208, the Italianate houses at 103 and 106 South Lake. Continue the tour along South Lake and Providence streets (entries 10 to 32). Then return to the corner of South Lake and Providence, and drive north on South Lake to the corner of Madison Avenue (begin with entry 38). Many prominent industrialists and business leaders built homes in this area at the turn of the century. End this part of the tour with entry 72.

Next, explore the Pine Hills neighborhood beginning with entry 88, a Queen Anne-style house at 527 Western Avenue, and continue through entry 154, the Lustron houses. Conclude with a visit to the campus of the State University (entry 155). Allow sixty minutes.

If all or part of a second day is available for touring, take a look at old Albany by stopping at Cherry Hill, built in 1787 for Philip van Rensselaer (page 56). Also visit the Schuyler Mansion, built between 1761 and 1764 for Philip J. Schuyler and his wife Catherine van Rensselaer (page 48). You may also wish to stop in at the Urban Cultural Park Visitor Center (page 248).

Early Albany:
Buildings before 1790

Paul R. Huey

An Italian scholar visiting Albany in 1785 recorded that "most of the houses are built of brick after the Dutch taste. . .with a very high peak to the roof, which slopes down sharply on both sides of the house." These, he said, "give Albany the aspect of one of those ancient cities or villages that we see represented in. . .paintings." Other descriptions of Albany published between 1785 and 1790 reported that the old Dutch houses were "both inconvenient and clumsy" and that the city lacked "beauty or elegance." Albany was already an old city by 1790; officially established by the Dutch West India Company in 1652, it had begun as a cluster of buildings north of Fort Orange, built in 1624.

Unfortunately, very few buildings constructed in Albany before 1790 remain standing. Only six houses or parts of houses from before 1790 are known to remain above ground within the present boundaries of the city, and none of these dates from the 17th century. A very visible and historically significant artifact in Albany, however, is the 17th- and 18th-century street plan of the colonial city, which still survives largely intact.

Aside from the few structures still standing, the most specific and reliable information about the buildings that were built in Albany before 1790 comes from old photographs and drawings or sketches made of some of them before they were demolished. It is on the basis of these surviving contemporary pictorial records, supplemented with a wide variety of other documentary sources and archeological data, that the following architectural history is presented. The area that is covered consists of the present city of Albany, which, of course, includes buildings that once were considerably outside the original limits of the town.

Of the buildings from before 1790 for which old photographs or contemporary drawings have survived, it is remarkable how few were lost by fire. Most were deliberately torn down. Two major losses occurred in 1798 and in 1806 with demolition of part of the Schuyler house on State Street and of the Reformed Church. Between 1833 and 1841, at least five historic structures were lost, and from 1864 to 1872 at least four more. The worst period may have been from 1882 to 1893, coinciding with the city's bicentennial in 1886, when six important buildings were lost. During World War II at least two more colonial houses were demolished. Much more research on these as well as on still-standing structures, of course, is required, and one hopes that other rare survivals remain hidden in the city, yet to be discovered.

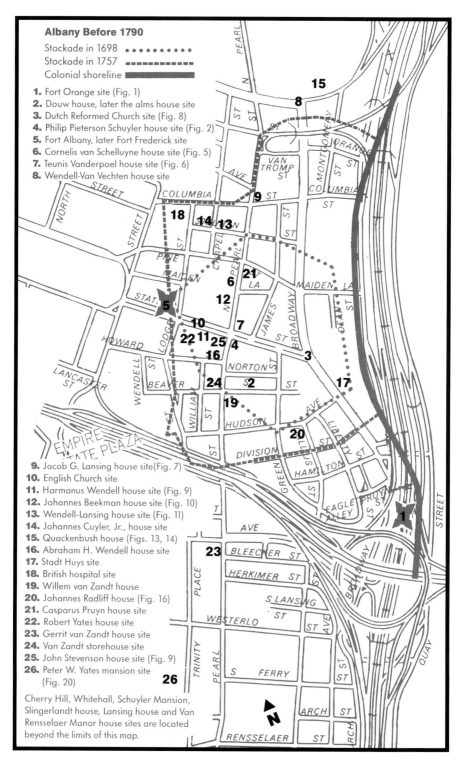

Albany Before 1790

Stockade in 1698 ●●●●●●●●●●
Stockade in 1757 ▬ ▬ ▬ ▬ ▬ ▬ ▬
Colonial shoreline ▬▬▬▬▬▬

1. Fort Orange site (Fig. 1)
2. Douw house, later the alms house site
3. Dutch Reformed Church site (Fig. 8)
4. Philip Pieterson Schuyler house site (Fig. 2)
5. Fort Albany, later Fort Frederick site
6. Cornelis van Schelluyne house site (Fig. 5)
7. Teunis Vanderpoel house site (Fig. 6)
8. Wendell-Van Vechten house site

9. Jacob G. Lansing house site (Fig. 7)
10. English Church site
11. Harmanus Wendell house site (Fig. 9)
12. Johannes Beekman house site (Fig. 10)
13. Wendell-Lansing house site (Fig. 11)
14. Johannes Cuyler, Jr., house site
15. Quackenbush house (Figs. 13, 14)
16. Abraham H. Wendell house site
17. Stadt Huys site
18. British hospital site
19. Willem van Zandt house
20. Johannes Radliff house (Fig. 16)
21. Casparus Pruyn house site
22. Robert Yates house site
23. Gerrit van Zandt house site
24. Van Zandt storehouse site
25. John Stevenson house site (Fig. 9)
26. Peter W. Yates mansion site (Fig. 20)

Cherry Hill, Whitehall, Schuyler Mansion, Slingerlandt house, Lansing house and Van Rensselaer Manor house sites are located beyond the limits of this map.

Early Dutch Settlement before 1652

In September, 1609, under contract with the Dutch East India Company, Henry Hudson sailed in the ship *Half Moon* from the Netherlands across the North Atlantic to the continent of North America. Arriving at the mouth of a great tidal river flowing from the north into the ocean at what is now New York City, Hudson sailed up the river and explored it northward, carefully recording the valley and thereby claiming it for the Dutch. The explorer found Indians eager to trade furs to the Dutch at the place where he finally anchored the *Half Moon*, nearly 150 miles above the river's mouth and just south of the future city of Albany. The river was later named the Hudson River.

As word spread in the Netherlands about Hudson's voyage, an intense rivalry soon developed among eager Dutch merchants who followed him. Early trade between the Dutch and the Mohawk Iroquois Indians was focused on the Normans Kill and on the low, flat alluvial island located at its mouth. Later known as Castle Island, it has been filled and covered with deep deposits of soil dredged from the Hudson in the 20th century and is occupied today by the Port of Albany. The first known non-Indian resident of the area was an intrepid, Dutch-speaking African-Hispanic trader named Juan Rodrigues. He arrived at Castle Island with other traders on a Dutch ship in 1613 and decided to remain there by himself during the winter of 1613-14 to trade with the Indians.

Early in 1614 returning traders began constructing a fort on Castle Island, possibly not far from present-day Island Creek Park. Known as Fort Nassau, it was a square redoubt armed with cannons and smaller guns, with walls fifty-eight feet in length surrounded by a moat eighteen feet wide; inside the fort was a building measuring thirty-six by twenty-six feet in plan. Despite continuous occupation, Fort Nassau was frequently flooded by the river and was soon in disrepair.

In 1624 the West India Company sent a number of families to New Netherland to establish a settlement two-thirds of a mile north of Castle Island on the west bank of the Hudson. Mostly French-speaking Walloons from the southern Netherlands, they planted grain, built dwellings, and erected a new fort called Fort Orange. The settlers were evacuated permanently to Manhattan in 1626 because of continuing trouble with the Indians.

The first Walloon dwellings were described as "hutts of bark," and evidently Fort Orange was also initially made of temporary, but strong, wooden construction. It had four bastions and, apparently, a moat around three sides. On the fourth side, facing the river to the east, was the entrance. The fort was perhaps 140 feet square excluding the bastions. It was located across Broadway, southeast of the present-day Econo Lodge motel and under Interstate 787, not far east of an 1886 tablet that has been remounted on the concrete retaining wall on the east side of Broadway.

This tablet has been moved twice since 1886 and is today closer to the probable site of the west curtain wall of the fort than its original location on the site of the northeast bastion.

In 1629 the West India Company gave permission to Kiliaen van Rensselaer, as a patroon, to develop an agricultural colony in the area, provided he did not interfere in any way with the company's trade monopoly or fortifications. His Colony of Rensselaerswyck occupied an area along the Hudson corresponding with much of present-day Rensselaer and Albany counties. One of the first tracts that Van Rensselaer acquired from the Indians included Castle Island, where, by 1631, he established a large farm with "a convenient dwelling, the sides and gable built up with brick, long and wide as required; in addition two hay barracks, each of five poles fifty feet high; also a barn and sheepcote and other necessaries." There was a saw mill on the nearby Normans Kill, and another one was built a few years later on the Fifth Kill, a stream near present Tivoli Street.

During the 1630s eight small structures for soldiers were built within Fort Orange, along with a large and elegant West India Company building, which was described as having a flat roof, balustrade, and "lattice work." In 1639, the company opened the fur trade conditionally to private traders; to protect his trade advantages, Van Rensselaer built a trading house as close to Fort Orange as possible, on the edge of the north moat. Floods, including a major one in 1640, forced the evacuation of the fort and probably damaged it, and in 1643 Fort Orange was described as "a wretched little fort. . .built of logs, with 4 or 5 pieces of Breteuil cannon, and as many swivel guns."

When archeologists excavated part of the site of Fort Orange in 1970 and 1971, remains of several structures from this initial period of occupation were uncovered, including several sections of brick foundation walls from a structure that must have stood just inside the fort near the east entrance. The east-west wall was constructed of alternating rows of dry-laid red brick of stretchers and headers that rested directly on the soft alluvial ground surface; this wall was at right angles to another wall built of larger, softer, and crumbly dry-laid red bricks, which also rested on the ground but were lined on each side with large cobblestones. (A similar use of cobblestones was uncovered in the foundations of a church built in 1617 in Jamestown, Virginia.)

By 1644 resident traders had taken over so much of the trade at Fort Orange that the company's "house of commerce," probably the elegant building with "lattice work," had closed. In 1647, Jean Labatie, a carpenter formerly employed by Van Rensselaer and now also a trader, was given permission to build a brewery inside the fort against the east curtain wall and south of the entrance. About forty-six feet long and twenty-two feet wide, the brewery evidently survived a flood in 1648 that almost entirely washed away the old wooden fort. The new director general of New

Netherland, Peter Stuyvesant, decided to rebuild the fort with stone and also encouraged the traders to build private houses inside the fort at their own expense. Archeological evidence suggests that quarried stone was used to build a stone ravelin protecting the south wall of the fort and that the curtain walls were built with horizontally stacked timbers above a moat faced with large, round cobblestones.

Private houses were to be built of brick to a height of twelve feet, and the rear walls were to form part of the fort's curtain wall. Archeological excavations revealed parts of three houses inside the fort that were evidently among those constructed beginning in 1648. They were erected above shallow cellars that had plank walls and flooring and were clearly not meant to be permanent structures. One, built by Trijntje Jochems, the wife of Abraham Staats, was about forty-four feet long and twenty feet wide. Another is believed to have been built by Hendrick Andriessen van Doesburgh; it was falling into ruins by 1660 and collapsed about 1664. The cellar was about four feet deep, and the structure was about twenty-one feet wide from the curtain wall of the fort to its opposite wall. Its length was probably no more than twenty-five feet. A small six-foot-wide section extended about four feet beyond the cellar wall and formed a small closet or cellar entry built of single plank walls near the corner with the curtain wall. The main ridge of the roof of the structure must have been parallel with the curtain wall of the fort; below the plank cellar floor were floor beams laid at intervals of about four feet and at right angles to the curtain wall. The plank floorboards probably were between twelve and twenty-one inches in width, but their remains were very fragmentary. Distances

Fig. 1 Fragment of wooden wall and floor boards of the Van Doesburgh cellar in Fort Orange. The small fireplace probably dates from 1664.

between the vertical posts framing the wood cellar wall below the gable end of the structure varied from four feet, three inches to five feet, three inches. Except for the plank wall of the extension, the wood cellar wall consisted of at least three alternating horizontal and vertical layers of wooden planks probably nailed together (Fig. 1).

Above its wooden cellar the Van Doesburgh house probably was constructed of red brick and was no more than a story and a half. There is evidence that the chimney was built of harder-fired, small yellow clinker bricks imported from the Netherlands as ship's ballast. The roof was covered with curved, red earthen pan tiles of the type also imported from the Netherlands. There was a plain, single wrought-iron beam anchor that most likely was located in the chimney of the end gable wall. Pieces of crown window glass, window lead and iron saddle bars provide evidence of leaded casement windows with fancy roundels having enamelled inscriptions and other decoration. Window painters and glaziers are known to have visited Fort Orange and Rensselaerswyck, and the trimmed scraps of crown window glass found in the excavations indicate that the glazing of windows was common in the fort.

The interior of the house was plastered, and blue-decorated delft tiles were evidently set around the fireplace or along the base of each wall. Red earthen tiles, some with clear lead glaze and others with green glaze, probably formed the hearth of the fireplace or perhaps an entire floor in a checkered pattern. The cellar of the house was filled with malodorous garbage even while the house was occupied, and its perishable construction indicates that it was clearly intended to be temporary. Yet, above ground, the house was constructed and furnished in an expensive, refined manner that corresponds with elegant Dutch houses depicted in numerous paintings of the period.

Meanwhile, conflict between the Colony of Rensselaerswyck and the interests of the West India Company had grown steadily. Van Rensselaer had claimed the ground on which Fort Orange was built as part of his colony and insisted on his right to build houses around the fort. When the new director of the colony, Brant van Slichtenhorst, arrived in March, 1648, there were three houses standing near the fort. By August, the patroon's trading house had become a church, and eight houses stood north of the fort in an area known as the *fuyck*, or hoopnet, named after the settlement's layout. Stuyvesant ordered all construction within a distance of a cannon shot to cease. The controversy increased as Van Slichtenhorst continued to erect a new building north of the fort, possibly near present Columbia Street, since he claimed that it was about half a mile from the fort. Soldiers pulled down some of the houses in the *fuyck*, but Van Slichtenhorst persisted. He laid out and leased six village lots; on one of them Rut Jacobsen planned to build a new house near the Rutten Kill, which flowed along present Norton Street and crossed Broadway between State Street and Hudson Avenue.

Farther up the Rutten Kill, other houses may have been standing as early as 1647. Archeological excavations between Norton and Beaver streets east of South Pearl Street exposed the cellar floor of a house owned by Volkert Jansen Douw, on which he seems to have paid rent as early as 1647. Fourteen-inch-wide floorboards were supported by beams that were spaced three to four feet apart and rested on thick, gray, undisturbed clay subsoil. The north-south orientation of the beams indicates that the gable facade of the house probably faced east. When the building was enlarged in 1686, the orientation was changed so that it faced north on Norton Street, and stone cellar walls were evidently added at that time.

In 1651 a bridge ''with railings and benches to sit on'' was ordered to be built to carry the present Broadway across the Rutten Kill. Another bridge was built at the north end of the settlement across the Vossen (Fox) Kill, which roughly followed the present Sheridan Avenue and the south side of Van Tromp Street. Plans were made in 1650 to build a school, and a lot was designated for an almshouse.

Although the highly profitable fur trade attracted settlers, Stuyvesant's claim to the area around the fort, including the settlement, deterred growth. For instance, Harmen Bastiaensen Visscher, a carpenter, was reluctant to build a house early in 1652 "at the place assigned to him" even though he had secured the lumber. The major buildings still had no more than thatched roofs.

Buildings in Dutch Beverwyck and English Albany, 1652-86

On April 8, 1652, Stuyvesant formally proclaimed that the West India Company would henceforth control the *fuyck* settlement, which was to be named Beverwyck and to be independent from Rensselaerswyck. The settlement at that time contained about one hundred houses. Today's State Street extended westward up the hill from a point about 1,500 feet north of Fort Orange and must have served as a market place and focus of activity. In 1652 and 1653 Stuyvesant granted lots along State Street, along present Broadway and along the Rutten Kill from Broadway to present South Pearl Street. The open space immediately around Fort Orange, south of Beverwyck, was reserved for gardens.

Nevertheless, the fort remained the administrative center for Beverwyck, and evidently in 1652 a wooden building about twenty-seven feet long and two stories high containing a guard house and court room was erected inside by Harmen Bastiaensen Visscher, the Beverwyck carpenter. The cellar was about nineteen feet wide and extended under the full length of the structure. The first floor was divided into two rooms, and the floor above was supported by eight beams resting on corbels. Upstairs was a single room used by the court.

During the Dutch war with England in 1652-54, attention turned to the defense of Beverwyck. A fortified redoubt was built on the Fifth Kill (Patroon's Creek) north of town, and by 1655 a guardhouse had been built on the hill near the head of State Street. Early in 1656, the inhabitants decided to build a second blockhouse at the foot of the hill, in the intersection of State Street and Broadway. The shortage of funds soon became apparent, however, and the inhabitants asked Stuyvesant to raise the money for this project in New Amsterdam (now New York City) by soliciting donations for the construction of a new "church." Built in 1656, the blockhouse, indeed, became known as the Dutch Reformed "blockhouse church." From it have survived an original brass or copper weathercock and several windows painted with coats of arms each dated 1656. The bricks and the roof pan tiles are believed to have been produced near the Vossen Kill. Other new buildings in Beverwyck included an almshouse built between 1652 and 1655 to which were added a ''poor farm'' in 1657 and a bleach field used to bleach cloth by 1658.

As locally produced lumber, brick, pan tiles, and other building materials became available, the quality of construction in Fort Orange and Beverwyck improved. A house built in 1658 was described as having a ''kitchen, cellar and a small chamber built up with brick; . . .the garret floor and the main floor laid; the gable of matched boards; a stairway to the garret and a stairway to the cellar; a bedstead in the chamber.'' A new brick courthouse was built in Fort Orange in 1657-58. It had two adjoining six-foot-deep cellars, each about twenty-one feet square, built of quarried stone and separated by a brick partition wall. On the first floor was a twenty-one-foot-square room, a five-foot-wide hallway, and a room sixteen by twenty-one feet in plan. Upstairs were two twenty-one-foot-square rooms. There were built-in wainscoted bedsteads, a winding stairway, an oval window upstairs, and a fully open attic space. At each gable end was a double chimney built of imported yellow clinker bricks and braced by forty-two anchors. The roof was covered with pan tiles, and it was probably the finest building in Fort Orange or Beverwyck. It is also the first known to have had a stone cellar. In 1659, Jeremias van Rensselaer had the cellar under his house rebuilt with stone, and he built a second cellar of brick ''toward the rear for a vegetable cellar.''

In 1659 the inhabitants of Beverwyck decided to build a defensive wall around the town ''against attacks by Indians in these dangerous times.'' It was built of posts and horizontal planks to a height of eight boards and had seven bastions; it was 3,100 feet long and surrounded most of the village. An additional length of wall was to be built along the river bank. The wall followed present Hudson Avenue westward to about Green Street before cutting diagonally northwest to State Street just above present South Pearl Street. From State it continued northeast, intersecting North Pearl Street between Steuben Street and Maiden Lane. Then it angled to Steuben, which it followed eastward to the river. Gates opened into each of the major streets. To pay for the wall, a tax of three guilders on every chimney was levied.

Intended as an effective defense against Indians, the wall was of no use in preventing the English from taking New Netherland, including Fort Orange and Beverwyck, during peacetime in September, 1664. Beverwyck was renamed Albany, and Fort Orange became Fort Albany. At the same time, a prosperous Beverwyck trader, Philip Pietersen Schuyler, purchased a prominent fifty-four-foot-wide lot on the south side of State Street at South Pearl Street and east of it. About 1659, Schuyler evidently had built a house on the east part of this lot. In 1667, when his title to the lot was confirmed, he apparently built a second house on the west part and replaced or remodeled the house on the east half to match. Across the front of both houses, facing State Street, he placed the bold iron figures ''ANNO 1667.'' The iron figures

*Fig. 2   Philip Pietersen Schuyler house,
originally dated 1667 on the facade.*

undoubtedly formed the ends of iron beam anchors used to fasten the brick wall of the house to its wooden framing members.

Margarita Schuyler, his granddaughter, moved into the west house about 1763. Anne MacVicar, the eight-year-old daughter of a British officer, later wrote that the "house was the most spacious and best finished I had ever entered. The family pictures, and scripture paintings, were to me particularly awful and impressive." In 1777, the east house was purchased by Henry Staats, at which time it was already held by Richard Cartwright, a tavern keeper and merchant who had been transported to North America as a convict in 1743. During the Revolution, Cartwright and Staats refused to cooperate with the Commissioners for Conspiracies. Angry mobs twice surrounded the house, destroyed and plundered Cartwright's possessions and abused him physically. After Margarita Schuyler died in 1782, the west house became the City Tavern, and in 1798 it was demolished in order to widen South Pearl Street.

The east house was photographed frequently (Fig. 2) before it was demolished in 1887 (it is the oldest Albany house of which a photograph has survived). Bricks, delft tiles and other souvenirs were saved. Old photographs show that the house had a very steeply pitched roof, with the ridge parallel with State Street. This configuration represents a startling departure from the traditional Dutch urban houses in Beverwyck, which had been built with the gable-ended front facade facing the street. This house may have been Schuyler's bold statement of his willingness to adapt to English ways. A house of this size, proportion, and orientation would have been entirely appropriate in many 17th-century English urban settings, but there was also a precedent for such houses in the southern Netherlands. Moreover, the Dutch tiles with pastoral and landscape scenes were of a type rarely used before 1660 and would have been a new and highly fashionable feature in 1667, not only in Dutch but also in English houses. The Schuyler houses, boldly emblazoned with their probable construction date (also the date of the proclamation of peace between England and the Netherlands) were a harbinger of the future wealth and power of the Schuylers and of other families allied with them by marriage.

Fig. 3 *Jeremias van Rensselaer house, built in 1667-68, from a drawing made about 1839 by Francis Pruyn.*

In the spring of 1666, a flood destroyed the farm of Jeremias van Rensselaer, the director of the colony of Rensselaerswyck, but he soon built a new house near the Fifth Kill, also called Patroon's Creek. It was near the grist mill and his new brewery, and it was, he wrote, "only straight and plain, of two rooms, but the cellar built of stone and further with a stone foundation." Construction continued through June, 1668, and in October, 1669, he sued two masons because the gable was settling badly (the masons were ordered to make the necessary repairs). Guests who visited Van Rensselaer's grandson there in June, 1744, "were handsomely entertained with good viands and wine. After dinner he showed us his garden and parks." This building served as the manor house for Rensselaerswyck until a large, new house was completed in 1765. The old house was recorded in a drawing made by Francis Pruyn just before it was torn

Fig. 4 *Leaded casement window from the Jeremias van Rensselaer house, now in the collection of Crailo State Historic Site.*

down in 1839 (Fig. 3). Pruyn also rescued a leaded casement window from the house (Fig. 4).

Pruyn's drawing shows a one-story brick house with iron fleur-de-lis beam anchors. The entrance was in the long side rather than in the gable end; the rooms were evidently arranged side-by-side. Farmhouses of this sort were a relatively new phenomenon in the southern Netherlands in the 17th century. Previously, stables, threshing floors and storage spaces had been attached to these side-entrance long houses under one long roof. Farmhouses built earlier in Rensselaerswyck were combined with a barn, though it seems unlikely that this Van Rensselaer house ever had an attached barn. Like the new Schuyler house in Albany, Van Rensselaer's new house, built in a modern style typical of the southern Netherlands but perhaps also consistent with English architecture, reflected his status.

By 1674, the town stockade had been moved farther west, where it intersected State Street just west of present Chapel Street. A guard house was built there, and a sentry was posted in it. Every householder was required to build a stone sidewalk eight feet wide in front of his or her house. In 1676 the court ordered that no new streets were to be laid out and no new houses were to be built until vacant lots on existing streets were occupied. Corner houses were to be built first. All new houses were to be two rooms deep and at least eighteen feet wide, with brick fronts and pan tile roofs. Meanwhile, old Fort Orange, renamed Fort Albany but still located south of the town, was abandoned, and a new Fort Albany was built on the hill at the head of present State Street just above present Lodge Street. It was a stockade with four bastions, two of which were apparently connected with the town wall, which was soon rebuilt with stockade posts twelve feet long. In 1678, water from a spring on the hill above was directed into the fort through conduits made of pine logs and oak posts, and in 1679 this water system was extended from the fort down the hill to the foot of State Street. A visitor in May, 1680, recorded that "the inhabitants have brought a spring or fountain of water, under the fort, and under ground into the town, where they now have in several places always fountains of clear, fresh, cool water."

Records have survived from two important urban houses built in this period. The first of these was erected about 1680 on a large lot north of Maiden Lane on the west side of North Pearl Street that had been granted in 1667 to Harmen Bastiaensen Visscher, the carpenter from Hoorn. Probably in 1680 or 1681 Cornelis van Schelluyne, a shoemaker and already or soon to be Visscher's son-in-law, occupied a new house on Visscher's lot. He was adding to the house in 1717, when he requested from the city a small piece of ground so "that he may build his house regular."

An old photograph of the Van Schelluyne house (Fig. 5) shows that it had a brick facade facing North Pearl Street, as required by the regulations of 1676, and side

Fig. 5   Cornelis van Schelluyne house, built c. 1680.

Fig. 6   Teunis Vanderpoel house, built in 1682.

walls covered with wood clapboards. A distinctive feature was its simple step gable, which was typically Dutch but was a type of gable used in Amsterdam mostly between 1600 and 1665. By 1680 in Amsterdam other gable types such as the spout gable, the neck gable, and the bell gable had replaced the old-fashioned step gable. The Van Schelluyne house had iron fleur-de-lis beam anchors that held the brick facade wall to a wooden frame. The photograph reveals traces of a large garret doorway that had been bricked in, and the trim around the doorway and the stoop appear to date from the early 19th century.

The Teunis Vanderpoel house, also with a step gable, was constructed at the northeast corner of present State and North Pearl streets in 1682 (Fig. 6). When Jacques Milbert, a French traveller and artist, visited Albany in 1819, he noted this house especially: "Noteworthy is the palace of the former Dutch governors, whose odd, characteristic architecture aroused my curiosity to such an extent I decided to draw it" (Fig. 6). It became known as the Lydius house, as Balthazar Lydius, "a very eccentric old gentleman," lived there until his death in 1815. The building was demolished in 1833, and later views based on Milbert's drawing showed it with the erroneous date 1657 across the front in iron numerals. The original drawing shows only a small tablet on front with "ANNO" and an indistinct date.

Buildings from the Initial Wars with France, 1686-1713

On July 22, 1686, having successfully persuaded the Van Rensselaers to give up their claim to the city, Gov. Thomas Dongan awarded the city of Albany its charter, with land extending due northwestward between parallel boundary lines for a distance of sixteen miles. The south boundary began at the north end of Castle Island, and the north boundary was near present Orange Street. Governor Dongan sought to fortify Albany against French encroachment on the Indian trade. In 1687 he reported that Fort Albany was constructed of fifteen-foot or larger pine logs and was armed with nine guns. He recommended rebuilding it with stone. Meanwhile, other improvements had occurred within the city. Present Norton Street was laid out in 1680 along the Rutten Kill south of present State Street. The Reformed Church purchased the old Volkert Jansen Douw house on the south side of Norton Street and rebuilt it as a new almshouse in 1686.

In 1689, the Albany stockade was repaired and rebuilt with new posts, and the fort was repaired and altered. The French attack on Schenectady in February, 1690, terrified Albany. Several houses just outside the Albany stockade were pulled down, and all fences and trees within three hundred feet of the stockade were removed. In 1692 the Reformed Church began construction of an expensive new parsonage for the Rev. Dellius on the east side of Broadway between Maiden Lane and Steuben Street.

In 1694 the northwest bastion of Fort Albany was rebuilt of stone in a semicircular plan, with a ''well arched'' magazine beneath it. A drawing made in 1695 by the Rev. John Miller shows that the other three bastions and the curtain walls were still a wooden stockade, while inside were separate quarters for the commander, officers and soldiers. The quartering of soldiers with inhabitants in the city created tension and trouble, and the Common Council soon requested that additional barracks be constructed and that blockhouses be modified to accommodate soldiers. In 1698, Col. Wolfgang Römer drew plans for a larger stone fort to replace Fort Albany at the same site and carefully recorded the existing fort with its fine ''Governor's House'' of two stories, parapet gables and end chimneys. Construction of the new fort was underway by 1703.

Römer's detailed map of the city, also made in 1698, shows that the south stockade wall followed Hudson Avenue southwest to Green Street, where it angled northwest to a blockhouse. From there it continued northward to the southeast bastion of Fort Albany. From the northeast bastion, the north stockade wall ran in a straight line eastward to present Steuben Street, which it followed most of the way to where it turned and went south parallel with the river. It followed Dean Street, and a section of that street still exists behind the 1930s post office. The city hall, which had replaced the courthouse in old Fort Orange, was located on lower Broadway, and the Lutheran church stood on South Pearl Street. Well outside the stockaded area, perhaps near the present Albany County Courthouse, stood the ''Indian Houses,'' built on the hill as early as 1660 to facilitate trade with the Indians. Early in 1699, at least four more Indian houses, each forty-five feet in length, were built on the hills to the northwest.

An old house that stood until the 20th century probably dated from this period. It was located at what was later 674 Broadway, between Orange and Quackenbush streets, now the present exit ramp from I-787, and may have been built by Harmanus Wendell, a shoemaker, as early as 1699 when he married Anna Glen. Perhaps not wishing to live so near the tanyards along the Vossen Kill, Harmanus built a new house with a step-gable facade in 1716 on State Street above South Pearl Street on former Glen property. Reuben van Vechten seems to have occupied the 674 Broadway house, and Wendell's son, Harmanus H., married Van Vechten's daughter. Harmanus H. Wendell then joined with Lucas van Vechten, his brother-in-law, in a profitable sloop and trading business. In 1824 Harmanus H. Wendell's heirs sold the house, and it was later occupied by the Albany Wood and Coal Company. The house was demolished in 1941. Photographs show that it had a brick gable facing the street and side walls with wide, overlapping plank siding. The brick front was held to the timber frame with fleur-de-lis beam anchors.

When the war with France resumed in 1701, Albany was daily in fear of French attack. A new blockhouse was built near the river to lodge soldiers. Nevertheless, Albany continued to develop, particularly north of State Street. In 1704 a market house was built in the middle of State Street. A stone "well" to supply water from the city's water system was later constructed a few yards downhill. Pearl Street inhabitants meanwhile requested permission to build a new system to carry water from the hills to the Pearl Street gate, near present Steuben Street.

The house bearing the date 1710 in iron numbers attached to the beam anchors that stood at the northeast corner of North Pearl and Columbia streets is traditionally associated with Jacob G. Lansing (Fig. 7). However, it appears that when two brothers, Jan and Cornelis Maessen Bloemendahl, acquired this lot in 1712, they had already made "improvements," which could have included the brick house. Records show that Jan Maessen Bloemendahl made bricks near this area, perhaps to build the house. In 1718 he married Rebecca Fonda and in 1722 was made the sealer of weights and measures for the city. He and his brother Cornelis were braziers, and they may have occupied the house as a residence and shop as late as 1761. In 1736 the city sold land south of the Vossen Kill to Jacob G. Lansing, but Jan Maessen Bloemendahl evidently continued to own and occupy the corner lot, which was opposite where the old blockhouse stood at the Pearl Street gate of the stockade. In 1736, the second ward inhabitants were permitted to build a market house in the street at this location. Jacob G. Lansing, born in 1681, had married Helena Glen about 1710. He was a baker, and early in 1711 he purchased a lot nearby on Broadway, where he built a house. The origin of his traditional association with the

Fig. 7 Jacob G. Lansing house, dated in the
gable 1710.

house at North Pearl and Columbia streets is unclear. He was also a silversmith, and
perhaps he used the building, with its braziers' facilities, as his shop. It is not clear
how Jacob G. Lansing acquired the property, but in 1824 his great-grandson conveyed the property to Ebenezer Pemberton, whose family operated a grocery store
in the building until it was demolished in 1893 for an addition to the Albany Business
College.

The parapet gable facade on Columbia Street had fleur-de-lis iron beam anchors
that held the brick wall to a timber frame. The brick, laid in Dutch cross bond, formed
a zigzag pattern called *vlechtwerk* (wicker work) along the upper edges of the
gable. The brick finial atop the gable was very similar to that on the Van Schelluyne
house. Both houses, as well as the Van Rensselaer house and probably the Vanderpoel house, had wrought-iron cranes in the gable for hoisting goods into the upper

floors. It is said that the Lansing house was constructed so that the floors of each room were separated by two or three steps up or down. The exposed ceiling beams were smooth and polished, and delft tiles with Biblical scenes surrounded the fireplaces.

Albany Architecture during the Peaceful Interlude, 1713-44

The Lansing house was evidently built outside the protective north wall of the city and therefore must have been in a somewhat more dangerous location because of the war with France. In 1713, however, the Treaty of Utrecht ushered in a period of peace which lasted thirty-one years. The population of Albany in 1714 was 1,136, of which ten percent were slaves. The new period of peace was an important one in

Fig. 8 "A View of the late Protestant Dutch Church in the City of Albany," drawn by Phillip Hooker and published in 1806.

Fig. 9 John Stevenson house, built c. 1770. To the right is the Harmanus Wendell house, dated on the gable 1716.

the development of Albany; new public buildings, as well as residences and commercial structures, were constructed.

The Dutch Reformed Congregation had become too large for the old blockhouse church, and in 1714 the city granted a license to rebuild the church. The new foundations were laid around the old building, and new stone walls were built up enclosing it. Services were continued as construction proceeded in 1715 and were interrupted for only three Sundays to allow for the removal of the old structure and completion of the new interior.

The old oak pulpit was installed in the new building, and the ceiling and the front of the meeting space were painted sky-blue. It is said the ground floor pews were reserved for women, while men sat in two elevated galleries along the sides. An engraving published in 1806 (Fig. 8) shows that the church had a pyramidal roof with a cupola on which was the brass weathercock that reportedly came from the old blockhouse church. A brick entry hall was built against the south wall, covering part of one of the tall, rounded windows; the entry hall facade also had a

*Fig. 10   Johannes Beekman house, built in 1725
and later known as the Vanderheyden Palace,
as drawn by James Eights in the 19th century.*

parapet gable and iron wall anchors. With the construction of a new church (the building that still stands on North Pearl Street south of Clinton Square) beginning in 1797, the 1715 church was no longer required. It was sold to the city and torn down in 1806. The pulpit and weathercock were taken to the new church on North Pearl Street, where they may still be seen. Several painted and dated windows, a piece of the bell inscribed "Anno 1601" and other objects were also saved.

Meanwhile, the congregation of the English church petitioned the city for a grant of land in the middle of State Street, above Pearl Street and close to the fort, on which to build a new church. The city aldermen strongly opposed this project, but, with the support of Governor Hunter, construction was begun in 1714. Infuriated, the city ordered the work stopped, but the foundation was laid nevertheless. The city arrested two masons for trespass, and delays ensued. Finally, the church was opened for services in 1716. It was a stone building forty-two by fifty-eight feet in plan. In 1751 a bell tower was added to the west end. It continued to serve as the English church (the predecessor of St. Peter's Episcopal Church) until a new building was constructed in 1803.

In contrast, Harmanus Wendell was completing a traditional Dutch house not far away, on the south side of State Street. A shoemaker and probable builder of the house at 674 Broadway, Wendell inherited this lot from his father-in-law, Jacob Sanders Glen. He constructed this new house in the old-fashioned Dutch step-gable style. On the facade were the iron figures 1716 and letters HW. The building was demolished in 1841, but it was recorded in a watercolor by James Eights about 1850 (Fig. 9).

Use of the step gable continued with the construction of a prominent dwelling in 1725 on the west side of North Pearl Street, just south of Maiden Lane. Later known as the Vanderheyden Palace, it was built by Johannes Jansen Beekman, whose father, a blacksmith, had purchased two lots there with a total width of about fifty-seven feet in 1685. Drawings indicate that the house was one and a half stories and had a brick front and wood side walls (Fig. 10). The roof ridge was parallel with North Pearl Street, but the street facade had two prominent step gables flanking the entrance. The brick facade walls had iron fleur-de-lis beam anchors and iron gable cranes mounted on brick finials. Beekman's two daughters continued to live in the house after his death in 1756. In 1778 Jacob Vanderheyden, a merchant, purchased the property. Washington Irving described the Vanderheyden residence as "in the Dutch style, with large iron figures on the gables, that gave the date of its erection." The interior was furnished "with good old mahogany," he wrote, and the parlor was decorated with many Indian relics. The house was demolished in 1833, but Irving secured one of the weather vanes (a running horse), which he then installed on his own house, Sunnyside.

New development continued to extend outside the stockaded limits of the town. In some places the stockade was moved to accommodate construction. An area around Gallows Hill, northwest of present Hudson Avenue and South Pearl Street, became an enclave of weavers after 1720. In 1729, Evert Wendell, a son of Harmanus, decided to build a dam and a mill with an overshot water wheel on the Beaver Kill in present Lincoln Park. Adjoining the mill was the miller's (or a baker's) residence, in which there was a bake oven in the end wall. Closer to town but south of the stockade eleven house lots were sold in 1730 in the space north of present Hudson Avenue between South Pearl Street and Green Street.

Fig. 11   Wendell-Lansing house, built c. 1718.

North of the town, buildings constructed just north of the stockade included two structures on Chapel Street north of Steuben Street. It is possible that Isaac Wendell built the house that stood at the northeast corner about 1718. Although the house was in poor condition by 1886, a proposal was made "that the building be removed to some other location and then 'restored.'" Fortunately, it was recorded in photographs (Fig. 11) and a sketch. The ridge of the roof was parallel with Steuben Street, and the front wall, built of brick, faced south toward Steuben Street. The gable end was of wood construction and had a garret door. The entrance was flanked by single windows. The extraordinary height of the substantial stone foundation wall and the position of the doorway six feet above grade suggest that the hillside had been graded away, leaving the building much higher than when it was built. The use of a side entrance suggests Flemish if not English influence. In July, 1886, a writer lamented in the *Argus* that "it seems strange that the bi-centennial year should witness the destruction of one of the oldest houses in the city, and yet such is the case. . . ." It was sold to the Young Men's Christian Association and demolished for construction of the organization's new building, which is still standing.

Directly across Chapel Street another old house survived to the 19th century. It stood on the corner lot sold by the city in 1730 to Johannes Cuyler, Jr., but he may have had a house on the lot since 1720. The Cuyler house was acquired by Harmanus Ten Eyck, who in 1776 married Margaret Bleecker. She was a daughter of Hendrick Bleecker, Jr., and Catalyntje Cuyler. In 1802 Ten Eyck sold the lot to the Albany Mechanics Society, which, in turn, sold the property in 1826. The Cuyler house was sometimes confused with the Wendell-Lansing house across Chapel Street, and it was also called the Glen house. An old engraving shows that the Cuyler house, likewise, rested on a very high stone foundation wall. The walls were a full two stories. The parapet gable faced south toward Steuben Street. Both the south and east walls, at least, were of brick, and the building appears to have had casement windows.

Because of growing competition over the Indian trade, there were rumors of a French attack on Albany. Plans were made in 1730 to build a new stone fort; new blockhouses were put up, and other measures taken to improve security. The city decided to purchase a fire engine. Later the blockhouses were fortified with "great Guns," and in 1734 construction began on a new wall around the city, which was expected to be "a work of some years and great expence." There was also a need to construct docks and fortify the waterfront, which was "very irregular and inconvenient for building," while the construction of a new jail and courthouse was expected soon to be "absolutely necessary." By 1735, some of the new wall was being built of stone, as was the new British fort, located where the old fort had stood at the head of State Street.

In 1736 or 1737 the Lutheran church built a house in Albany as a source of rental income, for which specifications survive. It was to be "20 feet long and 22 feet wide, with a shingled roof and a stone [brick?] front, or stones up to the point-beam; inside with stones and the outside with boards on all sides. Also a door at the front and the back, both cut in half, with steps, locks and bolts, also a cellar made of rocks from front to back, with a trap-door on the side of the road. Also two gutters, two stairs, one in the cellar, the other in two parts in the attic. Also in the east wall a cross-bar window with four panes of glass, in the attic one window with one pane, and in the south wall a cross-bar window with one pane. Also a mantel-piece with a border and an iron for the hearth, also with an arched roof of stones over the hearth.'' The

Fig. 12   Slingerlandt house, built c. 1732.

windows in this description may be early sash windows.

A house located at 922 Broadway (Fig. 12) may have been built about 1732 when Robert Dunbar married Cornelia Spoor. Dunbar may have conveyed the house to his half sister, Catherine, who in turn probably conveyed the house about 1764 to her recently-married step-daughter and son-in-law, Christina and Albert Slingerlandt. By 1767, he was listed as a resident of the West Manor of Rensselaerswyck, a large area that surrounded Albany but also included the land on which this house stood. Slingerlandt bequeathed his property to his son Teunis, a cabinetmaker, who sold the house and its lot of 31 by 248 feet in 1806. It was torn down about 1943.

With its brick and wood gable front facing the street, the Slingerlandt house was a typical Dutch urban house, even though it stood well outside of Albany. A story and a half with a steeply pitched roof, the facade consisted of brick for the first floor below an overhanging gable wall. The shingled gable originally had a garret door and a smaller window. The side and rear walls were covered with clapboards. The room arrangement shown in the 1937 HABS drawings may be original. The front door opened into a small, narrow hall, or *voorhuis*, that contained the staircase. The front living room was entered through the side of the hall. Directly behind the hall and separate from it was a small bedroom less than eight feet on each side; together they occupied the south side of the original, main section of this house. In the living room was a fireplace built against the original rear wall, which, like the front wall, was evidently of brick. From the living room a door adjacent to the fireplace opened into a slightly later rear wing addition, which contained a dining room, another very small bedroom and a large kitchen with fireplace at the back. The older, front part of the house was wider than it was deep. However, the plan of a *voorhuis* with a staircase and entrance door, a living room with small bedroom or bed box, and a rear kitchen addition with a bed box beside the door was being used on a larger scale in Amsterdam by 1670 for weavers' houses. The Albany house bears a remarkable similarity to the small wooden 18th-century houses, often with the front facade of the first floor built of brick, that are typical of a small area of North Holland immediately north of Amsterdam.

More substantial houses were built closer to Albany but still outside its protective walls. One of these is the Quackenbush house (Figs. 13, 14), still standing near the Clinton Avenue exit of I-787. Pieter Quackenbush, also known as Pieter Bout, was working as a brickmaker in Beverwyck by 1657. The brick and tile yards of Bout and other brickmakers were located north of the Vossen Kill and the tan yards and tan pits and apparently close to where this house stands. Quackenbush sold his pan tile kiln in 1687, but in 1683 his son, Wouter, had purchased land north of the Vossen Kill. It is probable that Pieter's great-grandson, Peter, born in 1706, built a new house on the property about 1736, soon after the death of his father. The new north city wall was not far to the south, and in 1735 the city paid damages to Peter Quackenbush for "loss he sustained by reason of the stones for building the city Wall were laid on his ground."

Fig. 13 Quackenbush house, built c. 1736 and extended c. 1782

Fig. 14 Quackenbush house, as it appeared in 1993.

Peter Quackenbush bequeathed the house to his son Henry, who added the rear extension soon after 1782. Henry's daughter, Anna Lansing, and her children continued to live in the house until about 1813, and her son Jacob, a distinguished judge, resided there through the mid-19th century. The structure housed a tavern in

41

1969 when it was scheduled for demolition for construction of I-787. The structure was saved, however, through the joint efforts of the New York State Historic Trust, the State Transportation Department, and the Office of State History. While the downstairs had been heavily remodeled as a tavern, a number of late 18th- or early 19th-century features survived, including a fireplace and mantel; floors and other woodwork upstairs appeared to be original. The Quackenbush house is a full two stories. The brick walls are laid in Dutch cross bond, and the less steep pitch of the roof may have been a new architectural development. With its gable fronting the street, the building nevertheless is characteristically Dutch.

Another old house, the Abraham H. Wendell house, which bore the date 1738, was apparently related in time and design to the Quackenbush house. It stood at 7 Howard Street, a short distance west of South Pearl Street. Built of brick laid in Flemish bond, the gable facade, which faced south, had shallow-arched windows. It was built directly behind the Harmanus Wendell house of 1716. Abraham H. Wendell, a son of Harmanus, probably built this house shortly before his marriage in 1740 to Elizabeth Wendell, a distant cousin. In his will dated 1793, Abraham left both houses to his children and a grandson. By 1802 his two younger sons had mortgaged the property to two printers, Charles R. and George Webster. In 1804 the property was conveyed to William James, who then conveyed it to John Barber and another printer, Solomon Southwick. Located south of the old Harmanus Wendell house, the Abraham H. Wendell house on Howard Street became Southwick's printing office, where the *Albany Register* was published. It appears that in 1809 the ancestor of the New York State Museum was opened in the building by Henry Trowbridge. For years afterward the building was known as "Henry's Old Museum." It was demolished for construction of the National Savings Bank, which still stands on the site.

Once the new stone fort on the hill was completed, the city turned its attention to repairing existing public buildings and constructing new ones. In 1740 the Common Council ordered repairs to two market houses standing in State Street and construction of a new building for the fire engine. In 1742 funds were allocated to shingle every market house.

Work on a new courthouse and jail started in 1740 and was probably completed by April, 1743, when iron hardware for the stocks was purchased. It was built on the east side of Broadway at a location in the present plaza, nearly opposite Hudson Avenue; an old marble stone still identifies the site. In 1744 Dr. Alexander Hamilton of Annapolis, Maryland, described the new building: "The great hall where the court sits is about 40 foot long and thirty broad. This is a clumsy, heavy building both without and within." However, Peter Kalm, the Swedish naturalist who visited Albany in 1749, described it as "a fine building of stone, three stories high. It has a small tower or steeple, with a bell, and a gilt ball and vane at the top of it.''

In 1754 this building was the meeting place of the first American colonial congress, called to unite the colonies with the Iroquois against the French. Delegates from each colony came to Albany to meet with the Indians, but they also focused their attention on whether a colonial union for mutual defense was desirable. In this building Benjamin Franklin, a delegate from Pennsylvania, presented his historic Albany Plan for a voluntary union of the colonies under a federal government, which the congress adopted but England and the colonial legislatures rejected. During and after the Revolution, the state Legislature met in the building, and from 1797 until 1807 it served as the state Capitol. In 1809 the building was auctioned and leased for a period of twenty-one years. The old bell was removed to the new Capitol built in 1806-09, but when the city's inhabitants complained that it was not rung regularly, the bell in the new Reformed Church was rung at the customary times instead. A dry goods store opened in the building in 1826, and in 1836 it was destroyed by fire.

The form of this three-story stone building with its twin chimneys at one end, its lower-pitched roof, pedimented gables and doorway, cupola, and sash windows embodied elements of the colonial early Georgian style. Architecturally, it was related to such buildings as the Old Colony House built between 1739 and 1741 at Newport, Rhode Island, and to earlier buildings such as Independence Hall at Philadelphia (1731) and the College of William and Mary at Williamsburg (1695). Though perhaps not as elegant as these earlier public buildings, the Albany courthouse was important both for its historical associations and as a local expression of early English, Georgian-style architecture.

Albany Architecture during the Final French Wars, 1744-60

With the dreaded renewal of war between France and England in 1744, the Albany traders desperately tried to keep the French Indians, as well as the New York Iroquois, neutral in the conflict. The next year French Indians attacked settlements in New England and at Saratoga, while Albany's attempts to persuade the New York Iroquois to join the British against the French consistently failed. In April, 1746, the Albany Indian commissioners angrily resigned when they learned that William Johnson, a Mohawk Valley trader and land manager, at the governor's request had successfully negotiated an alliance with the New York Iroquois and had taken over Indian affairs.

A rapid succession of French and Indian attacks on farms around Albany followed during the spring and summer. Farmers and cattle were killed, buildings burned, and many prisoners taken to Canada. The people of Albany had never before experienced such fear and terror. Farms everywhere were abandoned. Crops were left unharvested, and farm families crowded into Albany for protection. The city was "in great misery and distress," and a constant vigil against attack was maintained. The town seemed besieged, for no one could venture safely outside the walls. By this time the north stockade wall was located north of Columbia Street, and Albany's three market houses were converted into lodgings by the addition of fireplaces and chimneys for British troops arriving from New York.

The agony continued through 1747 and into mid-1748, when the war officially ended. A number of structures built on the south side of the city after 1750 have survived in photographs or are still standing. One of these was the ferry house located near the west landing of the ferry to Greenbush (now Rensselaer). In 1751, Bernardus Bradt and his first partner, Johannes Ten Broeck, were authorized to operate the city ferry and to charge the established fees. It seems likely that Bradt built the ferry house when he began to run the ferry in 1751, since he operated it continuously from 1752 until 1780, except for an interruption in 1756 and 1757. In 1780 the city decided that the location of the ferry was inconvenient and ordered the construction of a new residence nearby for the ferryman and the accommodation of travellers, to be located "adjoining or near the dwelling house of Bernardus Bradt." Construction of the new ferry house may have been delayed, for records from 1786 indicate that it was to be forty by fifty feet, of two stories each of seven feet, with four rooms on each floor and four chimneys at the gable ends, and built with brick-filled wooden walls. The 1794 De Witt map shows that it was at the northeast corner of Ferry and Church streets, in the newly developing south end of the city.

When Church Street was later extended south of Ferry Street, it cut off the entire west end of the Bradt house. A photograph shows that the new west wall of the truncated house faced Church Street and was covered with narrow boards, while the north side of the house was still covered with much older, wider clapboards. A photograph of the original east gable facade of the house, identified by Roderic Blackburn, shows that the brick was laid in Dutch cross bond, and the upstairs windows had swinging casements of wood. There was an ornate brick gable finial, and the parapet was finished with *vlechtwerk*. In 1886 the garret was described thus: "The rafters are of hewn yellow pine, about four inches square, and nearly five feet apart. The roof boards are also of yellow pine. . .They are from eight to fourteen inches wide. . .Originally the roof was covered by tiles; now modern shingles replace them." It appears that the building was demolished between 1900 and 1910.

Anticipating the inevitable renewal of conflict with the French, the city of Albany requested funding from the colony to complete the replacement of the city's stockade wall with a permanent stone wall, a project that had been started but not carried on. War resumed in August, 1754, with the French and Indian destruction of the settlement at Hoosick, New York. From 1755 through 1758 large British and

Provincial armies gathered at Albany as campaigns were waged against the French at Fort Niagara and Crown Point, and the presence of these armies permanently altered the character of Albany.

Construction of a new barracks for five hundred men began late in 1755 along the west side of Chapel Street, and blockhouses along the stockade wall also were converted into barracks. A British survey of the number of private dwellings in Albany the next year determined that 1,400 soldiers could probably be quartered with the inhabitants "without incommoding them." In an emergency, it was thought, the town could quarter two thousand troops in private homes. British engineers proposed elaborately improved town defenses, additional barracks, and other facilities. Thomas Sowers, an engineer, in his drawing of the stone fort, then called Fort Frederick, showed a single, long, two-story barracks inside the fort along one curtain wall and an equally long two-story "Governors House" along the opposite side of the fort.

Meanwhile, the city stockade wall had been enlarged to enclose a larger area. From Broadway, the south stockade followed Division Street to Green Street, where it turned north for a block to the line of the old stockade at Hudson Avenue. The stockade from here ran westward up Hudson Avenue and across South Pearl Street to a point near the south side of the present Knickerbocker Arena. There the wall turned north, following Lodge Street to Fort Frederick. North of the fort, the wall paralleled Lodge Street, turned eastward on Columbia Street, then ran north along North Pearl, crossed the Vossen Kill and turned eastward to the river along Orange Street and the present entrance ramp to I-787.

During 1756 and 1757 the British further enlarged the size of the city by expanding and rebuilding some of the walls. A new south wall along Division Street to South Pearl Street added a new block between Hudson and Division streets from Green to South Pearl streets. North of the fort, the wall was moved farther west from the line of Lodge Street. Within the additional space created north of Fort Frederick, a new hospital was built to accommodate four hundred sick. The main building had a cupola and balcony. Attached were four wings; the northwest wing included a kitchen, and an apothecary's shop was in the northeast wing. Nearby, along the west side of Chapel Street north of Maiden Lane, a new H-shaped barracks was also built to hold 740 soldiers. Other important new buildings included stables in the vicinity of present South Pearl Street between Beaver Street and Hudson Avenue and magazines in Maiden Lane and State Street near the Dutch church.

By November, 1757, plans had been made to quarter British troops at a number of different locations outside the protective walls of Albany. A large barracks traditionally believed to date from 1757 stood south of Albany near Whitehall Road west of Delaware Avenue. Known later as Whitehall, it was less than two miles west of

Fig. 15 Whitehall, originally a British
barracks, built c. 1757.

the Hudson and about a mile north of the Normans Kill. It was two stories high and had a gallery running its full length. Two wings on the ends, said to be later additions, gave the structure an H-shaped plan (Fig. 15).

The origins of this building are difficult to document. In December, 1760, Albany residents complained to Gen. Jeffrey Amherst about the quartering of British officers in their homes when available barracks could contain many more soldiers. Because Canada had fallen to the British, most troops could now be quartered in distant places. In February, 1761, Amherst was notified that no unnecessary labor was to be spent on "the Hudson river barracks," perhaps including the Whitehall building.

A map of Renssselaerswyck drawn in 1767 shows that Whitehall was then owned or occupied by John Bradstreet. At this time Bradstreet had leased Castle Island, located to the east on the Hudson River, from Stephen van Rensselaer, where as early as 1765 Bradstreet had been in command of the king's stables. Castle Island was also, however, a valuable farm, and about 1769 Bradstreet evidently allowed a number of immigrants under John Tunnicliff, from Derbyshire, England, to occupy the farm he had leased, including Whitehall. The old barracks would have been an especially useful structure for his laborers or other followers. Tunnicliff brought sheep from Derbyshire with him and was also able to produce excellent crops from especially unproductive land within five years.

When Bradstreet died in 1774, he left this farm to John Bradstreet Schuyler, the nine-year-old son of his closest friend, Philip J. Schuyler. In 1789, John Bradstreet Schuyler sold the Whitehall farm to Leonard Gansevoort. It contained 1,090 acres of land. In 1795 Gansevoort's daughter, Magdalena, married Jacob Ten Eyck, and they established the Whitehall mansion as their residence. He died there in 1862, and the mansion burned in 1883.

When part of the stockade was moved southward in 1756 and 1757, the space that became available prompted new development. A portion of a building constructed at this time is incorporated within a later building still standing at 36 South Pearl Street. This corner lot may have been conveyed to the Rev. Thomas Barclay as early as 1718. More likely, it was occupied by Willem van Zandt soon after he purchased from the city a lot along the south side of the Rutten Kill in June, 1757. His grandson Willem was living here in 1827 when the building was damaged by a fire that also destroyed the contents of a drugstore probably located on the first floor. The Van Zandt family were carpenters and woodworkers, and they must have profited from the construction underway in 1756-57, including the new British stables built just southwest of this house.

The brick gable of the rear wall of the Van Zandt house was discovered in 1981 when the building was being renovated. The sloping edges of the gable were laid in the Dutch *vlechtwerk* pattern, and near the peak there is a small round ornamental opening, probably one of two originals. The story-and-a-half house faced north toward Beaver Street and was constructed with bricks made probably in the nearby Rutten Kill brick kilns.

Another 18th-century house (Fig. 16) stands in an area that by 1756 had been enclosed by moving the stockade south to Division Street as far west as Green Street. It was most likely built by Johannes Radliff, a shoemaker and son of Lambert Radliff, who in 1733 had a small brick-yard west of South Pearl Street. Johannes married Elizabeth Wilkinson in December, 1759, at Albany, and he may have constructed this house shortly after their marriage. The neighborhood became concentrated with many shoemakers. With deerskins readily available, Albany had been a center for shoemaking since the 17th century.

Fig. 16   Johannes Radliff house, built c. 1759 and remodeled c. 1937, as it appeared in 1993.

By 1783 this house already needed repair. There had been two fires in the chimney of the cellar kitchen during 1782. In 1783 the chimney was in a ''ruinous situation,'' and Radliff was ordered not to use it. About 1790 Elizabeth Radliff, Johannes's daughter, married Samuel Norton, a mason. They evidently not only repaired but also enlarged the house: the date ''A D 1790'' appeared on the clapboard gable. The Nortons continued to live in the house until 1817. In 1835 Jared Holt purchased the property. Holt, a merchant selling leather and shoemaking equipment, developed an exceptional wax for smoothing the thread used in stitching boots and shoes. In 1879 he established a stitching-wax factory in the South End, but he maintained his store at 48 Hudson Avenue until 1892. The current owners, the Saul family, purchased the property in 1935. About 1937, the storefront facade was altered, and the second-floor windows were enlarged. Since 1989 the structure has been threatened by development proposals. However, since it is a rare survival of a wood-frame and clapboard Dutch urban house from the mid-18th century, it is hoped that the opportunity to preserve what may be Albany's only remaining Dutch wooden urban house on its original site within the original colonial street plan will not be lost.

Albany Buildings in the Era of the American Revolution, 1760-90

By 1760 the threats of French and Indian attacks on the Albany area were effectively eliminated with the British conquest of Canada. New farms could now be safely settled, and country homes could be developed outside the city walls.

In January, 1761, Philip J. Schuyler of Albany purchased land on which to build a new country house on the south side of the Beaver Kill, about a half mile south of the stockade (Fig. 17). The site was about a third of a mile west of the Hudson on a gentle bluff overlooking the fields adjacent to the river. Great-grandson of Philip Pietersen Schuyler, Philip J. Schuyler was born in 1733 in the old Schuyler house at the southeast corner of State and South Pearl streets. He married Catherine van Rensselaer in 1755; she was a granddaughter of Robert Livingston, Jr., and had lived in the brick Van Rensselaer house called Crailo, which is still

Fig. 17   Schuyler Mansion, built between 1761 and 1764.

standing across the river in the city of Rensselaer. Commissioned a Provincial officer in 1755, Schuyler served under William Johnson and then under John Bradstreet, a British colonel, who became Schuyler's closest, lifelong friend. In March, 1761, Schuyler sailed to England to settle Bradstreet's accounts with the War Office, leaving John Bradstreet and Catherine Schuyler to supervise construction of the new house.

While Schuyler was in London in 1761 and 1762, he purchased hardware, window glass, wallpaper and numerous other fine items for the house. When he returned to Albany in November, 1762, little more than the shell of the house was complete. Schuyler personally directed the finishing of the interior in 1763 and 1764.

The Schuylers' house is built of red brick made in a brickyard near the Rutten Kill and laid in Dutch cross bond. It originally had two flanking wings at the rear corners: one was a nursery with an adjoining kitchen, and the other was an office (raised gardens with stone walls outline the approximate locations of the wings). To the rear was a barn measuring eighty by fifty feet, larger than the mansion, which is sixty-two by forty-seven feet in plan.

The mansion was a bold architectural statement for Albany in 1761, just as the old Schuyler house on State Street had been in 1667. The new Schuyler house was as fine and modern as many English country houses of its time. It symbolized new cultural attitudes and values and, perhaps, the pride of Americans such as Philip Schuyler who had helped to expel the French from North America and believed the colonies had become equal partners in the British empire. Even so, Philip Schuyler may have deliberately incorporated a few subtle reminders of his Dutch heritage in his floor plan of the house. The central hall, for example, is nearly as wide as the flanking parlor and the living room (Georgian houses in the North generally did not have such wide central halls). The hall was Schuyler's public *voorhuis*. The house was decorated with delft tiles, probably around fireplaces.

John Bradstreet lived in the house with the Schuyler family until his death in 1774. Despite his association with Bradstreet, an unpopular British officer, Schuyler was commissioned a major general of the American army in 1775. In October, 1777, he entertained the captured British General John Burgoyne and his staff in the mansion, and in 1780 Schuyler's daughter, Elizabeth, married Alexander Hamilton there. Loyalist raiders attempted unsuccessfully to kidnap Schuyler from the house in 1781.

The balustrade on the roof of the mansion may have been added or replaced in 1808, and the hexagonal front entrance vestibule, perhaps designed by Philip Hooker, was added by 1818. After the Schuyler family sold the mansion in 1806, it was occupied by a succession of owners, and in 1858 the widow of one of the owners married former President Millard Fillmore there. In 1886 the mansion became the Saint Francis de Sales orphan asylum. The diocese was proud of the history of the house, and when it became necessary to move the orphanage, the diocese cooperated with several patriotic societies and individuals in arranging for preservation of the building as an historic site. In 1914 the property was turned over to the State of New York and is now a State Historic Site, open to the public.

Fig. 18   The Van Rensselaer Manor House, built in 1765 and remodeled in 1843.

A second great country mansion was built north of Albany in 1765 (Fig. 18) by Stephen van Rensselaer II, patroon of the manor of Rensselaerswyck. It was located near the Fifth Creek on the low flats along the river at a site east of Broadway just north of Tivoli Street. Built of brick, the house had a gambrel roof and a pedimented pavilion. The front entrance opened into the largest room, a central great hall, which was twenty-four feet wide, had a twelve-foot-high ceiling and extended the full depth of the house, almost forty-seven feet. At the west side of the great hall was a wide central arch with carved spandrels taken from a book of ornament by M. Lock and H. Copland. On the walls was hand-painted tempera ''Ruins of Rome'' wallpaper made in England in 1768 by Neate and Pigou and sent to Van Rensselaer by his father-in-law, Philip Livingston. At his father's death in 1769, the property passed to young Stephen van Rensselaer III. He married Margarita, a daughter of Philip J. Schuyler, in 1783. Flanking one-story octagonal wings designed by Philip Hooker were added in 1820. After Stephen van Rensselaer III died in 1839, the property passed to his son, Stephen van Rensselaer IV, and the entire house was extensively remodeled to designs by Richard Upjohn between 1840 and 1843.

By 1868, when Stephen van Rensselaer IV died, the mansion had become less desirable as a residence; factories, canals, and railroads were built nearby. In 1893, after more railroad tracks were laid closer to the house, it was demolished. Through the efforts of Marcus T. Reynolds, stone, bricks, and timbers from the old house were transported to Williams College, where Reynolds designed a new fraternity house resembling the old Van Rensselaer house and incorporated some of the materials. Members of the Van Rensselaer family saved the rare wallpaper and original wood-work of the great hall and later donated them to the Metropolitan Museum of Art. With these and other fragments, including the original doors donated by the Williams College fraternity, the museum recreated the Van Rensselaer Room in the American Wing, which was opened in December, 1931.

Gambrel roofs on two-story residences like the Van Rensselaer house were frequently used by builders of fashionable new Georgian style houses in the upper Hudson Valley after 1760. The gambrel roof, which was probably of English origin, was built in New York with proportions that distinguished it from the style of gambrel roof used in other colonies, and it came to be associated with the New York Dutch architectural tradition. The New York gambrel had short upper sections and longer lower sections. Gambrel roofs had been used on smaller Hudson Valley Dutch farm houses of less than two full stories since early in the 18th century, but their appearance on two-story houses was a new refinement.

One example was a small brick house at 39 North Pearl Street. As early as 1668 Frans Jansen Pruyn had owned property in this block. His great-grandson, Casparus Pruyn, a blacksmith, married Catharina Groesbeck in December, 1762, and probably Casparus built the house about that time. The house was torn down about 1872. A full two stories high and built of brick laid in Dutch cross bond, it had a typical New York Dutch gambrel roof, with its ridge line parallel with North Pearl Street, in the English manner. Two surviving two-story structures of this period with similar roofs near Albany are the rear wing (1762) of Crailo State Historic Site in Rensselaer and the old brick house at 524 First Avenue, above 112th Street, in the Lansingburgh section of Troy.

Casparus Pruyn's house represented a significant departure from the traditional Dutch urban house type in Albany, which had the gable end facing the street. The Pruyn house must have been distinctive in Albany in 1762. In 1778 it was the military headquarters of the Marquis de Lafayette. Years later, when Lafayette returned, he recognized the house from its curious brass door knocker, the figure of an animal hanging by its hind legs.

Meanwhile, friction over the continued British military presence in Albany had increased. In 1765 the city demanded the removal of not only the barracks but also the buildings in the streets of the town used by the British including the "great store house" near the Reformed Church. Late that year the British sold the "old barracks" and several other buildings including the "Old Provision Shed" on or near the site of Fort Orange just south of the city, where the British engineer intended to erect a new provision storehouse. However, the Reformed Church and Common Council refused to allow the new storehouse to be built on the Fort Orange site except under completely unreasonable conditions. In October, 1766, a mob collected in the streets, grew disorderly, and began to pull down the detested provision storehouse in the city. Many of the stores were looted from the building before a company of British troops arrived from the barracks to protect the remains of the storehouse and the provisions and to impose order.

During these troubled times the city continued to expand beyond the limits of the old stockade, while other new houses continued to be built among the older Dutch-style houses in town. On the south side of State Street, about opposite Chapel Street, for instance, Robert Yates occupied a house built perhaps about 1765, when he married Janetje van Ness. Described as "a man of great intellectual power," he became one of the first justices of the state Supreme Court in 1777 and chief justice in 1790. He died in 1801, leaving the house to his son, John van Ness Yates, who became secretary of state for New York. The house stood on a small lot about twenty-four feet wide and only eighteen feet deep. A drawing of the house shows that it was a two full stories and had a double hip roof. It was demolished in 1855.

Above State Street, west of Fort Frederick and the old stockade wall, a grid plan of new streets and large blocks of land for development was laid out in 1764. King's Street (now Washington Avenue) was the widest street and led "to Schoenctade and the Western Country of Indians." One block south was Prince (present State) Street. South of Prince Street between Duke (now Eagle) and Hawk streets were a new building and six and one-half acres of land designated by the city for a free school, overlooking "a fine Country along the River." King's Street later became known as

Lion Street, and the other east-west streets were also given names of animals. Of these names, only Elk Street still survives. The north-south streets were given names of birds. Hawk Street still retains its original 1764 name.

On September 5, 1765, the city granted lots along both sides of Washington Avenue from present Swan to Lark streets, including a large lot on the south side of Washington Avenue east of Dove Street, which was conveyed to John Hewson, a shoemaker. Hewson apparently built a house on this lot in 1765 or 1766. Most of the other lots remained undeveloped. The map of Albany by Simeon De Witt published in 1794 shows Hewson's solitary property with formal gardens and trees on it. The house at 144 Washington Avenue now stands on this lot, but it was not specifically indicated by De Witt in 1794 (he did not attempt to show every building on his map). The brick facade of the house is laid in Flemish bond. It is two stories with six-over-six windows on the second floor. The mansard roof was added probably in the early 1870s. The design of the original roof remains unknown, but like other new houses in the city, its ridge line was probably parallel with the street in the English manner. The property passed from Hewson's son to Thomas E. Hewson and then through the hands of other owners. The 1854 Albany city directory shows the house as the residence of William Rankin, whose business was boots and shoes; after ninety years, the house was still the home of a shoemaker.

Fig. 19 Christopher Lansing house, dated in the gable wall 1766.

Another house, similar to the Casparus Pruyn house and perhaps to the John Hewson house, was the Christopher Lansing house built north of Albany on Broadway (Fig. 19). It was constructed of brick, had a gambrel roof parallel with its three-bay-wide front and was dated 1766. It stood on land that was conveyed by Barent Wemp and the heirs of Sweer Teunissen van Velsen to Hendrick Lansing in 1694. The property passed eventually to his great-grandson, Christopher Lansing, who married Sara van Schaick in 1766. According to tradition, a messenger bringing news of General Burgoyne's defeat in 1777 to Albany tossed away near the house the willow twig he had used to lash his horse. Lansing's nine-year-old daughter, Alida, planted the twig in front of the house, and it grew into a large willow tree that lived for about a hundred years.

The Christopher Lansing house stood at the northeast corner of Broadway and North Lansing Street, which ran from Broadway east to the river. In 1799 the Lansings laid out thirty-four building lots between their house and the river. North Lansing Street was widened, and the area was developed rapidly. A block to the north was the new state arsenal designed by Philip Hooker, while on the riverbank was the new state prison. By the 1830s, the riverfront east of the Lansing house had become the eastern terminus of the Erie Canal. The house was torn down in 1882 for construction of the present railroad bridge across Broadway at North Lansing Street.

The Lansing house was built at a time when many other physical improvements were underway. In 1766 it was decided to construct three docks on the Albany waterfront. The wharves "abounded in Lumber," and huge rafts of timber were sent down the river. In 1767 a large lot on the Vossen Kill was given to the Dutch Reformed congregation for a new church. While most of the buildings in the city in 1769 were said to be still "shaped like the old Dutch Houses" with gables facing the street, the increased British influence had prompted new architectural styles, as well as other development in the arts.

A map of the city about 1770 shows that the stockade wall had been removed, and in April, 1771, the Common Council decided to erect twenty street lamps. The grid plan for westward expansion of the city had been established. Albany was becoming a more pleasant and efficient place in which to live and to conduct business. Property values increased. In 1770 Richard Cartwright sold to Samuel Judah for 600 pounds a house, the construction of which had cost Cartwright 548 pounds. The house, "as pleasantly Situated as any in town," was "19 feet by 35 two story a fine warm cellar under the whole with a good kitchen in the rear with a pleasant bed chamber over it. . .In the front is a neat Shop Completely fitted up [with a] Stair Case, behind which is a large Parlour well finished. . .above Stairs is very Pleasant, a bed place adjoining behind, behind [a] bed chamber and above two fine Garrets English fireplaces. . .Stabling for 3 horses & a Cow."

Other new houses were built in the south part of the city, particularly as expansion beyond the former stockade line became more convenient. One was built about 1770 at 137 South Pearl Street by Gerrit van Zandt, a younger brother of Willem van Zandt. Parts of the house survived until about 1982 and were recorded. It seems that the house was of two stories built of brick laid in Dutch cross bond. The floor beams were oriented east-west, and it appears that the house originally faced South Pearl Street with its roof line parallel with the street. The smoothly finished first- and second-floor beams in the interior had been exposed, as in a Dutch house.

Gerrit van Zandt, a merchant, owned several storehouses in Albany. He may have been a partner with his brother Willem, whose house was at the southeast corner of South Pearl and Beaver streets. On the opposite corner of those streets, Willem built a new storehouse apparently about 1770 just as Gerrit's business was expanding. This may be the house that the city gave Willem permission to build in 1770 on the Rutten Kill. The 1856 city directory shows that George Young operated a grocery here, and in 1867 he purchased the remaining property. It was torn down in 1870 to build a music hall, and later, about 1874, the Martin Opera House was built on the site. A photograph shows that the old storehouse was a plain, story-and-a-half building with its gable lengthwise, parallel with Beaver Street.

About 1770, when the Van Zandts were building along South Pearl Street, another prosperous Albany merchant, John Stevenson, constructed a large, elegant house on State Street (Fig. 9), probably on the occasion of his marriage to Magdalena Douw, daughter of the mayor of Albany. Stevenson was a successful businessman, selling bars of iron and steel as well as hardware on a large scale. When the house was completed, it created considerable comment in Albany. Standing In sharp contrast to the old-fashioned, adjacent Harmanus Wendell house, the Stevenson house was a modern mansion of two full stories with a gambrel roof. It had a Palladian window over the pedimented front entrance. One Albany resident recalled that "the Stevenson House was then a wonder in architecture, it being in a style quite different from any thing in Albany. It was purely English throughout, and it was known as 'The rich man's house.'" The house later became the Albany residence of Martin van Buren. It was demolished in 1841.

During the Revolution Albany was a center of military activity as American forces prepared to meet British attacks on the city from the north, west, and south in 1777. At the same time, growing numbers of inhabitants with Loyalist sympathies both within and outside the city were a source of increasing concern.

The old houses of Albany proved to be an important resource at this time, when lead for shot was in short supply. In July, 1776, when 1,500 pounds of lead were needed, the Albany Committee of Correspondence was ordered "to cause so much Lead to be taken out of the windows of the houses in Albany as to supply that quantity of Lead." A year later a member of the Albany Committee assisted "in taking all the Lead out of the Cesh [sash] Windows in the Houses in and about this City." He was directed "to use all the prudence and Caution in his power to prevent any Damage being done to the Windows Ceshes &c." The old British hospital also filled important wartime needs. Described in 1777 as "two stories high, having a wing at each end and a piazza above and below," it contained forty wards and was capable of accommodating five hundred patients, "besides the rooms appropriated to the use of surgeons and other officers, stores, etc."

In spite of the war, Peter W. Yates built a large new mansion house, probably between 1780 and 1782, south of the city near the Dutch Church pasture and just one thousand feet north of General Philip J. Schuyler's mansion. Yates was the son of a blacksmith and a nephew of William Waldron, the master mason who built the Schuyler mansion. In 1775, Yates was chosen to serve on the Albany Committee of Correspondence, but he was expelled from membership when he was suspected of being a Loyalist. He signed an oath of allegiance in 1777, after being threatened with imprisonment. He later moved to Catskill, again fell under suspicion, but signed a new oath of allegiance in May, 1779. By 1780 he had returned to Albany and was found to be loyal to the American cause.

On August 7, 1782, a new preceptor for an Albany school, Simeon Baldwin, arrived in town and lodged in the Yates home. Baldwin discovered that the Yates household was disorderly and increasingly hostile toward him. Mrs. Yates, he wrote, was "as cross as the Devil," and "the rough manners of the children would disgrace a family far less pretentious than theirs." Simeon Baldwin's rough sketch map of Albany made that same year seems to indicate the Yates mansion. Alexander Coventry, visiting Albany in 1785, recorded "a visit to P. Yates' new house" in his diary, and an English visitor commented in 1787 that the best houses in the area were the Van Rensselaer manor house and "those of General Schuyler and a Mr. Yaetes situated on the Rise of a hill to your right hand as you go out of town on the opposite side."

The De Witt map of 1794 shows that like the Schuyler mansion, the Yates house faced east toward the river. The grounds in front were landscaped with trees as far as South Pearl Street. On the north and south sides were formal gardens extending to Grand Street. A watercolor painted about 1795 (Fig. 20) shows that the Yates

Fig. 20   Yates-Kane mansion, built probably between 1780 and 1782.

house, like the Van Rensselaer manor house, had a pedimented central pavilion at the front. Like both the Van Rensselaer manor house and the Schuyler mansion, the Yates house had windows flanking the front door. Like the Schuyler mansion, there was a hipped roof and a roof balustrade. The prominent Palladian window over the entrance was similar to that of the Stevenson house. These houses exhibit characteristics of the Georgian style with the addition of classical detail from architectural handbooks such as James Gibbs's, and they are typical of the best houses built in the northern colonies during the third quarter of the 18th century.

The Yateses sold their home and five and a half acres of land to James Kane in 1809. In 1817, the state supreme court issued a judgment against Kane for $350,000, and the sheriff sold the house and about two acres. The property was leased to Gov. William H. Seward from 1839 to 1843. It subsequently served as the residence of the Albany Female Academy principal and as a girls' dormitory. Finally, it was sold to the trustees of the Ash Grove Methodist Church, who demolished it in 1864 to erect a new church. The former Philip Schuyler High School now stands on the site.

After the Revolution, the city made an effort to erase the reminders of military activity and to promote more orderly development. Old Fort Frederick, which was long in bad repair, was demolished, and in 1784 stone from the fort was appropriated for other public uses. In 1785 butchers were ordered to stop butchering in their own houses and to use the old military storehouse instead. It was decided in April, 1785, to dismantle the old military hospital building and lay out building lots on the site, but evidently the work was not undertaken immediately, for in December a visiting company of comedians was allowed to use two rooms in the hospital for their performances. The popularity of stoves had increased the dangers of fire, and in 1785 property owners were ordered to remove all stovepipes leading through windows and roofs. The city decided to stop the construction of tan pits along Fox Creek

Fig. 21   Cherry Hill, built in 1787.

(the Vossen Kill) to facilitate expansion northward and suggested to the Reformed Church in 1785 that the pasture south of the city be laid out into streets and house lots ''to promote the welfare of this City and the weal of the State.''

On March 15, 1787, Philip van Rensselaer contracted with Isaac Packard of Albany, a housewright, to build a new house (Fig. 21) where Van Rensselaer's old one had stood, on South Pearl opposite the north end of Castle Island. (Directly across the Hudson River was the old Van Rensselaer farm, now Crailo State Historic Site, where Philip's father, Kiliaen van Rensselaer, had been born in 1717.) The site of Philip van Rensselaer's new mansion had been occupied by the house and farm of Hitchin Holland, a British military officer, and his heirs in the 1750s and 1760s.

Van Rensselaer and his family may have moved to their new house, which they called Cherry Hill, in 1778 or 1779.

The 1787 contract with Packard specified that the house was to be a two-story frame building fifty-seven feet long and thirty-seven feet wide with a gambrel roof "well Boarded and Shingled." There were to be twenty-four windows with twenty-four panes of glass each, as well as two windows at each gable end and two hall windows of eighteen panes each adjacent to the east entrance door. Built into the side of a hill, the house was to have two kitchens in the stone cellar, with four windows in the front cellar wall. Doors "taken out of the old house" were to be used in the kitchens. The two upper segments of the gambrel roof were to be enclosed by a balustrade that ran along the north and south edges of the upper segments of the roof and lengthwise along the break between the upper and lower sections. Upstairs, the central hall was to be twelve feet wide, and there were to be four rooms on each floor.

Philip van Rensselaer prospered as a merchant, and by 1798 his Cherry Hill farm was said to contain nearly one thousand acres as well as a tannery and a brew house. Between 1768 and 1793 he and his wife had nine children who survived to adulthood. After Philip died in 1798, his widow remained at Cherry Hill until her death in 1830. The family owned Cherry Hill until 1963, when it became a museum. Much of its original 1787 appearance remains. A photograph from the 1850s shows the roof balustrade and a piazza. The two dormers were added between 1850 and 1880. The house is an important example of a late Georgian country mansion typical of the Hudson Valley on the eve of the Federal period.

Summary of Trends and Patterns in Albany Architecture before 1790

The earliest Dutch architecture of Albany seems to have included influences in particular from Flanders, Zeeland and elsewhere in the southern Netherlands, perhaps because refugees from those areas had dominated the West India Company, but such an explanation is not altogether satisfactory. The Old World prototype of the early buildings with wooden cellars of perishable, non-permanent construction remains unidentified. The Schuyler and Van Rensselaer houses of 1667 to 1668, the Reformed Church of 1715 and the Isaac Wendell house as late as 1718 seem to have been derived from buildings typical of Zeeland and adjacent areas; however, the influence of Amsterdam and North Holland can also perhaps be recognized in the step-gable Van Schelluyne, Vanderpoel, Harmanus Wendell and Beekman houses after 1680 and with the Slingerlandt house as late as 1732. For brick houses, Dutch cross bond was most common, but Flemish bond appeared about 1699 in the Wendell-Van Vechten house and was used occasionally later in the 18th century (the Abraham H. Wendell house in 1738 and the Hewson house of 1765). The influence of English Georgian architecture is evident in public buildings as early as 1740 with the courthouse and after 1760 in houses such as the Schuyler Mansion.

Life in Albany from 1690 to 1760 had been more or less dominated by fears of French attack and massacre. The fur trade had declined despite the city's trade monopoly under its 1686 charter. English styles and influence after 1760 took precedence over traditional Dutch designs in architecture, but the two-story houses with distinctively proportioned gambrel roofs and wide hallways with hall windows seem to have established a regional late Georgian style between 1760 and 1790. With an unprecedented influx of immigrants from New England and elsewhere and with the rapid development of expanded sections of the city, Albany experienced changes after 1790 even greater and more demanding than those after the victory over the French in 1760.

While much more research remains to be done to document, discover, interpret and verify the identities of Albany's earliest historic buildings, it is equally important to maintain and preserve those few structures that have been identified. It is hoped that future planners and developers will respect the integrity of these resources, including the original 17th- and 18th-century street pattern, which reflects in part the plan of the original fuyck settlement predating 1652. In addition to the six buildings or parts of buildings predating 1790, there are probably others still hidden within existing buildings that have been remodeled. It will become increasingly important, as development continues, to study each structure standing within the pre-1790 city area to identify presently unknown survivals of early buildings.

The Stonecutters' Art in Albany

Michael F. Lynch

Competition to reflect cultural awareness and "good taste" among Albany's rapidly growing community of governmental officials, entrepreneurs and social lions has left the city with an outstanding collection of architectural stonework dating from the early 19th century to the mid-20th century. Distinguished local architects including Philip Hooker, Albert Fuller and Marcus T. Reynolds were called upon to design houses, banks, churches, courthouses and commercial buildings. Architects of national renown—Richard Upjohn, Patrick Keeley, Russell Sturgis and H. H. Richardson—were drawn to Albany by commissions for prestigious projects. From this combination of talent the city emerged—an immovable feast in stone to be savored by residents and visitors alike.

It appears that most stonecutters who worked in Albany were trained or served their apprenticeships in Europe. A notable exception was Charles Hinton, who was born in Ithaca in 1869 while his English-born father, Louis, worked with a crew of stonecutters imported by Ezra Cornell to build his mansion, Llenroc. Charles trained with his father and continued his father's work at the Cathedral of All Saints in Albany. He was unusual in Albany: perhaps the sons of stonecutters found the work too hard and other ways of earning a living more attractive. There was no shortage of talent though, because skilled stonecutters continued to emigrate to America. The Albany city directories, starting in 1813, show a succession of stonecutters arriving from Scotland, England, Ireland, Germany and Italy.

With very few exceptions, little is known of individual stonecutters. For the most part they labored anonymously; architectural work was rarely signed. Occasionally a cornerstone or dedication plaque identifies the stonecutter, but even here a specific artisan's work is not credited. The plaque at the old Albany Academy, for example, cites Peter McNab as the stonecutter, but it is likely that others did at least some of the work, since his firm, known as McNab and Hamilton, employed up to ten stonecutters on this job.

Direct attributions are more likely to result from documentary evidence than from signatures. Louis J. Hinton's work on the New York State Capitol, the Cathedral of All Saints and other buildings is known because of a manuscript history he wrote in the 1920s. A few oral histories record stonecutters who worked on the Capitol, but for the most part, their specific work is not known.

During the 19th and early 20th centuries, the stonecutter was considered an artisan, not an artist. A true artist, such as a sculptor, practiced fine art and was responsible for design; an artisan, on the other hand, engaged in commercial enterprise and was responsible for production. It was rare that a stonecutter, even a master like Louis Hinton who designed, supervised and executed work, made the leap to sculptor. However, John Brines, a master stonecutter who worked on the Great Eastern Staircase of the Capitol, later studied in Italy and subsequently opened a sculpture studio in New York City.

Artists did busts, portraits and bas-reliefs. Stonecutters undertook the production of a wide array of commercial products (Fig. 1). The account book of Albany master stonecutter Peter McNab includes decorative architectural items such as door surrounds, window lintels, fireplaces and hearths, as well as the more utilitarian—stovepipe stones, stone sinks and paint stones for grinding pigment.

Most stonecutters were journeymen, moving from community to community as the market for their services demanded. They usually worked for an individual master or a company. For example, Duncan Stewart, a journeyman who worked for McNab in 1811, does not appear in the city directories until 1824, when he returned to Albany, probably as a master stonecutter, to work for Brainard and Bruce.

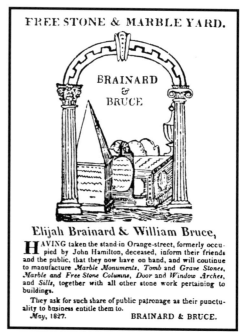

Fig. 1   Advertisement from 1825 Albany city directory.

For some, stonecutting was either a part-time occupation or was given up due to ill health, age, a poor economy or other interests. Loss of fingers and limbs often ended careers. A photograph of an elderly stonecutter shows that he was missing several fingers on each hand. Silicosis was a frequent killer, taking stonecutters relatively young.

Of the more than seventy-five stonecutters identified in the Albany city directories from 1813 to 1840, only seventeen remained longer than five years, and only six of those stayed longer than ten years. Business partnerships, too, seem short-lived, perhaps organized for the convenience of a large job. Later in the century, major institutional or government projects might employ stonecutters directly. In 1874, 219 stonecutters were recorded as being on the payroll of the New Capitol Commission.

Peter McNab was a stonecutter from 1802 to 1818, then became a merchant for four years before disappearing from the directories. James Robertson was a stonecutter from 1805 to 1816, then opened a grocery in 1817 but continued in the stonecutting trade until his death in 1825. Elijah Brainard first appears in Albany in 1820 as a pump and block maker. In 1824 he entered into partnership with grocer and stonecutter William Bruce to operate the stone shop formerly occupied by John Hamilton, but the partnership dissolved in 1827. Bruce continued as a stonecutter until his death in 1830. Brainard had several short-term partnerships until 1831, when he returned to the pump and block-making business. It is unlikely he was a stonecutter; he probably was a business partner but not an artisan. Several master stonecutters achieved levels of prominence in political and social organizations. Peter McNab was an officer of the Mechanic's Society in 1813-14 and of the Saint Andrew's Society from 1815 to 1819, and Joel Dickerman was Albany fourth ward alderman in 1839-40.

It is not true that old buildings have stone ornament because that is how things were done "back then." Stone was expensive. Clients would select as much carved stone as they could afford as a sign of both wealth and discerning taste. The costs for a major public building would, of course, be considerably higher than for a brick townhouse with a small amount of stone trim. The Bank of Albany paid Peter McNab over $3,350 in 1809-10 for what was obviously a large amount of stonework when workers' wages are considered: a laborer earned about $1 per week, a master stonecutter from $5 to $10 per week.

As artisans, stonecutters most often executed the designs of others. Architects frequently produced sketches for artisans to copy. Architects, builders and stone-cutters sometimes used published sources such as pattern books and technical journals for inspiration and to show clients. For more ornate work, sculptors were often commissioned to produce full-scale clay or plaster models that stonecutters then carefully copied. How prevalent this practice was in Albany in the early 19th century is not known, for there were few sculptors in the area. William John Coffee, a noted painter and sculptor, worked in Albany from 1827 to 1845. Previously he had produced designs for the ten pavilions at the University of Virginia. By 1846 Henry Kirke Brown had worked in Albany for two years during which time he pro-duced forty busts, and Erastus Dow Palmer was an active sculptor for a half-century. However, none of these artists is known to have produced designs for architectural use in Albany. It is possible that H. W. Snyder, an engraver who worked with Philip Hooker on the Albany Academy, could have provided models for stonecutter Peter McNab. In the absence of local artists, sculptors from New York City or other metropolitan areas were sometimes used. Later in the century Otto Baumgartel sculpted the plaster portraits that were carved by Killian Drabold in the Great

Western Staircase of the Capitol, and Maxfield Keck was the sculptor for the sunk-relief panels in the belt course of the Alfred E. Smith Office Building. In some cases the plaster models were produced in one location, and the stonecutting done in another. The plaster models for the 1930s Federal Building were sent to Vermont to be carved; then the stone was shipped to Albany for installation.

A third and very common source of designs was existing stonework known to the stonecutter or the client. An 1825 price list from New York City includes references to stonework "similar to Drake's Houses" and "similar to those on houses about St. John's Park." The doorway of 304 State Street in Albany is a scaled-down version of the entrance to the Albany City Hall. The Colonial Revival stone stoop at 54 Willett Street appears to have been copied from stoops in the Pastures, most notably 61 Westerlo Street.

Fig. 2   Detail of Great Western Staircase of the Capitol, carved from Scottish freestone.

The two predominant types of stone used in Albany in the early 19th century were marble and freestone. Freestone was commonly used to describe stone that could be worked easily, had no tendency to split in any preferential direction and was especially suitable for carving (Fig. 2). In Albany freestone was usually sandstone but sometimes granular limestone. Albany's location on the Hudson River provided ready access to stone from many sources. Records indicate that local marble came from quarries in Stockbridge, Massachusetts; Middlebury, Vermont; and Ossining, New York. The McNab account book records many shipments of marble from Philadelphia, and ads of the 1830s indicate European marbles were readily available.

The early sandstones were mostly New Jersey red sandstone, which was used to build the old Albany Academy. Unlike the Connecticut River valley sandstone used to construct brownstone rowhouses between the 1850s and 1880s, the New Jersey stone weathers extremely well. The carved detail on the exterior of the Academy appears as crisp and fresh as it was 175 years ago. The Connecticut River valley brownstone continued in popular use through the 1880s for entire facades as well as trim on brick buildings. In Albany it was the predominant stone used on religious, residential and institutional buildings. The Cathedral of the Immaculate Conception is a notable example.

After the Civil War, granite replaced marble as the material of choice for large government and commercial buildings. Prominent examples in Albany include the old Federal Building, City Hall, the Capitol and Union Station. Marble returned to popularity with the Colonial and Classical Revival styles and remained popular into the 1970s.

Two other types of stone saw limited use throughout the 19th and 20th centuries. Limestone was used for trim, steps and gravestones. Bluestone was used for window sills, foundations and sidewalk flagging, which sometimes required the cutting of splash blocks and gutters to conduct rainwater from downspouts.

Because decorative stone was costly, inexpensive imitations were often used. In the early 19th century the most common was sand-paint applied over wood: sand was dusted onto the surface of wet paint to create the surface look of stone. Marble and brownstone were convincingly copied in this way. Cast iron was used to duplicate the appearance of carved-stone ornament starting in the 1820s. Window lintels at 136-138 Green Street are the first documented use of cast iron for this purpose in Albany. In the mid-19th century entire cast-iron facades were built and painted to look like stone. Other popular low-cost imitators included cast zinc (poppyheads at 363 State Street), terra cotta (385-389 State Street), cast stone (Delaware and Hudson and Albany Journal buildings), rock-faced concrete block and stamped sheet metal (corner quoins at 96 South Swan Street). One imitation that was not a low-cost option is at 283 State Street, where the bricks were carved after the wall was built.

Until the second quarter of the 19th century, stonecutting was ranked among the top trades. But the status of stonecutters in New York State declined after 1828, when the inmates at Sing-Sing Prison in Ossining began providing stone for building projects. When marble produced at the prison was used at the Rensselaer County Courthouse, near-riots occurred at the site in 1834 as local stonecutters protested the cheap prison labor that was putting them out of work. The next year, when the Trade Union of Albany and Its Vicinity was organized, its founders included John McKeon, a stonecutter from Troy.

In the 1850s steam power was introduced at large stone yards to drive saws and polishing machines, and by the 1870s machines for carving simple flatwork were being introduced in this country. An advertisement in the 1882 Albany city directory noted that a local man, James Gazeley, was the "inventor, patentee and sole proprietor of the celebrated machine for cutting cylindrical forms of stone." Later, pneumatic-powered chisels replaced the hand-held hammer and chisel for much cutting and carving (Fig. 3). Louis Hinton complained in the 1920s about stonecutting machinery, saying "the trade has changed into something entirely different from what I knew it to be fifty odd years ago.''

The decline of construction during the Great Depression and World War II, followed by the distaste for ornament in modern architecture, almost brought an end to the practice of architectural stonecutting. Those stone yards that survived focused on gravestones and cemetery monuments or became regional suppliers for a large geographic area. The Adam Ross Cut Stone Company on North Broadway continues Albany's tradition as a producer and supplier of architectural stonework today.

Fig. 3   Stone carvers at Adam Ross Cut Stone Company, c. 1927.

Capitol Hill:
Summit of the City

Cornelia Brooke Gilder

New York State Capitol

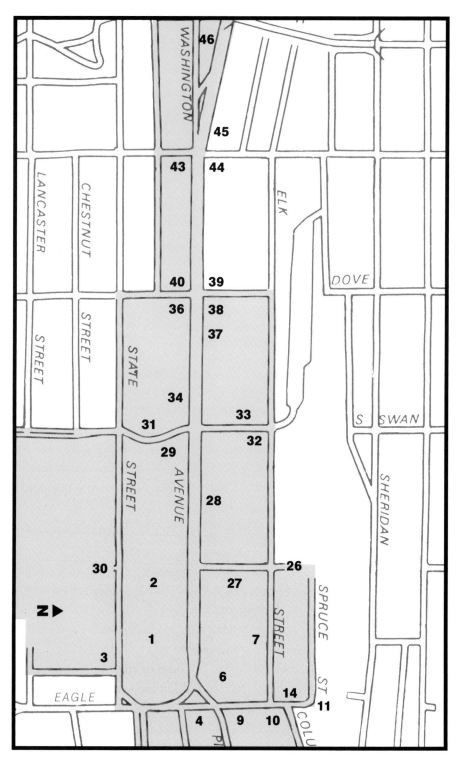

On the brow of the State Street hill stands a noble grouping of public buildings dominated by the late 19th-century state Capitol. In the 17th and 18th centuries Albany was concentrated along the riverfront north of Fort Orange and below Fort Frederick, halfway up State Street, not far from the present Saint Peter's Church. Being beyond the city confines, this pastoral summit, known in the late 18th century as the Public Square, was the site of celebrations. Here in 1788 a "Federal Bower," a temporary frame shelter, was built for a feast celebrating New York State's ratification of the U.S. Constitution. Albany's black population, slave and free, reveled here in the late 18th century during week-long, springtime Pinkster festivals.

Two deep creek beds flanked the hill. During the Revolution Tories were reportedly hanged and buried in the precipitous Sheridan Hollow, which still runs behind Elk Street on the north side of Capitol Hill. To the south, the Rutten Kill ravine has been the target of a series of great public works projects. In 1830 Philip Hooker, the indefatigable city surveyor and outstanding architect of his day, began to fill this gully and lay out streets to accommodate the expanding city. Today part of the area is spanned by the Empire State Plaza, built in the late 1960s and early 1970s.

As Albany grew over the course of the 19th century, the summit was developed. To escape "the noise of carriages and other interruptions" of downtown, a state and municipal committee chose a site on the Public Square near the northwest corner of State and Eagle streets for the first state Capitol. It was designed by Philip Hooker and completed in 1809. The land in front was fenced and exempted from further construction, but behind the Capitol a grid of streets was developed. In the 1860s and 1870s buildings behind the Capitol, between State Street and Washington Avenue east of Capitol Place, were swept away for the present Capitol. Hooker's building was demolished in 1883; a marker in Capitol Park, across from the telephone building, indicates the site.

Start at East Capitol Park.

Gen. Philip H. Sheridan Statue   1
East Capitol Park
John Quincy Adams Ward, sculptor, 1888-1906
Pedestal, Henry Bacon, 1914-16

Beyond commemorating a great Civil War
hero, this statue is a tribute to the determination of Daniel Chester French to see that his
tutor and colleague, John Quincy Adams
Ward, was finally recognized for his years of
work on a faithful representation of Gen.
Philip H. Sheridan, who had spent his early
childhood in Albany.

In 1888, the year of Sheridan's death, John
Q. A. Ward (1830-1910) was commissioned by
the Society of the Cumberland to make an
equestrian statue of the general for a site in
Washington, D. C. Highly regarded as the
dean of American sculptors, Ward had taken
American sculpture in the mid-19th century
from restrictive Neo-Classical models of
Greece and Rome toward realism. A mid-
westerner, Ward encouraged American
sculptors to find themes closer to home and
forgo European training.

With the Sheridan commission, though,
Ward's realism presented problems. Ward
painstakingly observed a cavalry horse in a
studio that allowed the animal free range. The
work went slowly as he modelled the heavy-
set, aging officer who had been his friend.
Eventually the Sheridan family lost patience
and in 1905 rejected Ward's latest model.
Irene Sheridan apparently wanted a more
dashing and youthful depiction of her husband. Disappointed, Ward saw seventeen
years of work come to nought.

After Ward's death, Daniel Chester French
(1850-1931) took up the cause when he learned
that Albany wanted to erect a monument to
Sheridan. In 1914 French urged Gov. Martin
Glynn to use Ward's design and offered to
supervise its completion without compensation.
French hired an assistant, Francis H. Packer,
to enlarge the working plaster model in Mrs.
Ward's possession and chose the John Williams
foundry to cast the statue. He brought in his
great friend, architect Henry Bacon (1866-1924),
to design the pedestal. At this time French and
Bacon were working together on the Lincoln
Memorial in Washington, D. C., and on the

1

Spencer Trask Memorial in Saratoga Springs.

The statue of the parading general in full
military dress, hat held in outstretched hand,
was dedicated in 1916 with Sheridan's widow
and daughter in attendance. A spokesman for
local veterans expressed hope that the statue
would inspire "the fever of patriotism" in
Albany schoolboys as they trudged up the
State Street hill within sight of the statue of
"the little Albany boy who made his name
known and honored in every part of the land
by his valorous deeds." The curving paths
around the statute had been laid out about
1898 by the Olmsted brothers, sons of
Frederick Law Olmsted. They also designed a
modest West Capitol Park, but it was engulfed
in a larger landscaping scheme of the 1920s.

New York State Capitol   2
1867-99
Head of State Street
Thomas Fuller, 1867-76
Leopold Eidlitz and
Henry Hobson Richardson, 1876-83
Isaac Perry, 1883-99

Politics and architecture have rarely been so
inextricably intertwined as in the design and
construction of this monumental chateau of
Maine granite overlooking the Hudson River.
The Great Pyramid at Giza may have been
constructed faster and the nation's Capitol
built at half the cost, but ultimately Albany was
graced with a Capitol that is a masterpiece of

civic architecture and decorative design.

This structure was one of the last 19th-century state capitols to be built in a central urban setting. Hampered by the lack of space on this restrictive, sloping, clayey site, Thomas Fuller (1823-98), the Capitol's initial architect, faced circumstances quite different from those in Ottawa, where he was at work on the rambling, Gothic Parliament buildings. For Albany, Fuller chose the Italian Renaissance style. Because the dome and central rotunda were never realized, the three grand interior staircases became focal points of the design.

A look at the exterior of the Capitol tells the story of the "Battle of Styles" and of the succession of architects involved in its construction. Fuller's Italian Renaissance design of the first two stories evolved into the Romanesque of the third and fourth stories, which signified the arrival of Henry Hobson Richardson. Fuller had been dismissed in 1876 after Lt. Gov. William Dorsheimer brought in a high-powered triumvirate—Richardson, Leopold Eidlitz and Frederick Law Olmsted—to examine the design and construction of the half-finished building. An energetic and aesthetically astute politician, Dorsheimer knew Richardson and Olmsted through their recent work in Buffalo. At that time Olmsted was at work on the city's park system, and he had planned the grounds of Richardson's Buffalo State Hospital, then under construction. Richardson had designed a house in Buffalo for Dorsheimer in 1869-71. Richardson and Eidlitz ignored an 1877 state law that required all work to continue in the Italian Renaissance style. They divided responsibility for the interior spaces, with Eidlitz taking the Assembly Chamber and the Assembly and Senate staircases and Richardson taking the Senate Chamber, Governor's Office, the Great Western Staircase and the State Library (burned, 1911). Eidlitz designed a chamber for the Court of Appeals (now known as room 250), but when the justices refused to use it, Richardson undertook a second one (moved in 1917 to the New York State Court of Appeals on Eagle Street).

Dorsheimer dreamed of making the Capitol a repository of fine art, but few of his commissions

were ever executed. William Morris Hunt's allegorical murals in the Assembly Chamber (1878) have been obscured since 1888, when the original vaulted ceiling was removed to correct structural faults, and a new wood ceiling was installed at a lower level.

2

2

The final phase of the construction (1883-99) was supervised by Isaac Perry of Binghamton, who came to the job as a provincial architect with a solid reputation. Appointed by Gov. Grover Cleveland, Perry managed to survive the vagaries of politics, finances, and engineering problems until the suspension of construction. Faced with structural problems, he suggested a lighter cast-iron tower in place of the Fuller and Eidlitz proposals, but it was never executed. An admirer of Richardson, Perry supervised the completion of many of his designs. In the case of the Great Western Staircase (completed 1897), Perry went beyond Richardson's concept, giving British master craftsman Louis J. Hinton the opportunity to design the extraordinary cornucopia of relief portraits and horticultural designs. Perry's contribution to the exterior is the Eastern Approach, a cascading stairway with elaborate stone carvings supervised by John Francis Brines and completed in 1897.

Perry and the skilled stone carvers had an influence beyond the Capitol itself. The stone carvers' art is found in many public and private buildings of the 1880s and 1890s in Albany (including the interior of All Saints Cathedral and 333 State Street). Perry took on at least two other state-related projects in Albany, the remodelling of the Thomas Olcott house on Eagle Street for the Executive Mansion (1887) and the construction of the New York State Armory on Washington Avenue (1889-91).

The Senate Chamber in the Capitol was restored to Richardson's design in 1978-81 by Mendel-Mesick-Cohen-Waite Architects. In the Senate lobby gates of mild steel, brass and bronze by Albert Paley and stained glass designed by Hilda Sachs and fabricated by Cummings Studio were installed. Tours of the Capitol are given daily.

Enter the Capitol from Washington Avenue, and walk through to State Street.

New York Telephone Building 3
158 State Street
Building A: McKenzie, Voorhees and Gmelin, 1914-15; Building B: Voorhees, Gmelin and Walker, 1929-31; Building C: Smith, Haines, Lundberg and Waehler, 1967

Standing in the shadow of state government buildings, this structure's architectural history is intertwined with that of its powerful neighbor. The first part of the complex, on the southwest corner of State and Park streets, is now known as Building A but was originally called the Albany Main Telephone Building. It was built in 1914-15 and designed by McKenzie, Voorhees

and Gmelin, a New York City firm founded by Cyrus Eidlitz. Between 1900 and 1910, sixty-two of the sixty-nine projects undertaken by the firm were telephone buildings, and the majority were designed for New York Telephone. Eidlitz retired in 1911.

The ten-story, terra-cotta clad Italian Renaissance structure on the corner is the work of Paul Gmelin. German-born and trained, Gmelin had been associated with Eidlitz since 1890. The pitched, tile roofscape acknowledges the contribution of Leopold Eidlitz, Cyrus's father, to the Capitol in the 1870s.

The 1931 and 1967 additions (Building B to the south and C to the west) are the work of successor firms. In 1929, as Building B was underway, forty shorers from a New York City subway project were brought in when the treacherous soil conditions of the hill caused two foundations to cave in. Building B has a grand Baroque doorway facing Park Street, now an insignificant side street. Like its predecessor, this handsome, ten-story building has a steeply pitched, green glazed-tile roof, terra-cotta cladding and classical detailing.

In the mid-1960s, when New York Telephone wanted to expand again, the adjoining gigantic Empire State Plaza project was in its infancy. The state mandated the size, fenestration and materials of the telephone company addition, and the Indiana limestone is a reminder of architect Wallace K. Harrison's initial choice of building stone for the Plaza. Nelson Rockefeller's directive to use marble came after the telephone wing was under construction.

Cut north across East Capitol Park, toward the tower of City Hall.

Albany City Hall 4
1880-83
NE corner of Eagle Street and Corning Place
Henry Hobson Richardson
Interior alterations, Ogden and Gander, 1917

On a frigid morning in February, 1880, Philip Hooker's Greek Revival City Hall of 1829-32 was destroyed by fire. Henry Hobson Richardson, the leading architect of the day, had been frequenting Albany for the past four years, working on the Capitol. "The Great Mogul,"

4

as his young assistant Stanford White called him, immediately secured the commission for the new City Hall.

This magnificent Romanesque building dates from the period generally regarded as Richardson's architectural peak. The banded arches, rhythmic fenestration, bold expression of materials and corner placement of the tower are characteristic of Richardson's style, in which he drew freely from a range of historical sources and disregarded archeological correctness. The exterior walls are rusticated Milford (Rhode Island) granite, with Longmeadow (Massachusetts) brownstone trim delineating the stories and accentuating the lintels and arches. The abundant, intricate carvings are nonetheless secondary to the massive simplicity of the overall design.

The Common Council chamber opens onto a loggia above the triple-arched portal. The mayor's office is located on the first floor of the tower. Designed for storage of city archives, the great 202-foot tower is accessible by a stairway in the adjacent turret. The carillon was equipped in 1927 with sixty bells made by the John Taylor Company of England. Enthusiastically financed by public subscription, it was the first city carillon in the United States.

Since the budget was limited, Richardson gave the exterior top priority. Consequently, his designs for the interior were very modest, and a Bridge of Sighs to the proposed jail was never built. The interiors, re-designed by Ogden and Gander and constructed in 1917, are disappointing, but in the mayor's office a fine Baroque frame designed by Marcus T. Reynolds surrounds a portrait of Albany's first mayor, Pieter Schuyler.

Statue of Gen. Philip Schuyler 5
1925
In front of City Hall
J. Massey Rhind, sculptor

Gen. Philip Schuyler (1733-1804), whose mansion still stands in the South End of Albany, was quartermaster general of the Northern Department of the Continental Army during the Revolution. He had the difficult task of supplying an army that was hampered by terrain, climate and disease in the wilderness of Quebec and the Champlain Valley. J. Massey Rhind (1860-1939) sculpted this noble likeness of Schuyler, which was presented to the city by George C. Hawley as a memorial to his wife, Theodora, in 1925. A third-generation sculptor, Rhind emigrated from Scotland to New York City in 1889. He is better known in Albany for his fountain of Moses Smiting the Rock (1893), dedicated to Rufus King, in Washington Park.

Proceed northwest into the park.

Academy Park and Lafayette Park 6
Bounded by Washington Avenue and
Eagle, Elk and Hawk Streets

These parks grew to their present dimensions in two stages, Academy Park first and then Lafayette Park almost a century later. Academy Park is the two acres to the east of the old Albany Academy. The park was laid out in 1833 and surrounded by a handsome iron fence similar to the fence around Capitol Park that had been designed by Philip Hooker. Here in the winter of 1864 an imposing temporary structure, designed by Walter Dickson, housed the Army Relief Bazaar, a Civil War event that raised nearly $82,000 for medical supplies. Huybertie Pruyn, who grew up on Elk

Street in the 1870s and 1880s, described the park in those days, when the gates were locked at ten each night, as a "wretchedly kept place" with "only one dim gas light in the center. . . we were warned never to go there after dark." In the 1920s Lafayette Park, the larger, western section, was created after more than thirty houses on the two blocks between Academy Park and Hawk Street were demolished.

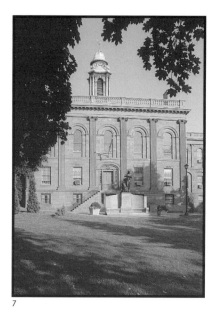

7

Joseph Henry Memorial   7
1814-17
Formerly Albany Academy
Academy Park
Philip Hooker
Alterations, Marcus T. Reynolds, 1935

Albany's oldest civic building, this elegant Federal-style structure originally housed the Albany Academy, a boys' school. Architect Philip Hooker presented himself in 1815 to the Academy's building committee as having the "experience of 25 years in building and a close application in the research of ancient and modern architecture." He was then the city's premier architect. Like Charles Bulfinch in Boston, he combined his talents as a private architect with those of city surveyor, transforming Albany with his graceful public buildings,

houses and commercial structures while laying out public spaces and taming the ridged topography to accommodate a city street pattern. In his lifetime Hooker would have the satisfaction of viewing two other major works from the steps of the Academy—the New York State Capitol (1806-09) and the City Hall (1829-32)—as well as the towers of four churches. He probably laid out the Public Square between the Capitol and City Hall, and the fence around Capitol Park was his design. Today, the Albany Academy and the Dutch Reformed Church on North Pearl Street are Hooker's only known surviving public buildings in Albany. The school building is the less altered.

Hooker's design for the Academy, with its classically detailed cupola and richly articulated facades of arcades and pilasters, shows the influence of Mangin and Macomb's City Hall in New York City completed four years earlier. Beyond the elegant detailing of the Nyack sandstone exterior (executed by William Murray, master mason, and Peter McNab, stonecutter), Hooker's architectural skill and refinement are evident in the beautifully proportioned and detailed second-floor chapel, one of the great Federal spaces in America, which survives intact. Seth Geer was the master builder, and Henry Farnham executed the carving of the original cupola and the interior.

When the Academy outgrew the building in 1930, the city purchased it. Albany architect and onetime Academy student Marcus T. Reynolds supervised the renovation, replicating the old wooden cupola in copper, modifying the center hall, and designing a new double staircase of marble. The building was renamed after its most illustrious professor, Joseph Henry, who discovered electrical induction while experimenting within its walls. The offices of the City School District of Albany now occupy the building.

Joseph Henry Statue   8

1927
Lafayette Park
John Flanagan, sculptor

This pensive statue of a forefather of electro-
magnetism, Joseph Henry (1797-1878), stands
outside the building where he discovered electrical induction in 1830. Then a young teacher
at the Albany Academy, Henry later taught at
Princeton University and in 1846 joined the
Smithsonian Institution as its first secretary. He
reminisced about his breakthrough: ''I arranged
around one of the upper rooms in the Albany
Academy, a wire of more than a mile in length
through which I was enabled to make signals
by sounding a bell.'' The henry, a unit of
inductance, recognizes his contribution. John
Flanagan, the sculptor of this monument, was
better known as a medalist; he designed the
George Washington quarter dollar in 1932.
The monument was cast by the Kunst Foundry.
    Return east to Eagle Street.

9

New York State Court of Appeals   9

1832-42
Formerly State Hall
NE corner of Eagle and Pine Streets
Henry Rector
Renovation and addition, Lewis F. Pilcher, 1916

Henry Rector followed Philip Hooker as Albany's
major architect. All of Rector's known works
have been lost except for this heavily altered
building and a row of houses he constructed in
1828-29 at 52-58 Westerlo Street. Originally
called State Hall, this imposing, domed
structure housed state offices. According to
architectural historian Talbot Hamlin, its construction ''proclaimed the complete victory of
the Greek Revival in the Albany region.'' Early

9

accounts describe five-foot-thick walls of marble
from Mount Pleasant, New York, foundation
stones that were ''the largest that could be
procured,'' ceilings arched ''to supersede the
use of timbers'' and make the building
fireproof, ''marble flag'' floors and stairs, and
a copper-sheathed roof and dome.

The building has undergone several remodelings. The most important occurred in 1916
when the state architect, Lewis F. Pilcher,

designed a rear addition to accommodate the
courtroom of the Court of Appeals, which was
moved here from the third floor of the Capitol.
This splendid, carved-oak room was designed
by Henry Hobson Richardson in 1881 and is
one of the finest 19th-century governmental
chambers to survive in America. Richardson's
work includes not only the decorative finishes
of walls, windows and fireplace but also the

desks, chairs, benches, clock and other movable furnishings. The reinstallation involved some modifications in the proportions and fenestration and a new plaster ceiling of a different design (the original carved-timber ceiling remains in room 315 of the Capitol). The dual preservation of a noble Greek Revival building and Richardson's sumptuous courtroom was an early triumph of historic preservation. The large cupola was added later. In 1958-59 the original cantilevered staircase in the entrance hall was removed, and the building was refaced with new marble.

Proceed north on Eagle Street.

Albany County Courthouse 10

1912-16
SE corner of Eagle and Columbia Streets
Hoppin and Koen

The design of this Neo-Classical county courthouse acknowledges that of its 19th-century neighbor, the state Court of Appeals. Hoppin and Koen, a prominent New York City architectural firm, won the county courthouse competition and supervised its construction at the same time that the state courthouse was being renovated. Hoppin and Koen's design was widely published in the architectural press of the day. Built on a sloping site, the granite and limestone-faced structure is four stories at the front and six at the rear. Two-story, engaged Ionic colonnades are found on the upper stories of both front and rear facades. The classically inspired doorways on all four elevations have huge bronze doors. On all sides stand handsome cast-iron lamps with acanthus leaf motifs. The interior is organized around a two-story light court with Doric columns of Caen stone on the ground floor, Ionic columns of variegated Belgian marble on the upper floor, and a vaulted, stained-glass ceiling. During the 19th century, two structures stood on this site—first an Egyptian Revival reservoir and later the Ruskinian-style Albany High School by Ogden and Wright (1875-76).

1-3 Columbia Place 11

This was sculptor Erastus Dow Palmer's studio and a focal point of the Albany artistic community in the 1850s. Initially a carpenter, Palmer (1817-84) came to Albany from Utica in 1846. He developed his skill at sculpting through cameo cutting. A painting in the Albany Institute of History and Art by Thomas H. Matteson shows Palmer in his studio here in 1857 surrounded by marble statues and three assistants—Launt Thompson, Charles Calverley, and probably Richard Parks—all of whom became noted Albany sculptors. Palmer lived here in the 1860s and later moved first his studio and then his home to two buildings on Lafayette Street, overlooking the west facade of Albany Academy.

Proceed, if desired, down Columbia Street, for side tour.

Columbia Street 12

This sloping, angled street is lined with 19th-century rowhouses, many of which date from the Greek Revival period. Never as grand an address as Elk Street, Columbia Street provides a glimpse of a more typical pre-Civil War residential streetscape in Albany. Numbers 83 and 85 have unusual bowed facades. John Meads, an important cabinetmaker, built 99 about 1829, probably to the designs of Philip Hooker. Its splendid concave entrance is preserved in the collection of the Albany Institute of History and Art. The interior has notable carving, probably by Meads. Number 98 was the lifetime home of Albany architect Marcus T. Reynolds (1869-1937), whose work had a profound effect on early 20th-century Albany, most dramatically in the Delaware and Hudson Building (1916) but also in many other imaginative commissions. Motherless at an early age, Reynolds grew up here with his father and widowed aunt, Laura van Rensselaer. He later bought the house and remodeled it. He died here in 1937. Reynolds's hand is found in a number of renovations in his own neighborhood. Scientist and teacher Joseph Henry lived at 107, originally two separate Federal-style houses.

Look at the Bar Center from Columbia Street and then walk west along Elk Street.

Elk Street   13

Elk Street was the home of an unusual assortment of notable Albany figures from bishops to merchants and, of course, politicians. The remarkable scale of the Elk Street houses of the 1820s and 1830s represents the first step as fashionable Albany moved up from the Pastures area near the Hudson River. Close to the corridors of power, the Capitol and City Hall, these houses are some of the finest Federal-style and Greek Revival residences surviving in Albany. Three served as governors' residences before the state purchased the present Executive Mansion on Eagle Street. The habits, eccentricities and daily lives of Elk Street inhabitants in the late 19th century are chronicled in Huybertie Pruyn Hamlin's book, *An Albany Girlhood*.

14

New York State Bar Center   14
1969-71
NW corner of Eagle and Elk Streets
James Stewart Polshek

James Stewart Polshek's New York State Bar Center integrates the fronts of three Elk Street houses with a modern office complex. In 1969 a major preservation dispute was resolved when it was agreed to retain these facades as a screen facing Academy Park. A compromise that permitted the demolition of the corner building gives a glimpse of the new wing behind, constructed around a courtyard leading to Eagle and Columbia streets. The project won an A.I.A. Honor Award in 1972. Appliqued fabric banners by Norman Laliberte (1971) that

hang in the central hall depict the world's great legal systems and the evolution of the state seal. In 1988, 5 and 6 Elk Street were incorporated as the Bar Center expanded. The facility is open to the public by appointment. Aside from being part of the center, each house is individually noteworthy (the following descriptions use the historic house numbers).

2 Elk Street   15
1827

In 1832-34, soon after this graceful house was completed, Gov. William L. Marcy made it his official residence. Like many early Elk Street houses, it is thought to be the work of Philip Hooker, architect of the Albany Academy across the street. Rufus H. King lived here in the late 19th century. As a child, his neighbor Huybertie Pruyn was fascinated by King's morning ritual. He would go down Steuben Street to see who went to New York on the 7:05 train and chat with Angel Booth, who punched the tickets. ''You could see the [two men] whispering confidently about why so-and-so was going to New York so soon again. . .After Mr. King had seen what he wanted to see, he would go to the restaurant and have his morning coffee. . .by 7:30 [he] could be seen returning by Steuben Street and vanishing into his house.'' The fountain in Washington Park of Moses Smiting the Rock is a memorial to this curious man's father.

3 Elk Street   16
1827
Facade remodeled, c. 1868

Built by Stephen van Rensselaer as speculative housing and sold to J. B. Plumb, president of the Bank of the Interior. This house was prob-ably remodeled by Gen. and Mrs. Frederick Townsend around 1868. Three brothers in the Townsend family had houses on Elk Street in the second half of the 19th century. Here at 3 Elk Street Huybertie Pruyn remembered amateur performances by the Albany Dramatic Club with the Townsend children.

4 Elk Street   17

c. 1830
Alterations, Marcus T. Reynolds, 1900

As a boy, author Henry James visited his aunt here. To him, Elk Street had a "vaguely portentous" ring as if inhabited by "beasts of the forest not yet wholly exorcised." James's Aunt Ellen was married to Smith Thompson van Buren, son of the President. In the late 1850s, Franklin Townsend bought this property. His furnace and machine shop were located at the top of this block, at the corner of Hawk Street. He was also president of the New York State National Bank. Mrs. Townsend, née Anna King, was a sister of Rufus King at number 2. The Townsends lived here for forty years, and another brother, Howard, and his wife later lived at 21. In 1900 Marcus T. Reynolds altered and enlarged this house for Curtis Douglas. Franklin D. Roosevelt lived here while state senator (1910-12) and left in 1912 to serve in the Wilson Administration as an assistant to the secretary of the navy.

5 Elk Street   18

c. 1827

U.S. Circuit Court Judge James Vanderpoel lived here from 1836 to 1843, and the Clarence Rathbones were residents in the 1870s. When a later occupant, Colonel Sweny, was sick, Huybertie Pruyn remembered Elk Street spread with tanbark to deaden the noise of the traffic. In 1897 Lt. Gov. Timothy L. Woodruff of Brooklyn moved into 5 Elk Street and caused a sensation on the block with his stylish clothes, fine horses, and elegant English coachman, who previously worked for the world-famous actress Lily Langtry. Richard Yaco's mural (1993) on the walls of the front parlor depicts Academy Park and its surroundings as seen from the house in the 1880s.

6 Elk Street   19

c. 1834
Alterations, Marcus T. Reynolds, 1906

Built for William Patterson van Rensselaer around the time of his marriage to Eliza Rogers, this red brick house and its mate at 7 Elk Street were two of Albany's finest Greek Revival houses. Although the architect is unknown, William and his half-brother Stephen, who were sons of Patroon Stephen van Rensselaer III, evidently had high architectural standards and took an interest in the minutest details. Stephen had hired Philip Hooker to design a house on Broadway in 1817. Some five years after William built this structure, he chose Frederick Diaper of New York City to design Beverwyck, his country house, which still stands across the river in Rensselaer.

Albany stove manufacturer Samuel Ransom occupied 6 Elk Street in the 1870s, and it served as the Episcopal Cathedral Deanery briefly in the 1880s. In 1906 Circuit Judge William Wallace engaged Marcus T. Reynolds to alter the house and add a fourth story. An 1885 painting by Walter Launt Palmer documents the interior as it appeared when occupied by Dean Frank Norton and his wife, Jennie.

7 Elk Street   20

c. 1833
Alterations, Marcus T. Reynolds, 1915

Built by William P. van Rensselaer on speculation, 7 Elk Street is almost as grand as his own house next door. During Elk Street's heyday, this house was owned by William and Adeline Pumpelly Kidd. Daughter of one-time owner of 1 Elk, Mrs. Kidd lived here until her death in 1914. Known for her acid wit, host of yapping dogs and many charities, she was the grande dame of Elk Street. Architect Marcus T. Reynolds was a pallbearer at her funeral and soon afterward undertook alterations here, including a new facade in Flemish-bond brick, for her nephew, Maj. Harmon Pumpelly Read. From 1941 to 1972 this building was owned by the Mohawk and Hudson River Humane Society.

From this point west, the Elk Street houses have odd numbers, for until the 1920s they faced a row of even-numbered houses, which were demolished for Lafayette Park.

17 Elk Street 21

c. 1845
Orr and Cunningham, builders
Addition, 1858

Standing on the largest and most central lot on the block, this Gothic Revival rowhouse was associated with Albany's distinguished Pruyn family throughout the second half of the 19th century. Numbers 17 and 21 were built by Albany masons Orr and Cunningham. A look at 21, which is the better preserved of the pair and has its Gothic doorway intact, gives a clearer idea of the original appearance of the Pruyn house. The windows of 17 still are framed with drip moldings, and the sash are overlaid with quatrefoils. Originally the houses were stuccoed and scored to resemble cut stone.

Irish-born David Orr began building in the Gothic style after his experience in 1842 working under architect Alexander Jackson Davis on Kenwood, Joel Rathbone's Gothic Revival villa on the outskirts of Albany. In 1845 Orr went into partnership with Andrew Cunningham, and they built this pair of houses on Elk Street: 21 for John A. Dix and 17 on speculation. They sold number 17 to a lawyer, Henry G. Wheaton, in 1846, and Wheaton sold it to John V. L. Pruyn in 1851.

John van Schaick Lansing Pruyn (1811-77) had attended the Albany Academy as a boy. An early advocate of railway travel and a lawyer, Pruyn was a consolidator of the New York Central System in 1853 with Erastus Corning, the uncle of his first wife, Harriet. The Pruyns had plans drawn up for another house on the lot to the east but decided instead to enlarge their existing house in 1858 with a dining room, kitchen and library behind and a piazza overlooking the garden. In the years following Harriet's death in 1859, Pruyn went into politics. He completed Erastus Corning's second term in Congress and became acquainted with Democratic leader Judge Amasa J. Parker. In 1865 he married Parker's daughter, Anna Fenn Parker, and returned to Washington, D. C., as a congressman from 1867 to 1869. Their daughter, Harriet, was born in 1868, and Huybertie, author of *An Albany Girlhood*, was born in 1873. Pruyn laid the first foundation stone of the Capitol in 1869, served as president of the Albany Institute from 1856 to 1877, was a longtime member of the New York State Board of Regents and from 1862 until his death was chancellor of the State University. Anna Pruyn lived here until she died in 1910. From 1894 to 1900 she was president of the Albany Anti-Suffrage Association, which then had about eight thousand members. Huybertie wrote nostalgically about her final hours in the family's house: "The place never looked so lovely, the grass so green, the goose fountain playing and the piazzas so cool behind their vines. And the view from the nursery window—goodbye—goodbye forever."

21 Elk Street 22

c. 1845
Orr and Cunningham, builders

This Gothic Revival house is the finest surviving example of the residential work of Albany builders Orr and Cunningham. The interior survives as well as the exterior. Inside, the octagonal entrance hall is enriched with Gothic woodwork, and the staircase in the separate stair hall is fitted with cast-iron balusters identical to those on the stoop. Number 21 Elk was built for lawyer John Adams Dix (1798-1879), who probably never resided here as he was elected to the U.S. Senate in 1845. It was rented to John V. L. Pruyn and later to Hamilton Fish, who lived here during his term as governor from 1849 to 1851. Years later, after a career of public service in Washington and New York, in the army and as U. S. minister to France, Dix served as governor from 1873 to 1875. By that time he had sold 21 Elk to Gen. John F. Rathbone. After the death of a child, the Rathbones moved to Washington Avenue (the site of the Albany Institute of History and Art) and in the 1870s sold 21 Elk to Stephen van Rensselaer for his daughter, Mrs. Howard Townsend. Her husband was a physician and brother of Frederick and Franklin, whose families lived at 3 and 4 Elk Street.

23 Elk Street 23
c. 1860s-1870s

This carved brownstone doorway flanked by Corinthian columns was once the entrance to the home of Edward Delavan. Above the four-story brick walls is a slate-covered mansard roof and iron roof cresting. Delavan was the proprietor of one of Albany's best known 19th-century hotels, the Delavan House, which stood on Broadway, well located for the growing railroad trade of the 1850s. A local Temperance leader, he eventually bent his principles for profit, much to the dismay of his colleagues.

25 Elk Street 24
c. 1860s-1870s

Politician and diplomat Daniel Dewey Barnard lived in this brownstone-trimmed brick house in the second quarter of the 19th century. He served briefly in the New York State Assembly (1838), four terms in Congress (1827-29 and 1839-45) and as U. S. minister to Prussia (1850-52). He also owned 1 Elk Street, built by Dudley Walsh, an ancestor of Barnard's wife, Catherine Walsh. Number 1 was occupied by a succession of governors: Enos Throop (1830-32), Washington Hunt (1851-52), and Horatio Seymour (1853-55).

29 Elk Street 25
1833

Beginning in 1869, 29 Elk was home to Albany's Episcopal bishops for almost a century. This Flemish-bond brick house, said to have been built for John Adams Dix in 1833, is trimmed with marble Doric columns on the first floor and Ionic columns on the second. Its best-known occupant was Albany's first bishop, William C. Doane, an indefatigable high churchman who began his lifelong service to the new Diocese at age thirty-six. Here he wrote hymns (including "Ancient of Days," still in popular use), directed an ambitious building program (including St. Agnes School for Girls at Hawk and Elk streets and All Saints Cathedral a block west), and was a dominant social and spiritual force on Elk Street where many neighbors were members of his flock. Huybertie

Pruyn remembered Doane as "very striking, tall and very jolly. . .who was never happy without a dog beside him and whose voice penetrated the thickest of walls." The house at 31 Elk was the mirror image of 29; their marble-trimmed doors stood side by side. Number 31 was long the home of Dr. Thomas Hun and later of his son, Marcus T. Hun, a lawyer.

At the junction of Elk and Hawk streets, look north across Sheridan Hollow.

Hawk Street Viaduct 26
c. 1888
Elnathan Sweet, engineer
Dismantled, 1970

Until the 1890s, residences on Capitol Hill were isolated from neighborhoods to the north by a deep ravine. After long debate, the Legislature approved the construction of the Hawk Street Viaduct in 1888, which linked the two sections of the city and became known as the "poor man's short cut to town." The one-thousand-foot-long bridge was a major engineering achievement and probably the first use of the cantilever arch in bridge construction. It was designed by the recently retired state engineer, Elnathan Sweet, president of the Hilton Bridge Construction Company of Albany. Regarded in its day as a daring experiment, the viaduct was copied in America and abroad. Only a segment of the south abutment of this historic bridge remains, below the northeast corner of the state parking lot.

Turn south toward the memorial in the park.

Vietnam Memorial 27
1986-92
Lafayette Park
Merlin Szosz, sculptor

A quiet and moving tribute to service in a troubled conflict, Albany's Vietnam Memorial was designed by Rhode Island sculptor-medalist Merlin Szosz. It was begun in 1986, the year after Szosz designed the city's Tricentennial medallion, and dedicated in 1992. The monument is in the form of a traditional Greek stele and has both classical and Asian influences. It

27

28

New York State Education Building

1908-12
Washington Avenue between Hawk
and Swan Streets
Palmer and Hornbostel

Hailed as the first major building in the United States to serve solely as headquarters for the administration of education, this grandiose temple to learning exudes the confidence and vision of the forceful first New York State commissioner of education, Andrew Sloan Draper. In the 1870s and 1880s Draper had built a reputation as a lawyer, Republican politician, and member of the Albany Board of Education. Returning to Albany in 1904 fresh from a successful building campaign at the University of Illinois, Draper launched a campaign for a separate education building to house the growing agency, as well as the State Museum and to provide fireproof quarters for the State Library, then located in the Capitol.

is made of pink Brazilian granite and has two bronze reliefs. The names of Albany County's dead and missing are inscribed in fluid, almost brush-like lettering designed by Szosz and executed by Alba Corrado. The reliefs are embellished with lush Southeast Asian vegetation, including a palm frond, a traditional symbol of victory, which here is broken. On the west side a soldier lifts a wounded buddy to safety. The memorial conveys the human compassion and sacrifices made by the unsung heros of the Vietnam War rather than military achievements; no weapons are in evidence.

Surrounding the monument are four bronze gas lanterns with lotus forms, designed by Szosz and fabricated by Reid Powers Mendenhall. The cast-iron and wood benches were originally designed by Szosz for the Washington Park Conservancy. Others can be found in Washington Park and other public spaces in Albany.

Turn west up Washington Avenue.

28

In 1906, after two years of negotiations with the Legislature, Draper secured appropriations for a building to be located on ''a suitable site near the Capitol.'' For years, land immediately west of the Capitol (now West Capitol Park) had been under consideration for that purpose. Draper ignited a ferocious church-state battle by snapping up this site on the north side of Washington Avenue while the unsuspecting Episcopal bishop, William C. Doane, was abroad. Doane, who had just finished the choir and Chapter House at All Saints Cathedral on South Swan Street, viewed the entire block as his manifest destiny. Now after Draper's coup, the cathedral was to be obscured by state government.

In 1907 the New York City firm of Palmer and Hornbostel won the architectural competition to design the building. Although the competition committee is said to have been divided about the selection of a classical design over "one embodying quite different principles," the top three entries—by Palmer and Hornbostel, Stokes and Howell, Miller and Pember—were all imposing Beaux-Arts designs. Since the new building was to face a solid row of buildings then standing across Washington Avenue, the restricted viewing angles may have influenced the selection of the uniform facade of Palmer and Hornbostel's block-long colonnade. The design is credited to Henry Hornbostel (1867-1961), who was trained at the École des Beaux-Arts in Paris. The R. T. Ford Company of Rochester was the builder.

Beneath the classical exterior is a steel structure worthy of Hornbostel's later reputation in New York City as a bridge builder (Queensboro Bridge, 1909; Hell's Gate Bridge, 1917). The massive columns have steel shafts clad with marble. The Corinthian capitals and other ornaments are terra cotta. The granite steps on Washington Avenue are flanked by two charming electroliers by Charles Keck, each with clusters of children absorbed in academic, artistic, and athletic pursuits, from tuning a violin to solving math problems. Keck also sculpted the bas-relief of Draper in flowing academic robes, located in the entrance lobby.

Inside, the architectural hub of the T-shaped building is the skylit Neo-Roman rotunda of Indiana limestone, at the junction of barrel-vaulted corridors and the entrance to the reading rooms of the former State Library. Here and along the staircase, allegorical murals by William H. Low depict the quest for knowledge. The central chandelier, encircled by draped female figures, is by Keck. The Paris-educated Hornbostel modelled the magnificent main reading room on the Bibliothèque Nationale in Paris. Its soaring fifty-foot-high space is spanned by lightweight

Guastavino tile vaults that rest on slender, iron Corinthian columns. The reading room is lit by high, arched windows. Chancellor's Hall, a nine-hundred-seat auditorium, fills the east end of the building.

The Education Building was to have been completed on January 1, 1911, but was not dedicated until 1912. The delay proved costly, for in March, 1911, a fire in the Capitol destroyed much of the library's collection. The State Library moved again in 1978 to utilitarian quarters on the upper floors of the Empire State Plaza's Cultural Education Center; in 1976 the State Museum left the top floor of the Education Building for more visible space in the CEC.

Turn south to the park behind the Capitol.

West Capitol Park 29
c. 1926-30
South Swan Street between Washington
Avenue and State Street
Sullivan Jones

Here on the west side of the Capitol, nothing remains of the original Olmsted Brothers' plan of 1898, which was only one-third the size of today's park. The present Beaux-Arts design was laid out during the late 1920s after years of planning and a succession of landscape schemes by state architect Franklin Ware (1911), landscape architects Brunner and Lay (1914), state architect Lewis F. Pilcher (1914) and Marcus T. Reynolds, who proposed a massive memorial colonnade. Designed by Sullivan Jones, the plan eventually adopted was to be a "Court of Honor." It combined ideas of the Ware and Pilcher proposals into a formal arrangement with a central tree-lined mall, a grand approach to the Capitol's west side, which up to that time had been hemmed in by 19th-century structures. To Jones, the towering Alfred E. Smith Building, then under construction to his designs, was the culminating feature of the park. Dwarfed by its surroundings, a statue of George Washington stands on the wide west steps of the park. One of hundreds of replicas of Jean Antoine Houdon's 1788 statue, it was placed here in 1932, the bicentennial of Washington's birth.

30

*Walk down State Street to opposite the south
entrance to the Capitol.*

Empire State Plaza   30
1962-78
South Swan Street between State Street
and Madison Avenue
Wallace K. Harrison
Justice Building: Sargent, Crenshaw, Webster
and Folley; Legislative Office Building: James,
Meadows and Howard; Swan Street Building:
Carson, Lundine and Shaw

Nelson A. Rockefeller's lasting architectural
legacy to Albany—the colossal grouping of
state office buildings known as the Empire
State Plaza—overshadows that of any other
New York governor. This was architect
Wallace K. Harrison's final monumental
commission in a long career associated with
the Rockefeller family. Beginning as a junior
partner on Rockefeller Center in the 1930s,
Harrison's designs, including the United
Nations headquarters (1953) and Lincoln
Center (1966) in New York City, frequently
consisted of complexes grouped around water.
But here in Albany the design is elevated and
separated from the city around it, covering a

vast space that was once forty city blocks.

The complex is said to have grown from
Nelson Rockefeller's embarrassment at driving
with Princess Beatrix of Holland in 1959
through the decaying streets of Albany from
the Executive Mansion to the Capitol. Never
mind that the bicycle-riding princess, now
Queen of the Netherlands, is known for her
love of simple things—Nelson Rockefeller was
not. He wanted noble architecture on a grand
scale. Committed to bringing state offices back
downtown, Rockefeller reversed a trend started
by Gov. Thomas Dewey with the State Office
Campus on the western fringes of the city.

The plaza is built on a massive, landscaped
superstructure with three lower levels of parking
and a concourse of shops and cafeterias. It
spans a hollow that the city surveyor, Philip
Hooker, began to fill 130 years earlier to allow
development to the south. In filling the old
ravine, Rockefeller wanted to create an effect
that had struck him on a visit to the Dalai
Lama's palace, where a great wall stopped the
valley. The mall, with its enormous platform
wall of Llenroc bluestone from quarries near
Ithaca, New York, was to be as separate from
its surroundings as the remote Tibetan palace.

From the time he made sketches on the back
of an envelope and handed them to Harrison
during a flight to Washington, Rockefeller was
directly involved in the design. He chose
marble over Harrison's proposed limestone,
conceived the "Egg" amphitheater, and
directed the landscape planning, which includes
allees of trimmed Norway maples like those at
Kykuit, his home in Pocantico Hills. The elderly
architect's good-natured comment was that
"I had a lot to do with everything Nelson
didn't do with the design of the thing."

During construction, from 1962 through
1978, the super-scale project was known first
as the South Mall. The construction of a five-
story superstructure a quarter mile long and
nine large, complex buildings was a feat of
logistics and engineering achieved by George
A. Fuller Construction Company and a host of
subcontractors. To stabilize ground conditions,
three million cubic yards of gelatinous blue
clay were removed, The four cantilevered
agency buildings (completed 1974) provide

three-quarters of the office space of the forty-two-story Erastus Corning Tower (1973), named for Albany's legendary mayor. Three of the four peripheral buildings were designed in detail by other architects subject to Harrison's approval—the Justice Building (1972) and the Legislative Office Building (1972), both on State Street, and the six-block-long Motor Vehicles Building on South Swan Street (1972). The Cultural Education Center (1977) balances the Capitol at the south end of the vast promenade, where Harrison had originally planned a triumphal arch. The complex is clad throughout with Vermont pearl white and Georgia Cherokee marbles, except for the exposed-concrete Egg (1975), housing a 983-seat theater and a 500-seat recital hall on a tripod pedestal. A printed guide to the stones used in the construction of the Plaza is available at the State Museum.

Over $2.5 million was spent on art to enliven the monotonous underground concourse. Here and outdoors are pieces by artists working in New York State in the 1970s—Robert Motherwell, Clyfford Still, Jackson Pollock, Alexander Calder, Mark Rothko, Morris Louis, Claes Oldenburg and David Smith. The cut-out aluminum figures in front of the Legislative Office Building are by Mary Buckley.

The plaza, concourse, and observation deck atop the Corning Tower are accessible to the public. Art tours are available by appointment through the office of the Plaza Art Collection.

Head west up State Street and then north along South Swan Street.

31

Alfred E. Smith Building   31
1926-30
SW corner of South Swan Street and Washington Avenue
Sullivan W. Jones and William E. Haugaard

This monolithic Art Deco building symbolizes the growth of state government in the 1920s. When built, the thirty-two-story granite and limestone structure was said to be the tallest building between New York and Chicago. Like the Buffalo City Hall (1929-31), also the work of Sullivan Jones, the Smith Building has a series of setbacks around a tall central tower.

Contemporary accounts lauded its "virile modern style" with "no monumental staircases and other architectural flourishes," a contrast to its ornate neighbors, the Capitol and the Education Building.

Sullivan Jones (1878-1955) came to Albany in 1910 as a junior partner with Palmer and Hornbostel to work on the imposing classical Education Building. Fifteen years later, Jones strove to preserve "the harmony of architectural treatment struck by the note of the Education Building" in the lower stories of the Smith Building. The main arched entrance, on South Swan Street, is monumental in scale, and a frieze running around the lower portion of the building is carved with names of New York State counties. Inside, Art Deco details include the bronze elevator doors, grilles and light fixtures. Construction of the Smith Building brought a host of state agencies under one roof and linked them to the Capitol by a tunnel. The top of the tower, once a famous outlook, is no longer open.

Cross Washington Avenue, and continue north along South Swan Street.

Cathedral of All Saints 32
1884-88
SE corner of South Swan and Elk Streets
Robert W. Gibson
Choir and East End, Chapter House: Robert
W. Gibson, 1902-04; West facade: Quacken-
bush, Wagoner and Reynolds, 1971

Inside a half-finished brick-and-stone shell is
one of Albany's hidden architectural treasures—
the magnificent Gothic interior of the Episcopal
Cathedral of All Saints. Albany's first bishop,
William C. Doane, was the driving force
behind its creation. Doane chose the design of
a little-known, young British immigrant over
the proposal of the famed H. H. Richardson in
a much-publicized architectural competition.
With his Albany City Hall underway, Richardson

32

had put forth what Henry-Russell Hitchcock
describes as "the most elaborate design of his
whole career" and was crushed when it was
rejected, although he apparently had made
little attempt to conform to the bishop's
requirements. On the other hand, the likable
young Englishman, Robert W. Gibson, had
worked with Doane on two projects at the
Albany Rural Cemetery, the Lodge (1882) and
the Chapel (1884).

At 320 feet in length (the cathedral for the

Diocese of Long Island completed in 1883 was
190 feet long), All Saints is the first Episcopal
cathedral in the United States conceived on
the scale of its European counterparts. It
marked the advent of Gibson's career as an
architect and the final chapter of the fruitful
life of master stone carver Louis J. Hinton.
Hinton's design and carving skills that are so
apparent on the Great Western Staircase of
the Capitol continue throughout All Saints in
the intricate, fluid designs for capitals, arch-
ways, bosses, and memorials of reddish pink
Potsdam sandstone. Assisted by his son,
Charles, and limited only by deafness, Hinton
spent his last years working his love of horti-
culture into the cathedral's stones. "One
generation shall praise thy works unto another"
reads the pillar near the baptismal font that
memorializes Doane's "blessed stone cutter."

The foundations were laid by the Norcross
Brothers, and builder John Snaith supervised
the first phase of construction from 1884 to
1888. The result was a provisional structure
that permitted immediate use of the entire
final floor area but at only one-fifth the projected cost of the completed building; the
masonry walls were laid up only to a height of
forty feet and covered with a temporary roof.
All towers, porches and exterior stone ornaments
were delayed. Nearly twenty years later,
Gibson, by then a successful architect in New
York City, returned to Albany to supervise the
second phase with builder John Dwyer—the
completion of the interior and the exterior of
the choir to its full height and details with
funds provided by J. Pierpont Morgan. The
Chapter House was also built. Envisioning
other Diocesan buildings on the grounds,
Bishop Doane gradually acquired options to
purchase adjacent property, but in 1906 while
Doane was in Europe, the commissioner of
education, Andrew Sloan Draper, succeeded
in acquiring the critical lots on Washington
Avenue for his own grand scheme, the State
Education Building. With his lifelong project
compromised by the power of the state, Doane
died in 1913.

Gibson's two great Gothic towers at the west
end were never realized. In 1971 the facade
was finally clad in Potsdam sandstone. John

La Farge designed the rose window at the west end, and the other stained glass is by Clayton and Bell of London.

62 South Swan Street 33
1866-70
Renovations, Marcus T. Reynolds, 1901-02

This Gothic facade of 1901-02 by Marcus T. Reynolds is a precursor of the masterpiece he created in that style during the next decade, the Delaware and Hudson Building at the foot of State Street. Reynolds renovated 62 South Swan Street for Canon George Carter and his wealthy wife, whom Reynolds found a difficult client. In 1923 William L. L. Peltz purchased the house from Clifford Sims. At that time the rear windows overlooked the lawns and gardens of the large Washington Avenue houses as far west as the Albany Institute of History and Art. Peltz later gave this house to the Institute, which in turn sold it to the diocese in 1957.

Return south to Washington Avenue, and proceed west.

Fort Orange Club 34
c. 1810
110 Washington Avenue
Alterations and additions, Albert Fuller, 1880
West lounge, Marcus T. Reynolds, 1907
Alterations and additions, Worthington Palmer, 1937

One of the last of a stately progression of grand houses that once lined Washington Avenue, the original, central portion of this structure was built for Samuel Hill, a hardware merchant, around 1810. The building has been much altered. For its first seventy years it was a private "mansion house" with gardens extending through the block to State Street. Its original Federal-style design has been attributed to Philip Hooker. The front hall and reception room have some of Albany's finest surviving Federal woodwork. Later, as the home of merchant George W. Stanton (1835-65), it took on an Italianate form with bracketed cornices, a cupola, and a bay window over the entrance. Bookseller E. H. Bender sold the

34

house to the newly organized Fort Orange Club in 1880.

Since then prominent Albany architects have left their mark on the club's elegant home. In his first known Albany commission, Albert Fuller made additions and alterations in 1880. A native Albanian who would become the city's leading architect, Fuller had just returned from a brief apprenticeship in Saint Louis. As a finishing touch, Fuller arranged for the imposing cast-iron lamps to be moved here from their original location at Philip Hooker's City Hall after the fire of 1880. Dating from c. 1830, these nearly fourteen-foot-tall lamps borne on crouching griffins are early examples of architectural cast iron in Albany. The *Albany Morning Express* reported on the new club soon after it opened that "There was nowhere in the country a clubhouse so well located, more appropriately and richly furnished or where the appointments were more complete." An Arts and Crafts-style room housed in a one-story addition, the west lounge was designed by Marcus T. Reynolds in consultation with co-member Fuller in 1907. In 1937 architect Worthington Palmer removed the ornate bay window and classicized Fuller's east wing. Edward Buyck of Slingerlands painted five murals of old Albany in the grill room.

150 Washington Avenue 35
1891
Edward Ogden and Son

This rusticated brownstone-front house was built for James McKinney (1825-1907) late in his career as Albany's leading manufacturer of architectural ironwork. By the time he moved here, McKinney's cast-iron storefronts, fences and architectural components—lintels, sills, capitals, railings and roof cresting—had become familiar features of buildings in and around Albany, and his often flamboyant wrought-iron railings adorned many newer houses around Washington Park. However, for his own dwelling, designed by architects Edward Ogden and Son, McKinney limited the ironwork to a few elegantly restrained features—medieval-inspired hinges, door knobs and escutcheon plates; a modest, low railing supported on twisted iron bars; and a latticework gate to the basement. When he died in 1907, McKinney was remembered fondly in the *Iron Molder's Journal* by an employee as "a man of wealth who thought molders were human and showed it by his kind acts and unselfish ways . . . He never entered his foundry, but he would walk to every man's floor and greet him with a 'good morning' and a kind word . . . Every time there was an advance in wages asked for, it was granted in a way that was satisfactory to both sides."

The house remained in the McKinney family through 1920. Since 1930 it has been the home of the Saint Andrew's Society, a benevolent organization for the welfare of Scots founded in 1803, whose headquarters on Howard Street was sold to make way for the De Witt Clinton Hotel. Former president David C. Lithgow, a Scottish-born Albany artist, designed the architectural and decorative scheme of the society's new meeting room. Lithgow also sculpted the Spanish-American War Memorial in nearby Townsend Park.

152 Washington Avenue 36

1934-35
Harold Fullerton
Annex, 1937-38; wing, 1952

This Colonial Revival building, designed by Harold Fullerton in 1934 for the New York State Teachers Association, is the most recent of the four landmarks at this intersection. Fullerton is said to have incorporated into it the 1899 brownstone of Dr. James Boyd on

Washington Avenue and another house on Dove Street. Fullerton used brick laid in Flemish bond, which complements Albert Fuller's Harmanus Bleecker Library across the street. The iron railing is similar to the balconies of the Arnold house several blocks west on State Street. The annex, with its two large arches, was added in 1937, and another wing in 1952. The Teachers Association occupied the building into the 1960s. In 1981 it became the headquarters of the Business Council of New York State.

37

Albany Institute of History and Art 37

1907-08
125 Washington Avenue
Fuller and Pitcher
Auditorium, 1925

In 1906, five local architects competed anonymously for the design of this museum. The winning firm, under the name of "Yesterday," was Fuller and Pitcher, the city's leading architects. The Institute had grown out of a merger in 1900 of the scientifically oriented Albany Institute and the Albany Historical and Art Society. In 1904 the group purchased the old Rathbone house and L-shaped lot running through to Elk and Dove streets. From his house next door, William Gorham Rice led the fund-raising campaign for the building.

The Beaux-Arts structure, of buff-colored brick trimmed with Indiana limestone, was completed in 1908. The *Albany Evening Journal* predicted that its rather severe exterior might one day be embellished, but it remains little changed. The building was set back one hundred feet "as a matter of honor" to preserve the old trees (and incidentally the outlook from the Rice house). The formal, rectangular building looks deceptively small from the front. The double staircases in the octagonal lobby were manufactured by the McKinney iron works, indicative of the long link between the Institute and the McKinney family. James McKinney lived just across Washington Avenue; Edward, his son, was a member of the building committee, and the library is named after James's grandson, Laurence. The auditorium was added in 1925.

39, 38

135 Washington Avenue   38
1894-95
Now part of the Albany Institute of History and Art
Richard Morris Hunt, Richard Howland Hunt
North wing, James Shattuck, 1940

Known for his sumptuous private houses (Marble House, Newport, 1892; Biltmore House, 1895), Richard Morris Hunt was America's most fashionable architect when two Albany newlyweds, Harriet L. Pruyn and William Gorham Rice, commissioned him to design this house in 1894. Hunt died the following year, but his practice was continued by his son, Richard Howland Hunt, who was involved in the Rice design. However, Harriet Pruyn Rice credited her husband, not the notable architects, with the finished palazzo that they first occupied in 1895; she wrote that "William went almost daily to it and it stands in its perfectness in every detail as a result of his tireless watching."

The house faced Dove Street, but the Rices used 135 Washington Avenue as their address (the number is carved over the former entrance on Dove Street). The Beaux-Arts structure of yellow, Roman brick has a rusticated, raised basement and an elaborate cornice. Railings and window grilles were supplied by James McKinney and Son.

The month before they moved in, William Rice was sworn in as U. S. Civil Service commissioner, and the Rices spent most of the next three years in Washington. But on their return, 135 Washington Avenue became their home for the next forty years. A Democrat, Rice ran unsuccessfully for mayor and lieutenant governor and served two terms on the state Civil Service Commission. He was active in the Albany Institute next door and was a trustee of the Dudley Observatory. Rice wrote several books on carillons and raised money for the set of bells in the Albany City Hall tower. In 1937 the Rices moved into the De Witt Clinton Hotel, and the Mohawk and Hudson River Humane Society, an organization dear to the heart of Harriet's sister, Huybertie, acquired the house. James Shattuck designed the wing to the north in 1938 for the Humane Society. In 1955 the building was sold to Blue Cross-Blue Shield. The Albany Institute acquired the house in 1966 and converted it to offices and a library in 1970.

University Club   39
1924-25
141 Washington Avenue
Albert Fuller

The University Club was Albert Fuller's last major commission in his formidable forty-five-year career, which had begun with alterations to the Fort Orange Club in 1880. The University Club was founded in 1901 and first rented an elegant Federal house that stood at 99 Washington Avenue. The club was founded as an all-male institution to "cultivate and maintain University spirit in the City of Albany." In 1907 it bought a turreted Victorian house on this corner and in 1914 added a substantial two-story wing on the north. The main house was gutted by fire in 1923, but the unscathed new wing was incorporated into the new building.

Fuller's Colonial Revival structure, unlike its predecessor, was oriented to Dove Street, with the entrance facing the front door of the Rice house. Like the library constructed opposite at the same time, the University Club is built of brick on a raised stone basement. The first-story windows are recessed in arched openings, and the portico is supported by clusters of attenuated columns. The building has several dining rooms, a billiard room, and a bowling alley, as well as rooms for residents. To tide itself over during the Depression, the club broadened its membership to men who had not attended college and to members' wives. In 1983 women were accepted as members. A Frederick Remington painting, "The Lone Scout," hangs in one of the small dining rooms. A series of Walter Launt Palmer landscapes of American and Italian scenes hangs in the main dining room.

156 Washington Avenue 40

1923-24
Formerly Harmanus Bleecker Library
Fuller and Robinson

This Beaux-Arts structure was hailed as "the last word in library construction" with light, air, comfort, and all other library essentials. Named for Harmanus Bleecker (1774-1849), a lawyer, state legislator, U.S. congressman and a leading citizen of old Dutch stock, the library was built with funds raised through the sale of a nearby theater, Harmanus Bleecker Hall (1889), which had been constructed with a bequest from Bleecker to the people of Albany. The new library was designed by Albert Fuller and William Robinson with J. H. Johnson and George Gleim. The Flemish-bond brick building has a raised basement, and large arched windows light the upper-story reading room. In 1977 the library was moved to a renovated office building one block west.

182 Washington Avenue 41

1891

This Romanesque Revival, pink sandstone facade of 1891 has richly foliated stone carving that is indicative of the talent of stone masons in Albany during the later years of the construction of the Capitol. The facade was part of a remodelling of an earlier brick house for knitwear manufacturer James Holroyd, whose Derby ribbed underwear was known throughout the United States and Europe. Holroyd began his business in Albany in the 1860s and built a large factory at Hudson and Lake avenues overlooking Washington Park in 1886. Behind the iron fence made by Michael Mahony's Troy Architectural Iron Works is a remnant of the Holroyd's garden, including the charming, conical-roofed, polygonal conservatory.

188 Washington Avenue 42

1869

This house conveys the atmosphere and architectural scale of mid-19th century Washington Avenue, when this was Albany's most elegant residential street. A substantial, free-standing brick house faced with brownstone, it was built for produce dealer Walter Merchant and remained in his family through the 1920s.

Key Bank, Park Branch 43

SE corner of Washington Avenue
and Lark Street
New facade, Albert Fuller, c. 1920-22

The present brick and brownstone facades with massive granite columns flanking the doorway are a later work of Albert Fuller. A bank has been located here since the late 1890s, when the Park Bank of Albany converted several dwellings for its use. This bank merged with the Union Trust Company of Albany in 1902, and in 1920 Union Trust consolidated with National Commercial Bank.

44

New York State Armory 44

1889-91
NE corner of Washington Avenue
and Lark Street
Isaac Perry

Albany's grand Romanesque Revival armory is one of forty designed by state architect Isaac Perry in the 1880s and 1890s. Many were built after 1884 legislation spurred their construction. Most of Perry's armories—most notably the one in Buffalo for the 74th Regiment—were castellated structures, but here in Albany, where he was at work on the Capitol, the spirit of H. H. Richardson prevailed in this massive, turreted structure trimmed with rusticated sandstone. Perry's love of stone carving is evident in carved decoration on the lively front facade—at the termination of gables, at the springing of arches. A row of small, conical towers descend along the Lark Street facade. A scornful contemporary account likened them to a row of candles being snuffed out and declared the side view "not nearly so agreeable" as the front.

4 Central Avenue 45

1872

This imposing Italianate commercial structure was long associated with furniture companies, most recently Mayfair, one of the first major Albany furniture stores to flee to the suburbs. This property was built for Charles, Frank and Martin Senrick, who were cabinetmakers. In 1877 William Appleton, a Yorkshire-born grain merchant, maltster, and owner of a river barge line, bought the building. In 1906 the Helmes Brothers, tenants since 1886, acquired the building. They operated their furniture store here until it was bought by the Mayfair Company, which left in 1975.

Continue up Central Avenue to Henry Johnson Boulevard.

Spanish-American War Memorial 46

1928
Townsend Park
David C. Lithgow, sculptor

This striding soldier on a granite base at the west end of the park is the work of Albany artist David C. Lithgow. Better known as a painter and portraitist, he painted murals for the State Bank of Albany and Saint Andrew's Society and at the old State Museum in the Education Building, where he painted the dramatic backgrounds for the Indian exhibits. A painting of Lithgow in his studio at 57 North Pearl Street is owned by the Albany Institute of History and Art.

Aside from the Parade Ground, such slivers of shade and lawn as Townsend Park were the city's only parkland before Washington Park was developed. The 1884 *Albany City Handbook* dryly commented that these little triangular parks throughout the city were "simply better than no parks." The handbook also noted that when Townsend Park was "first inclosed with a fence, in 1833, it was proposed to call it Washington Park and erect there a statue of the Father of his Country; but he escaped the honor." Instead banker John Townsend, who served as mayor in 1829-30 and 1832, was memorialized.

35, 36, 37   North Pearl Street

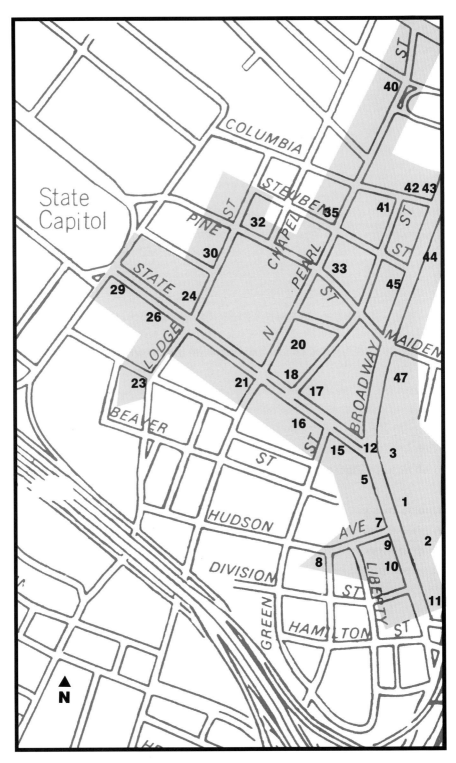

History and architecture come together in downtown Albany in a glorious display.
Albany began here as Beverwyck, a village created in 1652. The Dutch Reformed
Church became the physical as well as the spiritual focus of the community in 1656,
when the congregation built a house of worship near the middle of the intersection
of State Street and Broadway. Lining the streets around the church were brick and
timber houses, most with gables facing the street. A log stockade surrounded the
town.

By the second half of the 19th century, the city had become an established
commercial and transportation crossroads, and downtown Albany was a nerve
center of the Northeast. The blocks between Broadway and the Hudson River were
lined with tall, narrow warehouses stocked with goods being shipped on the river
and the Erie Canal and by railroad. Docks were so crowded with river craft that
water was barely visible in the harbor. Wires of telegraph, telephone, and trolley
lines formed webs above the streets. The pulse of the regional economy rose and fell
with the health of the many banks along State Street, and influential Albany
newspapers were printed on Beaver Street, a block south. The buildings of
downtown Albany have changed dramatically over the past three centuries, but the
pattern of narrow streets between Broadway and the Capitol affords a tangible
presence of the early settlement.

Start at the Plaza, on Broadway at the foot of State Street.

The Plaza   1
1912-18
Broadway at the foot of State Street

At the turn of the 20th century, the City Beautiful movement swept the United States with the idea that city vistas and architecture should excite the senses of those who lived and worked there. The construction of monumental structures in historical styles and the arrangement of urban spaces to create attractive approaches and focal points were some of the ways in which City Beautiful ideals were achieved.

In 1912 congestion and decay in certain parts of Albany prompted civic leaders to hire noted urban planner Arnold W. Brunner of New York City. In Brunner's words, ''a tangle of mean streets and wretched buildings'' on the waterfront that were visible from the top of State Street hill—and perhaps more significantly, from the Capitol—was too visceral a sight to ignore, and redevelopment of this area became a cornerstone of Brunner's work in Albany.

The irregular, medieval character that had defined downtown Albany since the 17th century was at the center of the new development ideas for State Street east of Broadway and the adjacent waterfront. The medieval cities of Europe, which Albany had grown to resemble, often had broad, centrally located plazas surrounded by densely built public and commercial buildings. For Albany, Brunner proposed a very long building at the foot of State Street angled to create a large plaza facing Broadway; the new building would replace the warehouses and block the unsightly view of the waterfront. The plaza would also act as a turning loop for streetcars. Brunner's proposal was enhanced by the fact that the plaza would face handsome, existing structures—the Old Post Office and Federal Building, the former Albany Trust Company with its curved facade at the corner of State Street and the commercial buildings along the west side of Broadway south of State. Once Brunner's plan was in place, what was needed was a design for the new building and an owner to foot the bill.

2

Delaware and Hudson Building   2
and Albany Evening Journal Building
1914-18
Now State University of New York Central Administration Headquarters
Broadway south of State Street
Marcus T. Reynolds

The Delaware and Hudson Railroad, which had outgrown older headquarters on North Pearl Street, decided to build the greater part of the 660-foot-long structure planned for this site. In 1914 warehouses east of Broadway and along the waterfront were cleared, and during the next year, the Delaware and Hudson Building began to rise by the riverside. The Albany Evening Journal, the mouthpiece of the Republican party, constructed the adjoining building at the south end for its headquarters. When the Journal Building was completed in 1918, it overshadowed the headquarters of the Argus, the Democratic newspaper, across the street.

The architect commissioned to bring Arnold Brunner's plan for this site to reality was Marcus T. Reynolds of Albany. Reynolds had already shown his love of historical styles and flair for the picturesque in other Albany projects. For the railroad and newspaper headquarters, he was inspired by the massing and the pinnacled tower of the 13th-century Cloth Hall in Ypres, Belgium. The exteriors of the Albany buildings are lavished with symbolic details relating to printing and the history of Albany. The copper weathervane atop the central tower represents Henry Hudson's ship the *Half Moon*. Symbolic animals, such as the beaver, which alludes to the early fur trade of Beverwyck, are inter-mingled with Gothic foliation. Printers' marks decorate panels on the Journal Building. The overall effect is an homage to medieval Europe, but inside is a steel frame.

The *Journal* was defunct by 1926, but the railroad stayed in the building until 1974. Then, the State University of New York, under Chancellor Ernest L. Boyer, renovated the structure as offices for its central administra-tion. The top of the Journal tower at the south end of the complex, once the penthouse of Republican boss and *Journal* founder William Barnes, was remodeled to serve as a residence for the chancellor. The streetcar and bus loop in front of the building was eliminated, and the arcade was enclosed. Designed by William Hall Associates, the work was completed in 1978. The structure remains the largest adaptive-use project undertaken in Albany.

Old Post Office and Federal Building 3
1879-83
Broadway at the foot of State Street
William A. Potter, James B. Hill

After the Civil War, the United States Treasury Department built many post offices and fed-eral courthouses across the country to designs by officially appointed architects. A High Victorian Gothic-style building was proposed in 1875-76 for Albany by William A. Potter, a native of Schenectady who was serving a brief term as a supervising architect of the Treasury. During a three-year delay in construction, James B. Hill succeeded Potter. Hill preferred the Renaissance Revival style, which was reaching grand proportions in the construction of the New York State Capitol at the top of State Street. He kept the basic massing of Potter's design but transformed the fenes-

tration and detailing and substituted gray granite for Potter's proposed polychromatic stonework. The cornerstone was laid in 1879, and government officials began moving in in December, 1883. Federal emblems on the exterior include a band of shields and stars. The building is now part of the State University of New York headquarters.

3

4

Plaza Row 4
West side of Broadway from State
to Division Streets

A great fire in 1848 leveled nearly all of down-town Albany from Hudson Avenue south to Herkimer Street. The Albany *Argus* reported that upwards of five hundred buildings had been transformed into "one indiscriminate mass of smoldering ruins, tottering walls, rickety chimneys." Just three days later, prop-erty owners along this stretch of Broadway directed a committee "to draw up a plan of improvement." As part of the redevelopment, Broadway was widened and straightened. In the blocks south of State Street, there was a flurry of remodeling and new construction, and the new brick facades with storefronts, evenly spaced windows and simple cornices created a homogenous streetscape. Some fronts were later updated with bracketed Italianate cornices while others—thrust into the limelight when the opposite side of Broadway was cleared for the Plaza in 1914—acquired entirely new fronts. As it now stands, Plaza Row displays nearly 120 years of architectural tastes, the simple and the ornate all telling a part of the story.

Coulson's News Center 5
1814-15
420 Broadway
Addition, 1850s

Among the New England immigrants who settled in Albany after the Revolution was Spencer Stafford, who became a leading hardware and stove dealer. He built this brick structure in 1814-15, and people came to know his business by the gilt stove hanging over the door. In the mid- and late 19th century, hardware and saddlery firms sold their wares on the ground level, while the upper floors were used for manufacturing. The original four stories of the facade are laid up in Flemish bond, with alternating rows of headers and stretchers; atop the windows are flat brick arches. Ghost marks on the exposed north side of the building reveal the outlines of an early gable roof and a round window. Goods were hoisted up the front of the building with the help of a pulley and swung inside through doorways in each center bay. Today only the doorway in the fifth story, added in the 1850s, remains. The Coulson family has operated a newsstand here since the 1940s.

Walk south along Broadway.

Argus Building 6
c. 1830s
408-412 Broadway
Addition, 1871

Curved corners were a feature of several Greek Revival buildings in downtown Albany, but this is the only example remaining. This building was well known as the home of the *Argus*, the city's official Democratic newspaper, which was published here surrounded by competing papers from the mid-19th century until its demise in 1921. This structure may date from the 1830s, when a "Law Building" housing shops as well as lawyers' offices was located on this site. In 1871 the *Argus* added the mansard roof and dormer windows. The corner clock replaced a large letter A.

400-402 Broadway 7
Additions, 1890-95

These two, narrow buildings appear to have been built early in the 19th century, for the width of the facades is indicative of the dimensions of building lots laid out in 17th-century Albany. Elisha Dorr made and sold hats at number 400, while William Fowler sold fine leather goods at 402. Brushes were manufactured at 400 from 1867 to 1939. Large portions of an early 19th-century facade, including splayed brownstone window lintels, remain at number 400. In the early 1890s, the fourth floors of both buildings were added.

Look up Hudson Avenue to number 48, the one-and-one-half-story building facing the parking garage.

Radliff House 8
c. 1759
48 Hudson Avenue
Additions, 1790s, c. 1838

About 1756, the southern wall of the Albany stockade was expanded a block south from what is now Hudson Avenue to Division Street, thereby opening the south side of Hudson Avenue for development. It was probably at about the time of his marriage in 1759 that Johannes Radliff, grandson of a 17th-century immigrant to Beverwyck, built a small, wooden house for his family at what is now 48 Hudson Avenue. The building was enlarged in the early 1790s to accommodate a daughter and her family. The orientation of the gable toward the street, a typical urban Dutch building practice, appears to have been retained from the older house. A storefront was inserted c. 1838 for

Jared Holt, who pioneered the manufacture and marketing of a new wax for stitching leather goods. Asphalt siding and a parapet wall were added a century later. These changes disguise one of the last surviving examples of a Dutch gable-fronted house built in the United States.

388 Broadway 9
New facades, 1882

A cornerstone of Plaza Row, 388 Broadway is enriched with decorative brick arches and panels, a corbelled cornice and terra-cotta ornaments. John Knower had these new facades installed on an earlier structure in 1882 when Hudson Avenue was widened. He kept the property as an investment and rented it to a wholesale confectionery and grocery. Walter Woodward's carriage and saddlery business, here from 1908 to 1919, was suc-ceeded by the more up-to-date Franklin Car and Truck Company and by H. S. Braun, dealers in auto accessories.

R. B. Wing and Son Building 10
384-386 Broadway
Facade, Walter H. van Guysling, 1914

The R. B. Wing and Son Building is an archi-tectural jewel of Plaza Row. The Wing com-pany began business on Quay Street in 1845, selling provisions for sloops and later dealing in supplies and machinery for contractors and industry. In 1912, when the firm's shop at 385 Broadway was scheduled to be demolished for the construction of the Delaware and Hudson Building, Charles C. Wing bought this proper-ty across the street and hired architect Walter H. van Guysling to design a facade appropriate for this newly prominent location. Van Guysling created this whimsical interpretation of Baroque buildings in the Low Countries, surely a nod to his own heritage and to that of Albany and perhaps to the Hudson River Day Line Ticket Office across the street, on which he collabo-rated seven years earlier. The iron sailing ship and dolphins were fabricated by James McKinney and Son of Albany.
Continue south along Broadway.

11

L'Auberge Restaurant 11
1907
Formerly Hudson River Day Line Ticket Office
351 Broadway
Charles G. Ogden and Walter H. van Guysling

A century after Robert Fulton traveled up the Hudson River to Albany in his pioneer steam-boat *North River* (later erroneously called the *Clermont*), the Hudson River Day Line, one of America's most successful steamboat passenger lines, built this structure as a ticket office. Albany architects Charles G. Ogden and Walter H. van Guysling collaborated on the design of the building, which was con-structed in 1907. Their references to Baroque gables and scrolls and the stucco walls create a picturesque composition. The ticket office originally stood about one hundred feet to the north and was moved here when the Delaware and Hudson and the Albany Evening Journal buildings were built. The ticket office was con-verted to a restaurant in the early 1960s.
Walk north to State Street.

State Street 12

The generous width of State Street, which planner Arnold Brunner compared in 1912 to celebrated thoroughfares of European cities, had modest origins. The present street was within the area laid out as the town of Bever-wyck in 1652. The Dutch Church built a house of worship at the foot of the street in 1656, and the English built a church midway up the hill in 1715. By 1800 the street was paved, and a number of prominent Albanians had erected ample houses on both sides. The New York State Bank located its stylish new headquarters on State Street in 1803-04, and the first state Capitol was completed in 1809 at the top of the hill. These factors established State Street as a prestigious address that continued to attract large residences, stores, offices, and nearly every bank that has ever done business in downtown Albany. Many fine 19th- and 20th-century structures remain.

the 1830s. Reynolds, who had a keen interest in the history and architecture of his native city, retained the curved configuration and made it the focus of the new building by locating the primary entry at the corner and placing a domed tower high above it. The facade is ornamented in rich, Renaissance Revival detailing. Similarly styled but less ornate extensions were later added to both the State Street and Broadway facades. Inside is a circular banking room. The stonework, windows and doorways on the ground floor are the result of later remodelings.

14, 15

13

Albany Trust Company   13
Now Key Bank
NW corner of Broadway and State Street
Marcus T. Reynolds

In 1902 the Albany Trust Company commissioned Marcus T. Reynolds to design a new bank building for this prominent site, which had had a rounded-corner building on it since

Hampton Plaza   14
1887
Formerly National Commercial Bank
38 State Street
Robert W. Gibson
Alterations, Marcus T. Reynolds, 1904-06

The banking business in early 19th-century Albany was closely allied with the city's gains in commerce and transportation and enhanced by the proximity of state government, and Albany is still an important regional financial center. The Commercial Bank (now Key Bank) opened for business here in 1826 and in 1887 built anew on the same site. The architect was

Robert W. Gibson, an Englishman who began his career in Albany in 1881. Gibson was an unabashed fan of Henry Hobson Richardson, the nationally prominent architect who had designed the Albany City Hall and portions of the state Capitol. Among Richardson's trademarks were polychromatic patterns of alternating blocks of rough-faced brownstone and granite and richly detailed carving. Gibson created an artful combination of these elements for the front of what was by then called the National Commercial Bank. The upper part of the facade dates from 1904-06, when the building was converted to the Hampton hotel. Architect Marcus T. Reynolds sensitively added two stories by raising the cornice and small gables and tucking compatible stonework and windows in between. Among the noteworthy interior features accessible to the public are a domed main banking room with mosaics, a leaded-glass skylight and a pedestal clock.

Walk west along State Street.

16

Jack's Oyster House   15
1875
42 State Street

This granite facade has a cornice with brackets and modillions, quoins and segmental-arched windows, features typically associated with the Italianate style. This building was built in 1875 for Stephen van Rensselaer Gray, the proprietor of a well-known book and stationery store. A proverb once on the facade—"the fear of the Lord is the beginning of knowledge" —helps to explain why the building was long called Gray's Bible House. Jack's Oyster House has been at this location since 1937.

Key Bank   16
1901-03
Formerly National Commercial Bank
60 State Street
York and Sawyer

National Commercial Bank merged with two other banks in 1901 and had this handsome edifice built between 1901 and 1903. The architects, York and Sawyer of New York City, were nationally recognized specialists in the

design of banks, colleges and hospitals; they were at work on a new building for the New-York Historical Society when this bank was underway. The bold Neo-Classicism of the granite facade with its Ionic portico presents a sharp contrast to the bank's earlier polychromatic Richardsonian Romanesque building at 38 State Street. The entrance originally had bronze paneled doors. An admirer wrote in 1904 that the main banking room had "a general altitude of 45 feet" and was "wainscoted with the choicest marbles most elaborately matched."

Mechanics' and Farmers' Bank   17
1874-75
41 State Street
Russell Sturgis

This building was designed for Mechanics' and Farmers' Bank by Russell Sturgis of New York City and built in 1874-75 by James Eaton. Sturgis became noted for his mastery of the Ruskinian Gothic style, and he produced three important early examples in Albany, including the Learned and Norton houses at 298 and 300 State Street (1873) and this bank, which is one of the best surviving commercial examples of the style in the United States. Sturgis combined brick walls, stone trim, a turret, a rose window and an arched doorway into a handsome corner composition.

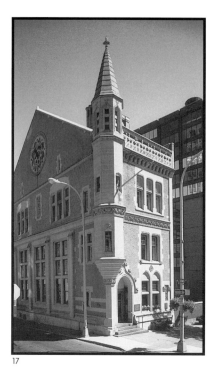

17

Fleet Bank 18

1927

Formerly New York State Bank

69 State Street

Henry Ives Cobb

The New York State Bank was incorporated in 1803 and immediately located its headquarters on this block, making it one of the oldest financial institutions in the nation and the oldest in the United States to occupy the same site continuously. Early in 1803, Albany architect Philip Hooker was commissioned to design its banking house, and his refined, Adamesque treatment placed the new building among the most sophisticated in Albany when it opened in 1804. The carved brownstone details of the surviving facade include rosettes, swags and medallions modeled after the obverse and reverse of an 1803 silver dollar.

More than a century later, recognizing that the original building was an important symbol of the bank's history, the bank's directors and Henry Ives Cobb, a Chicago architect of national renown, decided to incorporate the Hooker facade into a new, sixteen-story office building

and banking house, which was constructed in 1927. After the rest of Hooker's 1803 structure was demolished, its facade was carefully dismantled and moved thirty-seven feet west along State Street so that it would be at the center of the new building. The use of brick and brownstone, Federal-style motifs, and rustication in Cobb's new building echo Hooker's facade. The banking room is decorated with murals by David C. Lithgow, an Albany painter, depicting events in the city's history.

Walk north on North Pearl Street.

18

11 North Pearl Street 19

1927

Formerly Home Savings Bank

Denison and Hirons

Eleven North Pearl Street was completed in 1927 for Home Savings Bank, which had been incorporated in 1871. The flat surfaces of the brick-and-stone Art Deco exterior, designed by Denison and Hirons of New York City, are enlivened by panels of abstract foliation and cast-iron trim. Bronze was used extensively in the lobby. This building is well known in the Albany skyline for its colorful reliefs of European soldiers and American Indians.

19

story Corinthian pillars and a ceiling decorated with acanthus leaf and other classical motifs. The building was the first in the city to have automatic signal-controlled elevators.

21, 22

15 North Pearl Street   20

1937

Formerly S. S. Kresge

When this structure was built as an S. S. Kresge store in 1937, North Pearl Street was an important retail thoroughfare, as popular as today's suburban shopping strips where Kresge now operates as K-Mart. Terra-cotta panels at the top of the facade are marked with the Roman numerals V, X, and XXV, a symbolic and rather elegant way of saying that goods could be bought here for a nickel, a dime or a quarter.

Return to State Street and continue west.

National Savings Bank   21

1929-30

Now Key Bank

90 State Street

Halsey, McCormick and Helmer

National Savings Bank was the fourth high-rise bank built at or near the corner of State and Pearl streets just before the Great Depression. The large arched entrance and two tiers of shops at the ground level add character to this landmark. The elegant lobby retains marble-faced walls, a coffered ceiling, and bronze doors. The lofty banking room has two-

100 State Street   22

1901-02

Formerly Albany City Savings Institution

Marcus T. Reynolds

Addition, Marcus T. Reynolds, 1922-24

Marcus T. Reynolds designed an eight-story bank and office tower with a high, hipped roof in 1901 for the Albany City Savings Institution, which after a merger with the Albany County Savings Bank became known as City and County Savings Bank. The original three-bay-wide structure was expanded by Reynolds in 1922-24 with a six-bay addition to the west with a tower and tiled mansard roof. The granite exterior is lavished with generously-scaled stone ornament—winged lions, cartouches, swags of fruit, scrolled brackets and urn-shaped finials. The main banking room has a vaulted ceiling supported by marble Corinthian pillars.

Walk south on Lodge Street.

23

Ogden's Restaurant   23

1903
Formerly Home Telephone Company
SW corner of Lodge and Howard Streets
Charles Ogden

The designer of this building, Charles Ogden, took full advantage of an irregular site and utilized a variety of architectural devices—two-story arched openings , boldly detailed ornament and a corner entrance—to attract the attention of pedestrians on State Street toward Lodge Street. The building was built in 1903 as the headquarters for the newly established Home Telephone Company. Much of the interior woodwork remains. The name of the restaurant is a salute to the architect.

Return to State Street.

Saint Peter's Church   24

1859-60
NW corner of State and Lodge Streets
Richard Upjohn
Tower, Richard M. Upjohn, 1876

Anglican services were first held in Albany in 1708, primarily for British soldiers and their families. The first church was a gambrel-roofed, masonry structure built in 1715 in the middle of what is now State Street just below Lodge Street. It was replaced by a larger building, designed by Philip Hooker, on this site in 1802. When that structure became seriously deteriorated, Richard Upjohn of New York City was hired to plan a new edifice on the same site. Upjohn was well known as the designer of Trinity

Church in lower Manhattan and as an American pioneer in using the Gothic Revival style for religious structures.

The first phase of the construction of Saint Peter's was completed in 1860. The large blocks of Schenectady bluestone of the exterior walls have weathered to subtle tones of green and red that compliment the sandstone trim. When church member John Tweddle died in 1875, he provided a bequest for a bell tower, which was designed by Upjohn's son, Richard M. Upjohn, and built in 1876. Among the prominent details are three gargoyles, each of which weighs three tons and extend eight feet beyond the walls. A painting of the tower by Edwin Austin Abbey, the celebrated muralist, is in the collection of the Albany Institute of History and Art. The interior is richly decorated with works by leading designers. The Weaver Window (1880) was designed by the English artist Edward C. Burne-Jones and fabricated by the William Morris Company of London. The alter and reredos (1885) were designed by Richard M. Upjohn; Louis St. Gaudens, brother of Augustus St. Gaudens, sculpted the angels on the reredos. In 1885

24

Robert W. Gibson oversaw the redecoration of the walls and in 1886 designed a new pulpit. The chancel windows were made by Clayton and Bell of London in 1885, and the rose window over the State Street entrance was made by the Tiffany Company in 1892. The guild house, choir house and rectory are attributed to Albert Fuller.

109 State Street   25
1914-15

In 1914-15, a residence on State Street and a building to the rear were consolidated and remodeled by contractor Arthur Sayles to house the Matthew Bender and Company publishing company. The firm had sold law books since 1887, and their success in both publishing and selling soon brought them a national trade. The office was located in this building until 1952. The cast-stone facade is filled with graceful Gothic Revival arched panels, and the slender pilasters terminate in ornaments that incorporate open books.

25, 24

126 State Street   26
1915
Formerly Municipal Gas Company
Marcus T. Reynolds

Architect Marcus T. Reynolds gave the offices of the Municipal Gas Company a monumental quality by using large-scale rustication on the first- and second-story facades and three-story Ionic columns. Above, carved on the entabla-

ture in Roman numerals, are two dates—1841, the year that the first gas company in Albany was incorporated, and 1915, the year that this building was under construction. Originally, giant metal torcheres stood at each end of the cornice as symbols of the company's energy products.

26

Hotel Wellington   27
1923
136 State Sreet

The Hotel Wellington, a hostelry popular with state legislators, boasted of offering five hundred rooms when this building opened in 1923. The facade recalls elements of its 19th-century predecessor—the division of the front into four bays, stone lintels and sills that contrast with the brickwork, and a classically inspired entranceway.

Elks Lodge No. 49   28
c. 1911-13
138 State Sreet
M. L. and H. G. Emery

This Beaux-Arts structure was built for an Elks lodge whose membership had grown from eighteen at its founding in 1886 to one thousand when this building was dedicated in 1914. Two Corinthian capitals are embellished with elk's heads, and each cartouche bears an initial of the Benevolent Protective Order of Elks. Brothers Marshall and Henry Emery worked in New York as well as Albany. Henry later practiced in Nyack, New York.

De Witt Clinton Hotel 29
1927
SE corner of State and Eagle Streets
Kenneth Franzheim and C. Howard Crane

Named for an important governor, the De Witt Clinton opened for business in 1927. Designed by Kenneth Franzheim and C. Howard Crane, it has red brick facades with details derived from American colonial architecture. The paneled lobby is decorated with murals of Albany's early history by Victor White. Now used for apartments, the building helps to enclose the open space of Capitol Park and frame the view along State Street.

Walk down State Street, and walk north on Lodge Street.

30

Masonic Temple 30
1895-96
NW corner of Lodge Street and Corning Place
Fuller and Wheeler

Freemasons first established a lodge in Albany in 1737, and in 1768 a lodge was built on this corner. The present building was erected in 1895-96 to the designs of Albany architects Fuller and Wheeler and incorporated such Italian Renaissance-style elements as rusticated stonework, a loggia with Ionic columns and wide eaves. The entry is flanked by polished columns with orbs and protected by a

handsome wrought-iron gate. The bust honors James Ten Eyck, a prominent Albanian and grand master of New York State Masons.

Saint Mary's Centennial Hall 31
1898-99
SW corner of Lodge and Pine Streets
Albert Fuller

This yellow brick Romanesque Revival building was erected as a parochial school to celebrate the centennial of the founding of Albany's first Roman Catholic church. Architect Albert Fuller of Albany incorporated a corbelled cornice, arched windows and doorways, quoins and pilasters into the design of the facades.

32

Saint Mary's Roman Catholic Church 32
1867-69
NE corner of Lodge and Pine Streets
Nichols and Brown
Tower, 1894

Three buildings for Albany's first Roman Catholic church have stood on this block since the first cornerstone was laid in 1797. The second church was designed by Philip Hooker and built in 1829-31. The present brick building with white marble trim was designed by the Albany firm of Nichols and Brown and built in 1867-69; the bell tower was added in 1894. The boldly arched openings in the belfry and the weathervane with the archangel Gabriel blowing his horn are visible from many vantage points in the area. Notable inside are frescoes by Italian artists dating from 1891-95.

Walk east along Pine Street to North Pearl Street, and head north.

33

51-53 North Pearl Street   33
1861
Architectural Iron Works of New York
Addition, c. 1906

Albany's only surviving example of a cast-iron-fronted building dates from 1861, when this facade was made at the Architectural Iron Works of New York, whose owner, Daniel Badger, was a leading proponent of the architectural use of cast iron. He recommended cast iron for its strength, relatively light weight, incombustibility, and durability. The lower two

stories of this building have been altered, but the third and four floors show how using a cast-iron facade made it possible to have windows larger than those in traditional masonry structures and how the iron elements were fashioned to resemble more expensive, carved stone. The B. W. Wooster Furniture Company, which occupied the building from 1884 to 1888, advertised that elevators would carry passengers to the upper floors. The top story was added about 1906 for Julius Saul, operator of a men's clothing store.

59 North Pearl Street   34
c. 1792
Remodeled, 1879

North Pearl Street was considered a prime residential area when merchant Goldsbrow Banyar bought the lot at this corner in 1791. His residence and other Classical Revival houses along the street gradually replaced the earlier, Dutch-influenced dwellings. Although a storefront was inserted on the North Pearl Street front and a fourth floor was added, vestiges of the early facade, including the raised brownstone basement and Flemish-bond brickwork, survive along Steuben Street. From 1819 until his death in 1828, this building was the home of Gov. De Witt Clinton, the major political figure behind the creation of the Erie Canal.

Steuben Athletic Club   35
1886-87
Formerly Young Men's Christian Association
NW corner of North Pearl and Steuben Streets
Fuller and Wheeler

This was Albany's first YMCA building. The architects, Fuller and Wheeler of Albany, subsequently became nationally known as specialists in this building type and were even consulted on the construction of the YMCA in Paris. This building has blocks of contrasting, rough-faced sandstone and granite on the first story, while the upper facades were built of brick with sandstone trim. Of particular note are the broad Romanesque arch at the entrance, the fine stone carving, and the turret, which has lost its conical roof. The building was completed just after the game of basketball was created at the YMCA in Springfield, Massachusetts, and that team's first away game was played here. The building was vacant and seriously deteriorated before it was converted to a club and restaurant in 1982.

Pruyn Building 36
1879-80
70 North Pearl Street
Potter and Robertson

Robert Hewson Pruyn—an Albany attorney, state legislator, banker and U.S. minister to Japan—commissioned New York City architects William A. Potter and Robert H. Robertson to design this store and apartment building, which was constructed in 1879-80. The firm also designed houses at 38 and 44 Willett Street for Pruyn's sons. Potter and Robertson were pioneers in using the Queen Anne style in America, and this facade bears its hallmarks—contrasting materials, highly ornamented gables, paneled chimney stacks, terra-cotta ornament and small panes of glass in upper window sashes. One of the original, elegantly curved storefronts survives. The architects' names and the construction date are inscribed in small panels beside the storefronts, and there is a balcony with delicate ironwork at the third story.

Kenmore Hotel 37
1876-78
74 North Pearl Street
Ogden and Wright
Addition, 1890s

As the state capital and a hub of commerce and transportation, Albany has had a long tradition of hospitality, and this hotel was long a landmark for visitors and residents alike. The architects, Ogden and Wright of Albany, created a brick-and-stone facade rich with High Victorian Gothic elements, including red brick walls, contrasting window lintels, bands of stone, a gable with geometric motifs, and iron balconies and roof cresting. Adam Blake, Jr., a wealthy African-American with a long

history of hotel management in Albany, was the first proprietor of the Kenmore. In the 1940s, the Rain-Bo Room was a popular nightclub that attracted "big bands" on the travel circuit and its most famous patron, gangster Legs Diamond. Like many local adaptive-use projects, the Kenmore sat empty for many years before it was converted to offices in the 1980s.

Columbia Street 38

A look up Columbia Street reveals an attractive streetscape. The 1750s stockade ran up the hill here. Built on a fairly steep incline at the south edge of the ravine now known as Sheridan Hollow, the earliest surviving houses stand west of Chapel Street. The rowhouses east of Chapel were built in 1878, just after the Kenmore Hotel was constructed and given the now obsolete address of Kenmore Place.

79 North Pearl Street 39
1887
Formerly College Place
Ogden and Wright
Addition, 1893

This building at the corner of Columbia Street was constructed for the Albany Business College in two phases. The ten northernmost bays were built in 1887, and the rest was completed in 1893. The architects, Ogden and Wright of Albany, who had designed the polychromatic facade for the Kenmore across the street a decade earlier, chose here to adapt more features associated with the Richardsonian Romanesque—rough-faced brownstone trim, arched windows and a short tower with a conical roof above the rounded corner bay. Founded in 1857, Albany Business College trained men and women for executive and secretarial positions and had a special department for state and federal civil service jobs. The school remained here until about 1933, when it moved to 130 Washington Avenue.

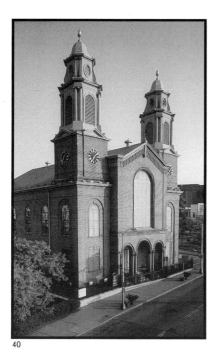

40

First Church in Albany   40
1797-99
SW corner of North Pearl and Orange Streets
Philip Hooker with Elisha Putnam
Remodeled, Von Steinwehr and Hodgins, 1857

This is the fourth church building erected for
the Dutch Reformed Church of Albany, which
was organized in 1642. The design, by Albany
architect Philip Hooker, resembles 18th-century
churches in England and may have been
adapted from Charles Bulfinch's Hollis Street
Church in Boston. The dignity of the building
lies in its delicate and graceful treatment of
late Georgian-style elements, particularly on
the towers, where there are small pediments,
oval vents, Baroque scrolls and acorn finials.
Although the towers are essentially original in
appearance, the portico was added in 1858,
by architects Von Steinwehr and Hodgins, who
also remodeled the interior. Hooker's 1798
portico had a triangular pediment decorated
with swags and supported by columns. The
pulpit dates from 1656 and was used in the
congregation's first building, at the foot of
Broadway. In 1910 the interior was extensively

redecorated by the Tiffany Company, which
installed the present stained-glass windows.
   *Return south on North Pearl Street, and turn
down Columbia Street.*

48 Columbia Street   41
1834

Columbia Street was once lined with elegant
19th-century townhouses. Many still stand west
of Chapel Street, but commercial development
east of North Pearl prompted many owners to
insert storefronts in former residences. This
building is a rare survivor that has retained its
original entrance. It was built in 1834 for
Catharine Visscher, a widow, and her children.
The entry has fluted Ionic columns, egg-and-
dart molding and delicate grilles over the
sidelights and transom. The rear parlor has
curved corner closets, a popular motif in
Albany houses built in the 1820s and 1830s.

41

Kennedy Garage 42
1925
45 Columbia Street

The facade of the Kennedy Garage, built in 1925, resembles those of commercial buildings of the same era, and it blends in well with its surroundings. Originally it also housed the offices of the Kennedy Construction Company.
Walk east to Broadway.

43

United Traction Company 43
1899-1900
600 Broadway
Marcus T. Reynolds

Now called the Pieter Schuyler Building, this structure exemplifies how the monumental Beaux-Arts style was used successfully for smaller buildings. The design was prepared by Marcus T. Reynolds for the offices of Albany's streetcar system, the United Traction Company. Built in 1899-1900, the facades of buff Roman brick are enriched with fluted, banded columns, cartouches, window and door surrounds and garlands. The interior has paneled ceilings and marble floors.

Union Station 44
1899-1900
Now Pieter D. Kiernan Plaza
575 Broadway
Shepley, Rutan and Coolidge

The New York Central and the Hudson River railroads were among the most successful American rail lines in the 19th century, because they were centrally located in the most industrialized section of the country and because they provided a quick, water-level route without grades to the West. Cornelius Vanderbilt consolidated the two lines in 1869. Another major line, the Boston and Albany Railroad, was added to the New York Central system in 1899. Their juncture was at Albany, and Union Station became the symbolic focus of the new system. Upon its completion in 1900, this imposing granite structure was the passenger station for the New York Central and Hudson River, the Boston and Albany, and the Delaware and Hudson railroads; it also housed division offices.

As the successors to H. H. Richardson, the Boston-based firm of Shepley, Rutan and Coolidge had designed numerous train stations, initially following Richardson's precedents but favoring the Beaux-Arts style by the turn of the century. In the firm's design of Albany's Union Station, passengers entered and left the building through great arched openings that led into the lofty, 110-foot-high waiting room.

The last train left here in December, 1968, and a small station was built across the Hudson River in Rensselaer. During the 1970s, Union Station suffered from small trees growing from its roof, falling plaster and vandalism. Government and corporate cooperation saved the building when Peter Kiernan, head of Norstar Bancorp, decided to convert it to the holding company's headquarters. Renovation began in 1984 under the direction of Einhorn, Yaffee, Prescott Architects and was completed two years later. Few changes were needed outside, but inside the original waiting room space was changed by raising the floor one story in order to accommodate computer equipment and

44

moving the walls with the cast-iron galleries forward. In conjunction with this project, the city of Albany created Tricentennial Park across the street, which features an interpretation of the city seal by political cartoonist Hy Rosen.

Arcade Building   45
1928
488 Broadway

Built in 1928, the Arcade Building has yellow brick walls and panels of abstract, Art Deco-style foliation. Within, shops open onto a wide, central hallway. A shopping arcade is a commercial building type that dates to the early 19th century in the United States; a much expanded version is the modern suburban mall.

472-478 Broadway   46

Numbers 476-478 were occupied for many years beginning in 1860 by Strong Brothers, "importers and jobbers of dry goods." About 1884 Cotrell and Leonard moved into 472-474 and in 1897 took over 476-478. They advertised in 1884 that theirs was "the most complete" hat and fur store in the United States. Today the buildings are vacant, but they are rare examples of large-scale mercantile houses that were once common in downtown Albany.

U.S. Post Office, Courthouse   47
and Customshouse
1932-34
SE corner of Broadway and Maiden Lane
Electus D. Litchfield, consulting architect
Gander, Gander and Gander
Norman R. Sturgis

This splendid Art Deco structure was conceived and constructed as a solid and dignified symbol of the presence of the Federal government at the center of downtown Albany. Executed in fine materials worked with excellent craftsmanship, the building represented the best efforts of its designers—Electus D. Litchfield, a distinguished New York City architect, and two Albany firms: Gander, Gander and Gander, the architects of record, and Norman R. Sturgis, associate architect. The design shows the influence of Philadelphia architect Paul

46, 45

47

Philippe Cret in the careful integration of classical and modern design elements and the axial organization of the plan with grand public entrances and generous circulation spaces.

Completed in 1934, the steel-frame building has Vermont marble facades with eagles carved over the two main entrances and an eight-foot-high frieze, also sculpted by Albert T. Stewart, depicting the activities of the post office, customshouse and federal court. Inside, the lobby walls and floors are finished with colored marbles and mosaics, and the ceiling of the 186-foot-long main hall is decorated with maps of the continents and likenesses of famous Americans who had appeared on postage stamps. Many original light fixtures, railings and other metalwork survive.

The preliminary outline and text for this tour were prepared by Douglas Sinclair and funded by the Architecture, Planning and Design Program of the New York State Council on the Arts.

107

Pastures and Mansions
of the South End

Anthony Opalka

10 Madison Place

The northernmost part of Albany's South End underwent significant changes after 1960 with construction of the Empire State Plaza and Interstate 787. As interest in historic preservation grew in the 1970s and 1980s, the Pastures Historic District and the Mansion Historic District were established. The following history examines the development of these two areas. The first part of the tour covers the Pastures Historic District. The second part explores the hillside Mansion District.

The Pastures Historic District takes its name from the earliest use of the land as a common grazing area. Almost the entire tract of land east of South Pearl Street between what is now Madison Avenue and the former south boundary of the city at Gansevoort Street was deeded to the Dutch Reformed Church in 1687, just one year after the Dongan Charter created the city of Albany. At that time, the Dutch Reformed Church was one of the most powerful institutions in the city, and there was little separation between church and state.

Throughout the 17th and most of the 18th centuries, most settlement in Albany was located within the stockade and centered around what is now State Street and Broadway in downtown Albany. South Pearl Street was a land route to the south, and prior to the 1780s, a road led from South Pearl Street through the pasture to a ferry slip. The ferry to Greenbush (now part of the city of Rensselaer) was for nearly two hundred years the principal means of crossing the Hudson River for residents of Albany.

In 1789 South Ferry Street was opened. It ran perpendicular to South Pearl Street and divided the area into upper and lower pastures. South Ferry and South Pearl determined the orientation of the other streets in the former pasture, which were laid out in a grid pattern forming small blocks in 1791. Since the Dutch Reformed Church wanted to maximize its profits, no provision was made for public squares or open spaces. Most building lots faced the east-west streets, and most streets were named for ministers of the Reformed Church. North of South Ferry Street, only Westerlo Street retains its original name. The lots were sold at auction after 1791, but it appears that little if any construction took place in the area until after 1800. No 18th-century buildings survive.

After 1800, the city's population began to grow as New Englanders migrated westward. With the introduction of the steamboat in 1807 and completion of the Erie Canal in 1825, Albany became an important river port and commercial center. The growing population created a housing boom, and the city expanded southward.

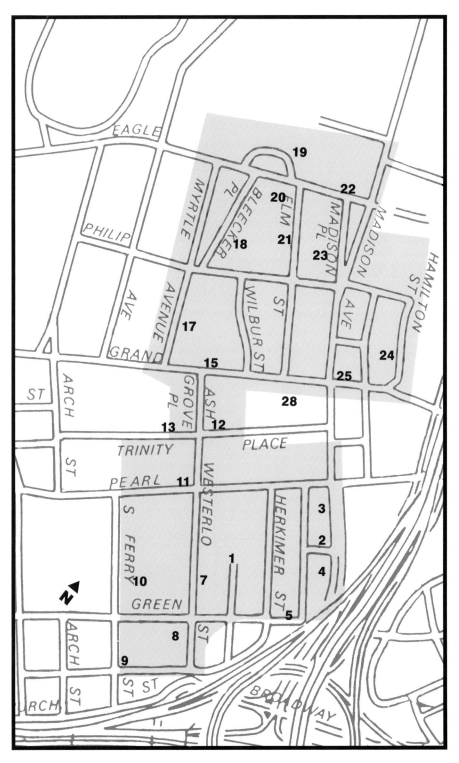

By 1850, the area as far south as Gansevoort Street from the river to beyond South Pearl Street was almost completely built up.

West of South Pearl Street, in the area now called the Mansion Historic District, development patterns were very different. Instead of one large tract of undeveloped land, there were large land holdings owned by individuals, often with a mansion house on each parcel. As urbanization fanned out from downtown in the 19th century, the estates were broken up and subdivided. Many of the speculators who purchased lots were masons or builders (unlike speculators in the pasture area, who typically were not engaged in the building trades). Among the more important developers in the Mansion District were Bradford Hand, who built houses in the late 1830s and early 1840s; Andrew Cunningham and David Orr, who were active in the 1840s and 1850s; and James Eaton, who seems to have begun his career here in the 1850s and became one of Albany's most prolific builders. Development began in the late 1830s and was essentially complete by the late 1870s, with most construction occurring just before the Civil War. Architecturally, the Mansion Historic District evolved from the late Greek Revival through the Gothic Revival and early Italianate, unlike the former pasture, where the Federal and Greek Revival styles predominated.

Like neighborhoods in other cities prior to the Civil War, this part of the South End was characterized by mixed land uses: residences, churches and synagogues, schools, breweries, large factories and a host of smaller industries existed in close proximity to one another. Families of different income levels, occupations and races lived in the same neighborhood and were employed in the nearby factories and shops and in businesses related to the bustling river trade.

Beginning in the 1840s, European immigrants began to change the character of what is now the South End. While most buildings had been constructed for individuals with Dutch or English surnames, Irish and German immigrants occupied them later in the century. After 1880, eastern European Jews joined the German-Jewish families who had lived in the South End beginning in the 1840s. Soon after 1900, the ethnic character changed again, as Italian immigrants made their homes there. After World War II, a number of black families moved from southern states to the South End.

Long periods of disruption caused by construction of the Empire State Plaza and the arterial highways, demolition carried out for urban renewal, and the erection of housing projects to the south brought more changes to the South End in the late 1950s and early 1960s. Construction of Interstate 787 and the spur to the Plaza formed new northern boundaries. The Pastures Historic District—bounded roughly by South Pearl and South Ferry streets and Dongan and Madison avenues—contains only about one-quarter of the original area of the pasture and today only a fraction of the historic buildings that once stood there. There has been much less demolition in the adjacent Mansion Historic District, which is delineated by the Empire State Plaza on the west and 1960s high-rise public housing to the south. Designated an urban renewal area in the early 1960s, the entire Pastures Historic District was acquired by the Albany Urban Renewal Agency in the 1970s. Originally scheduled for total demolition, it instead became one of Albany's first large-scale historic preservation projects, with "homesteading" initiatives for individual homeowners and subsidized housing in other buildings; the remaining structures were rehabilitated as condominiums and apartments. New housing on the east side of South Pearl Street was constructed in the late 1980s. As a result of the investment of federal Community Development and private funds, the Mansion Historic District also contains many rehabilitated houses, and both areas are viable neighborhoods that tell an important part of the story of Albany's development.

Pastures Tour

Start at Herkimer and Franklin streets.

Congregation Beth El Jacob   1
1907
90 Herkimer Street

Although Albany had a Jewish population as early as the 17th century, the first congregation was not formed until 1838; known as Congregation Beth El, it was made up mostly of German immigrants who lived in this area. Three years later, some members formed a new congregation known as Beth El Jacob and in 1907 had this new temple constructed. It has a rusticated stone foundation, yellow brick walls and matching towers. In 1974 Congregation Beth El Jacob merged with the Sons of Abraham to form Beth Abraham Jacob and sold this building to the Saint John's Church of God in Christ, its current occupant.
    Walk north on Franklin Street to Madison Avenue.

1

96 Madison Avenue   2
c. 1811

This three-and-one-half story brick building, attributed to Albany architect Philip Hooker, was constructed around 1811 for John Stafford, a hardware merchant, who lived in the house until his death in 1819. Joel Munsell, a 19th-century Albany historian, described it as

"the most elegant private residence of its size in the city." Joseph C. Yates rented the house in 1823 and 1824, while serving as governor, and remodeled portions of the interior. Later owners included a prominent Albany lawyer, James King, who occupied the house in the early 1830s and sold it in 1836 to Obidiah van Benthuysen, a well-known Albany printer and the publisher of the Albany *Argus*. After 1888, the first floor was converted to commercial use, and the storefront was added. From 1905 until the 1970s, Murray's Confectionery occupied the first floor.

Architecturally, this is one of the most outstanding buildings in the Pastures. The walls are laid up in Flemish bond, and the sandstone entrance is carved with Greek frets, rosettes, bellflowers, garlands and wreaths. Upper windows have carved sandstone lintels, and the Franklin Street elevation has two oval windows, a feature popular in finer houses of the Federal period. The front second-story windows originally had false balustrades similar to those at the Ten Broeck Mansion. The gabled roof is visible from Franklin Street. The sheet-metal cornice of the later storefront is stamped with wreaths and swags.

100 Madison Avenue 3
1808

The oldest surviving structure in the Pastures Historic District and one of the oldest remaining in Albany, this house was constructed in 1808 by Spencer Stafford, a wealthy Albany merchant. Originally it was a freestanding structure, five bays wide with a gabled roof, surrounded on either side by open land and Stafford's gardens. Following Stafford's death in 1844, his heirs sold the adjacent parcels. The Greek Revival house at 102 Madison,

which retains its original carved sandstone entry and door trim, was constructed shortly thereafter by John J. Hill, an attorney. The Stafford residence was sold to Isaac Wyckoff, pastor of the Middle Dutch Church, and in 1868 to Patrick Wallace, who enlarged it and converted the first floor to a liquor store around 1869. A third story, an Italianate cornice and storefronts were added, but the Flemish-bond brickwork of the original second story is still visible. The buildings at 98, 98½, and 104 Madison were constructed in the second half of the 19th century.

Walk east on Madison Avenue toward Green Street.

82-94 Madison Avenue 4
c. 1814, 1827

Constructed around 1814, these rowhouses are among the earliest buildings in this neighborhood. Four were initially owned by Dudley Walsh, a prominent Albanian. He was a founder of Union College and the Albany Academy, president of the Bank of Albany and partner in Walsh and Staats, dealers in ''domestic products, imported articles and landed property.'' Up until the Civil War, the other houses were rented to individuals involved in Hudson River shipping or to members of Albany's burgeoning mercantile class.

2 - 4

Number 82, built in 1827, was the home of bookseller Oliver Steele for about ten years. In the later 19th century, as the socio-economic and ethnic character of the neighborhood changed, some buildings were converted to stores and apartments. Owners and occupants at the turn of the century included eastern European Jewish tailors, merchants and jewelers; they were followed by Italian-born restauranteurs, laborers and barbers. The earlier buildings exhibit many characteristics typical of Federal-period rowhouses, such as high, stone basements, brick walls laid in Flemish bond, round-arched doorways with spring blocks and keystones, and gable roofs with ridges parallel to the street. Numbers 82 and 88 retain dormers, another feature commonly identified with Federal and Greek Revival rowhouses.

Walk south on Green Street.

103-111 Green Street 5
1819

In the original subdivision of the pasture, most building lots faced the streets that ran east-west. However, many speculators immediately reconfigured their property to face Green Street, thereby causing it to develop as a major throughfare and increasing the value of their lots. In 1819, a prominent Albany lawyer, John Lansing, Jr., had these five buildings constructed on land he had recently purchased. Lansing served as military secretary to the Revolutionary War general and Albany native Philip Schuyler and as speaker of the state Assembly, delegate to the Constitutional Convention, member of Congress and mayor of Albany. Among the early occupants on this block was Philip Hooker, generally considered to be Albany's first architect.

Around 1868, Thomas O'Connor purchased the row and operated a grocery store at 103. Numbers 105 and 107 were converted to commercial uses after 1900. The Italianate storefront and cornice at 111 may date from around 1879, when the house was sold to Joseph and Emily Ruelle, natives of Germany, who converted it to a saloon, liquor store and pool room; like other buildings in the

neighborhood, it became an Italian grocery around 1920. The Blue Note Cafe, operated by John and Louella Dozier, occupied 111 Green Street between 1953 and 1965. The row is a good example of modest Federal-period residential architecture. It retains Flemish-bond brickwork, some original arched doorways, gable roofs and simply tooled, splayed sandstone lintels over the upper windows.

132-138 Green Street 6
c. 1830

These four structures are typical of speculative housing that characterized the development of the pasture area. Originally part of the six-building row, they were constructed about 1830 for William James, a wealthy Albany businessman and grandfather of novelist Henry James and philosopher William James. The elder James leased five of the buildings as residences and 138 as a grocery with living quarters above. The high basements and stone water tables, six-over-six window sash, gable roofs and dormers are typical of Federal-period buildings in Albany. The lintels are one of the earliest uses of architectural cast iron in this area.

Throughout this historic district, several buildings retain their original double-parlor first-floor plans, as well as decorative woodwork and molded plasterwork. In a few buildings, curved corner closets in the rear parlors, an element common to more prestigious residences, can be found.

Turn west on Westerlo Street.

7

48-66 Westerlo Street 7

1828-31

Henry Rector and Darius Geer, builders

This part of the block was sold as unimproved lots in 1793 and again in 1827, after the speculator-owners reconfigured them into smaller parcels. In 1828 innkeeper Thomas Thomas constructed 48 and 50 Westerlo as rental property. Henry Rector and Darius Geer, two men then identified as carpenters, purchased the lots at 52 through 58 in 1828 and then built and sold the buildings in 1829. Rector, who became one of Albany's leading architects, designed the State Hall on Eagle Street, now the home of the New York State Court of Appeals, as well as many residences and churches around Albany. The house at 54 Westerlo was once occupied by Seth Geer, builder of Colonnade Row on Lafayette Street in New York City and Albany Academy. The remaining four buildings were constructed in 1830-31; the doorways were made even more elegant with the addition of fretwork lintels. Three elliptical windows grace the west side of 66, and the doorway has more elaborate, Ionic capitals. This is the longest Federal-period row remaining in Albany.

8

Saint John's Roman Catholic Church 8

1903-08

SE corner of Green and Westerlo Streets

Charles Ogden

This imposing limestone church was designed by Albany architect Charles Ogden and constructed between 1903 and 1908, after the congregation had outgrown a smaller building a block to the south. Original plans called for much taller, matching spires, which would have given the building a grander appearance. This is the second building constructed for the parish. As population shifted after World War II, this parish was merged with Saint Ann's to the south. This building has stood vacant awaiting reuse since the late 1970s.

Walk south on Green Street to South Ferry Street, then east on South Ferry to Dongan Avenue.

9

Saint John's School 9

1828-29

Formerly Saint Paul's Episcopal Church

NW corner of South Ferry Street and Dongan Avenue

Philip Hooker

This two-story limestone building was designed by Albany architect Philip Hooker and constructed in 1828-29. Described as an example of "the Gothic order of architecture" with lancet-arched windows and entrance, it originally housed Saint Paul's Episcopal Church. Saint John's, Albany's second Roman Catholic parish, was founded in 1837 and purchased this building two years later. Some remodeling was carried out, but the essential form was retained. As the Catholic population of the South End swelled with new immigrants, a larger church was built on Green Street, and this building was remodeled into Saint John's School. The windows were changed at that time.

Walk west on South Ferry Street.

59-61 and 65-71 South Ferry Street   10
c. 1815-32

Along this block of South Ferry Street are several Federal-period houses developed by James Boyd and others between about 1815 and 1832. Boyd owned the Arch Street Brewery, which stood directly across South Ferry Street and extended a full block south to Arch Street. He had founded the brewery in 1796 and around 1815 built a house for himself at 73 South Ferry Street (which no longer stands) along with five buildings at 67-71 and 75-77 South Ferry, which he conveyed to his five sons in 1822. Some were partners in the brewery, while others were merchants and landowners and retained the properties for rental income. William Fowler, a merchant, had the house at 59 constructed in 1827, and in the same year Robert Boyd, son of James and a partner in

10

the brewery, built a nearly identical house, with similarly paneled window lintels and doorway, next door at 61. Number 61 has a fine wrought-iron railing with Gothic tracery, probably made by Albany blacksmith Amos Fish. The Italianate style house at 63 with the richly sculpted entrance dates from the 1860s; it was once a Turkish bath.

The high-style brick townhouse with the ornate wrought-iron railing at number 65 was built by Russell Forsyth, a merchant. When completed in 1832, it was described in the tax rolls as a "superb dwelling" with "back buildings and gardens." Thomas Schuyler, president of First National Bank, purchased the house from Forsyth around 1850 and lived there until his death in 1875. It was later converted to apartments. The three-story houses at 59, 61, and 65 are notable for the use of white marble on their basements and stoops. Number 65 has freestanding columns at the entry and is the only building in the neighborhood with a pressed-brick facade. The smaller houses constructed by the Boyds also have Flemish-bond brick facades, cut stone foundations and splayed stone lintels.

Robert Boyd was active in religious circles and erected the Rensselaer Street Mission Sabbath School a few blocks south of his residence. This institution later moved to 77 South Ferry Street, the former home of Rabbi Isaac Mayer Wise. One of the founders of Reform Judaism, Wise conducted services in his home around 1850 and founded Albany's Congregation Anshe Emeth, the fourth reformed congregation in the United States. The corner building at 71 was converted to a synagogue by Congregation Agudas Achim in the early 20th century. Founded by eastern European Jews, this congregation merged with Beth El Jacob on Herkimer Street in 1959. The building retains a Star of David window.

Walk north on Franklin Street to Westerlo Street, then west on Westerlo to South Pearl Street.

South Pearl Street   11

South Pearl Street was one of the earliest roads leading south from Albany. Once known as Washington Street, it led into the Bethlehem Turnpike after 1800 and separated the former common pasture from the large properties to the west, including the Van Zandt, Kane, Schuyler, and Van Rensselaer (Cherry Hill) estates. With the breakup of these parcels in the early 19th century, the lots along the street were developed. The first horsecar line in Albany was constructed here in 1862. As immigrants from Ireland, Germany and eastern and southern Europe poured into the South End between the Civil War and World War I, South Pearl Street became a thriving commercial neighborhood. Virtually every building along the street housed small retail enterprises, such as bakeries, butcher shops, and clothing stores at street level, with residences above. After World War II, South Pearl Street lost its commercial vitality, and in the late 1970s the east side of the street was demolished for urban renewal. Within the past decade, residential and commercial uses have returned to rehabilitated historic buildings and new rowhouses have been built on the east side of the street.

12

Mansions Tour

Start at Ashgrove Place, at the northwest corner of Trinity Place and Westerlo Street.

2 Ashgrove Place   12

37-45 Trinity Place
1839

The residence at 2 Ashgrove Place and the adjacent row at 37-45 Trinity Place were constructed in 1839 by Alexander Gray and his son William, stone masons and owners of a nearby stone yard. They lived in the row for a time and later sold it. The rowhouses exhibit Greek Revival features, including high stone basements with curved stoops; simple lintels and sills; recessed entries with pilasters, sidelights and transoms; and brick frieze cornices. The corner building at 2 Ashgrove Place is much more highly decorated and has white marble trim. From 1848 to 1894 it was the home of Samuel Schuyler, a ship captain, who was one of the city's wealthiest and most prominent men. By 1857 he extended the original

three-bay-wide house westward, and he evidently added the spectacular belvedere, which provided sweeping views of the city.

Visible on the west side of Trinity Place to the north is the now-vacant Trinity Church, constructed in the early 1840s to the designs of James Renwick, architect of New York City's Saint Patrick's Cathedral. While the church has been vacant for the past several years, Trinity Institution, a social services agency, has been active since the early 20th century.

Philip Schuyler High School   13
1914
69 Trinity Place
Walter H. van Guysling

This imposing Collegiate Gothic building, designed by Albany architect Walter H. van Guysling, was constructed in 1914 as Public School 14 on the site of the Ashgrove Methodist Church, which in turn had replaced the Revolutionary War-era mansion house of James Kane. The school's prominent tower is visible from many parts of the adjacent neighborhoods. The tower is flanked by three-story wings with grouped windows under Tudor arches and separated by prominent buttresses. Separate girls' and boys' entrances, once a common arrangement, were provided at the north and south ends. During the 1930s,

13

the building was converted from an elementary school to Philip Schuyler High School, which closed in the early 1970s. After standing vacant for more than ten years, it was adapted to apartments and condominiums.

13-19 Ashgrove Place   14

These four buildings were constructed in the late 1860s following the demolition of the mansion that stood on land now occupied by the former Philip Schuyler High School. The three easternmost buildings were built as income property by Samuel Schuyler, owner of 2 Ashgrove Place. Schuyler's buildings have some of the most elaborate ironwork in the neighborhood—full-width balconies on the parlor floors, molded door and window lintels, and at number 13 fluted balusters intended to look like carved stone.

Walk west to Grand Street.

Grand Street   15

Grand Street was originally known as Hallenbake Street, after the farm and burial ground of the Hallenbake family. Once the area was subdivided in the late 1830s, rows of brick townhouses sprang up. Its relatively narrow width and fairly uniform building types make this one of the neighborhood's most cohesive streetscapes.

115 Grand Street   16

1840s
New facade, Gander, Gander and Gander 1927

Constructed as a residence during the 1840s, this building was the Albany Eye and Ear Infirmary by 1876. In 1927, it was converted to the Masterson Day Nursery, a day-care center operated by the Albany Catholic Diocese that served the nearby immigrant population. In the 1960s, it became the Saint Charles Lwanga Center, a residence for recovering alcoholics. The new facade was erected in 1927 to the designs of Gander, Gander and Gander.

Walk south to Myrtle Avenue, then west along Myrtle Avenue to Philip Street.

3-23 Myrtle Avenue   17

1873-74

The north side of Myrtle between Grand and Philip streets was developed in 1873-74 with three sets of slightly varied Italianate-style brick rowhouses built for middle-class families. All of the buildings feature high basements, cast-iron window and door trim and bracketed cornices, but the ornamental details on each group are slightly different. Although not individually distinctive, they make a striking composition as they climb the street.

Walk up Bleecker Place to Eagle Street.

Bleecker Place   18

The oblique path of Bleeker Place deviates from the grid of other streets because it follows the south boundary of land once owned by the prominent Bleecker family. After the estate was subdivided around 1850, frame cottages were constructed by wagon makers, coopers and other tradesmen. While no two houses are identical, all exhibit simplified Greek Revival details. Pilasters surround doorways at 11 and 27, and shouldered and battered doorway and window architraves are present

18

at 9, 13, 15, 17 and 25. The modestly bracketed cornices, like that at number 7, signal the onset of the Italianate style.

Executive Mansion 19

c. 1856
138 Eagle Street
Alterations, 1860s
Alterations, Isaac G. Perry, 1886

The Executive Mansion was constructed around 1856 as a private residence by Thomas Olcott of the Mechanics' and Farmers' Bank; he was the son of Thomas W. Olcott, who owned the Ten Broeck Mansion. The Italianate-style Olcott house had a gabled roof, an impressive wrap-around porch and elaborate wooden detailing. Since the state did not provide its governors with an official residence, Gov. Samuel Tilden rented this house from Robert L. Johnson, who had purchased the house from Olcott. Johnson remodeled it in the 1860s in the then-fashionable Second Empire style, adding a mansard roof with dormers, an impressive tower, large porches on either side, and a stone entrance portico. In 1877, under Gov. Lucius Robinson, the state

purchased the property from Johnson for use as the Executive Mansion. Isaac G. Perry, hired in 1883 to complete work on the new Capitol, was commissioned to overhaul and expand the mansion in 1886. He completely changed its appearance, adding Queen Anne details.

Turn north on Eagle Street.

139-145 Eagle Street 20

1891-92

These three-and-one-half-story residences were constructed in 1891-92. The two north-

19

20

ernmost buildings were owned by Timothy Sullivan, manager of Albany Brass and Iron, and his wife, Sarah. They lived at 139 and rented 141 to Albert Marx, a merchant tailor, until 1904, when the building was sold to Frederick Grey, one of the owners of Welsh and Grey, lumber dealers. Sullivan's and Grey's widows occupied the houses until after 1920. The southern buildings were owned for many years by Eugene Wood, a clerk, who occupied 145 and rented 143. These rowhouses are the only examples which remain of the Richardsonian Romanesque style in this part of Albany; they have heavily rusticated sandstone fronts, foliated carving and oriel windows. The original wrought-iron railings are intact.

Turn east on Elm Street.

21

48-68 Elm Street 21
1858
James Eaton, builder

These eleven buildings were constructed as speculative housing in 1858 by James Eaton, whose career included the construction of over five hundred residences as well as service as superintendent of construction of the Capitol, a post he held from 1874 until 1883. Each slightly projecting pavilion is capped by a false

gable and bracketed cornice. The round-headed windows of the third floor are another typical Italianate characteristic. Numbers 48, 58, 60, 62 and 66 retain their original iron railings and sandstone stoops. This rowhouse design must have proven popular, for Eaton in 1859 built an identical group around the corner on Philip Street.

Return to Eagle Street, and walk north to Madison Place.

Cathedral of the Immaculate 22
Conception
1848-52
SW corner of Eagle Street and Madison Avenue

The Cathedral of the Immaculate Conception was constructed between 1848 and 1852. It was the second Roman Catholic cathedral built in the state and was erected to house the seat of the Albany Diocese. Formed in 1847, the Albany Diocese stretched west to Rochester and north to the Saint Lawrence River. The cathedral was designed by Patrick Keeley of Brooklyn, one of the foremost architects of Catholic churches of the period and later the architect of Albany's Saint Joseph's Church on Ten Broeck Street in Arbor Hill. The inspiration

22

for the design was the Cologne Cathedral in Germany, which was then nearing completion.

Some thought that this hilltop site was too far away from the rest of Albany; the parish where it was located was described as being "exceedingly small, and the land about the church unsettled." Soon, however, the neighborhood began to grow up around it, and the building loomed over its small-scale neighbors. The dedication was held in 1852, although many interior details remained unfinished, including the main altar, which had not yet arrived from Rome. The building is constructed of brick faced with Connecticut sandstone and is a Latin cross plan. Lancet-arched stained-glass windows depicting biblical scenes are arranged along the north and south walls. The five-bay-long nave is articulated by flying buttresses on the exterior and by clustered columns on the interior. The foliated capitals and ribbed vaulting are plaster, made to resemble stone. The cast-iron fence was made by the Albany firm of Haskell and Orchard, which cast its name on the gateposts.

6-10 Madison Place 23
1845-48
David Orr and Andrew Cunningham, builders

Just one block long, Madison Place faces Bleecker Park, which was laid out in 1835. Numbers 6-10 were built a decade later, between 1845 and 1848, by David Orr and Andrew Cunningham. Orr, one of the wealthiest men in Albany in the mid-19th century, developed vast tracts of land in what is now the Mansion Historic District, Lincoln Park and the Empire State Plaza areas. The six buildings that he and Cunningham, a mason, built along Madison Place have high-style Gothic Revival features more usually associated with freestanding cottages—not surprisingly since the inspiration was Kenwood, the Rathbone house designed by Alexander Jackson Davis, and built by David Orr about a mile and a half south of here. Gothic tracery in wood and cast iron abounds—around the entrance, atop the windows, on the doors and in the railings. These Gothic Revival elements make this one of the most unusual collections of rowhouses in

the United States. The partners were also responsible for 17 and 21 Elk Street, just north of the Capitol. James Eaton built the house at 1 Madison Place as his personal residence about 1855; the small building directly behind it is believed to have been his shop and office.

Walk east on Madison Place to Philip Street, north on Philip to Hamilton Street, then east on Hamilton to Grand Street.

Hamilton Street 24

This stretch of Hamilton Street between Grand and Philip streets offers another glimpse of the mid-19th century residential streetscapes that graced much of downtown Albany prior to construction of the Empire State Plaza and the associated highways. It is also the only location where the tracks of Albany's once extensive electric steetcar system are still visible.

Walk south on Grand Street, cross Madison Avenue, and continue south on Grand.

24

57-65 Grand Street 25

145 Madison Avenue
1840
David Orr and Bradford Hand, builders

This row and the adjacent corner building at 145 Madison Avenue were constructed in 1840 by builders David Orr and Bradford Hand. For several years afterwards, 145 Madison Avenue was Orr's family residence and office, but the other buildings were sold shortly after construction. The buildings were designed in a severe Greek Revival Style, with undecorated stone basements, lintels and sills and simple, recessed entries with pilasters, sidelights and transoms. Some buildings retain their original masonry stoops and simple brick cornices. These buildings may be the oldest surviving examples of Orr's work.

25

146 Madison Avenue
1828

26

This two-and-one-half-story brick building is one of the oldest structures remaining in this neighborhood. Constructed in 1828, it has housed a grocery store in the basement for virtually its entire history. Owners have included Samuel Martin (1828-57), Daniel Eaton (after 1859), J. Gifford (1891-1904), Francis Thornton (1904-20), the Ciani family (who operated the Grand Street Cash Market between 1920 and the late 1970s) and now the Panetta family. It is a fine example of Federal-period architecture in the district, with its five-bay-wide facade of Flemish-bond brick, high stone basement, gabled roof and dormers.

Saint Anthony's Roman
Catholic Church
1908-15
SE corner of Grand Street and
Madison Avenue
Charles Ogden

27

Saint Anthony's was built between 1908 and 1915 to accommodate the large Italian population that had recently taken up residence in the South End. The building was designed by Albany architect Charles Ogden, whose new home for Saint John's Church on Green Street was completed in the same year. This parish remained strong throughout the mid-20th century, and Italian street festivals were held on Grand Street through the 1950s. When construction of the Empire State Plaza

scattered the Italian population, Saint Anthony's declined, and the church was closed in 1974. Since then, several attempts have been made to convert the building to an Italian cultural center.

Walk south on Grand Street.

78-92 Grand Street
1853

28

Constructed in 1853, these eight buildings originally had identical Gothic Revival facades. They may be the earliest surviving work of James Eaton, who put up other rows in this neighborhood and sold them to individuals. Much simpler than the high-style Gothic Revival row on Madison Place, these buildings nevertheless have similar finials, drip mouldings over the openings and projecting bays.

Center Square and Hudson-Park Neighborhoods:
Between Parks and Public Spaces

Cornelia Brooke Gilder

284 - 290 State Street

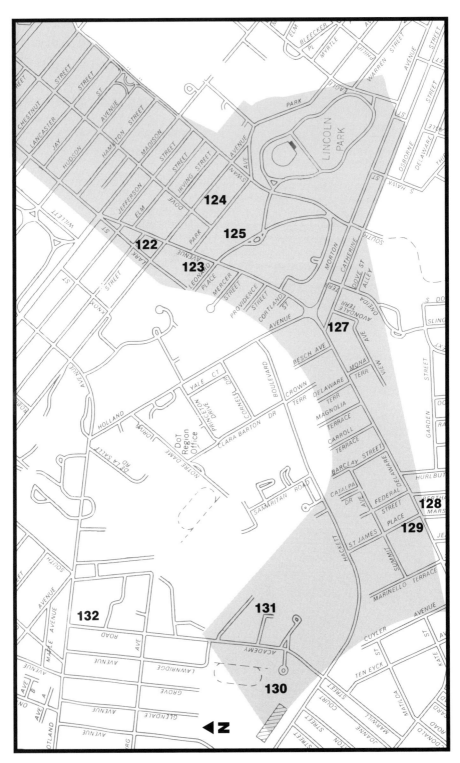

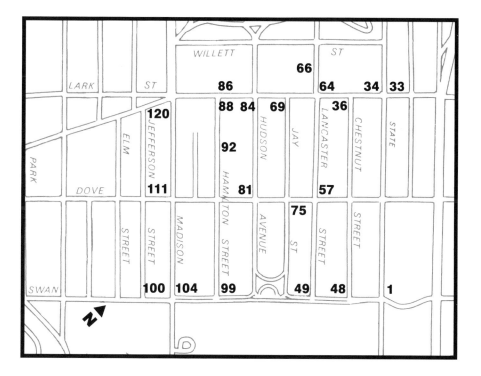

These twenty-two residential blocks are bounded by the Empire State Plaza on the east, Washington Park on the west, Lincoln Park on the south, and Washington Avenue on the north. Most buildings date from Albany's prosperous years between 1850 and 1900, but the terms Center Square and Hudson-Park are relatively recent. In 1957, even before the specter of the Empire State Plaza loomed, the Center Square Association, named by a small group of concerned residents, was formed to encourage preservation of the six blocks between State and Lancaster and later the north side of Jay Street. Sixteen years later, after the Plaza was completed and as commercial pressures were mounting on its fringes, a second group, the Hudson-Park Association, took on the larger fourteen-block expanse south to Lincoln Park.

This tour describes only a sampling of the wealth of architecture in these two neighborhoods. Beyond Center Square and Hudson-Park a driving tour describes scattered sites in and around Lincoln Park and along Delaware Avenue.

Start at corner of State and Swan streets, and walk west.

State Street 1

At the turn of the century, Albanians called this fashionable residential thoroughfare "Little State Street" to distinguish it from the broad commercial avenue down the hill, "Big State Street." Little State Street began with the block facing the Capitol, but the 19th-century streetscape began to be demolished in the 1920s for the New York Telephone Company and then in the 1960s for the Empire State Plaza. The street today, beginning at Swan, is a fascinating exhibit of mostly late 19th-century architecture. Here are lavish and original houses designed for leading Albanians by the city's greatest architectural talent—Charles Nichols, Albert Fuller, Ernest Hoffman, Alexander Selkirk, Walter H. van Guysling and Marcus T. Reynolds. Prosperous builders like James Eaton and Morris Ryder also left their mark. A few frame and brick survivors from the 1830s and 1840s are reminders that many of the houses are either the second on their sites or were given new facades in the course of the 19th century.

In the 19th and early 20th centuries fashionable Albany families often rented a house in town each winter but owned a summer house on the outskirts—Loudonville, Altamont, Slingerlands and Selkirk. This pattern changed during the Depression, when landlords pressured tenants "to buy or get out." Polly Peltz Schultze wrote that "our fathers updated furnaces, bought storm windows, laid in supplies of tire chains and mud hooks, and we all moved permanently into what had been our summer homes."

Fort Frederick Apartments 2
1915
248 State Street

One of Albany's greatest engineering feats was the task of moving this apartment building in 1926. When the state government condemned land on Swan Street for the construction of the Alfred E. Smith Building, the site included the Fort Frederick Apartments. The fated structure stood on the corner of Swan Street and Washington Avenue facing the Capitol and had been completed just nine years earlier. J. W. and J. P. Eichleay of Pittsburgh jacked the eight-story structure up two feet and placed it on several hundred steel rollers laid on railroad tracks. It was then gently propelled 350 feet south by two teams of horses and two winches at a rate of seventy feet a day. Complete with interior furnishings, the building was lowered onto new foundations without the loss of a single pane of glass. The grand entrance, which originally faced Swan Street, is now ignominiously hidden down an alley on the east side of the building. The original builder was John Askey and Son of Pittsburgh.

249-255 State Street 3
c. 1881
Charles Nichols

Around 1881 when E. H. Bender sold his Washington Avenue house to the Fort Orange Club, the State Street frontage of his lot was developed with these four pressed-brick and brownstone Queen Anne rowhouses designed by Charles Nichols. Once known as Malcomb Row, they have been altered, but 255 with its carved brownstone doorway is the most intact. Nichols was a leading mid-19th-century Albany architect. He and his sometime partner Frederick Brown probably designed Westminster Presbyterian Church across the street in 1861 and were responsible for Saint Mary's Church downtown (1867-69). In 1869 Nichols was briefly in partnership with Canadian Thomas Fuller, the first architect of the New York State Capitol.

261 State Street 4
1897
Alexander Selkirk

Built for Dr. Edward G. Cox, this townhouse was designed by Alexander Selkirk and constructed of the narrow Roman yellow brick that builder Morris Ryder favored in this period. Many of the windows on the State Street and west facades have stained-glass transoms. The copper cornice is decorated with lions' heads.

5

Westminster Presbyterian Church 5

1861-62
260 State Street
Interior rebuilt, 1928-30

Originally called the State Street Presbyterian Church, this brick-and-brownstone Gothic structure is attributed variously to architect William Hodgins and to the firm of Nichols and Brown. James Eaton (1817-91), the mason who built this church, later became a major Albany builder.

The church was renamed Westminster in 1919 after a merger of the congregation, which then had no minister, and the downtown Second Presbyterian Church on Chapel Street, which could not pay its fuel bills. In the course of roof repairs in 1928, a fire started by a spark from a blowtorch gutted the interior. The 1862 baptismal font, designed by Albany sculptor Erastus Dow Palmer, was unscathed as was the original Meneely bell. The interior was rebuilt with a carved reredos by Irving and Casson of New York City and stained glass by Wilbur Herbert Burnham of Boston. The education building facing Chestnut Street was added at this time.

Emmanuel Baptist Church 6

1869-71
275 State Street
Woollett and Ogden
Tower completed, 1883

Seven years after the Presbyterians built on the south side of State Street, the Baptists began this structure of rusticated Onondaga limestone. It is one of the few surviving works of the partnership of William L. Woollett and Edward Ogden. The church was dedicated in 1871, and in 1883 the tower was completed as a memorial to deacon Eli Perry, three-term mayor of Albany. The imposing marble baptistery is the focal point of the interior, and the pulpit can be lowered to give the congregation an uninterrupted view of baptisms. In 1928, the year of the rebuilding of the Presbyterian Church across the street, Emmanuel Baptist was redecorated and re-roofed, and the religious education building was added. The original stained glass was replaced in the 1960s. Both Woollett and Ogden were succeeded by architect sons, so their names were associated with Albany buildings for much of the 19th century.

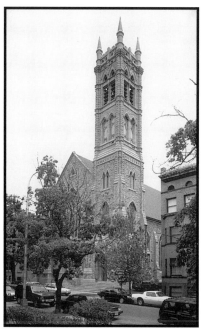

6

274 State Street 7
1870s

An imposing brownstone that has seen better days, this house was probably built for provisions merchant Luther Palmer, who moved here in 1873 and whose family occupied the house for the next thirty years. In the 1920s Dr. Andrew McFarlane redecorated the interior in a Japanese style. The exterior is vaguely Gothic with the wide arched doorway. The original cresting survives on the mansard roof.

276 State Street 8

This three-story brownstone facade is decorated with carving at the door and the third-floor window. Such carving was the glory of Albany in the 1880s, when there were many highly skilled stonecutters at the Capitol. The facade may have been added to an earlier house.

278 State Street 9
c. 1847

Set back from the street, this two-story brick house is one of the few early survivors on the block. The rope decoration around the door is a familiar mid-19th-century motif. Franklin White, a cattle dealer, lived here.

281 State Street 10
c. 1880

This grand brownstone may have been built for grocer Albert Wing, who moved here in 1882 from a large house on Madison Avenue. In 1896 the new owner, Dr. Samuel Ward, had these flamboyant wrought-iron railings installed. Made by the James McKinney and Son iron works of Albany, the ironwork combines ribbon-like scrolls and twisted bars.

283 State Street 11
c. 1881
Albert Fuller

This is one of architect Albert Fuller's first commissions in Albany. Although he tended toward the Romanesque Revival style at this time, he decorated this pressed brick-and-brownstone house generously with classical detailing—scrolled pediments, a swag and rosettes.

284 State Street 12
c. 1860

Chauncey Pratt Williams was president of the Albany Exchange Bank, and his wife, Martha, was legendary for her Friday Morning Club. From 1866 to 1956, the Williams family occupied this imposing brownstone, which has a five-bay-wide facade with a recessed center doorway and elaborate drip moldings. The cast-iron railings, typical of the period, have balusters and newel posts intended to look like carved stone.

286-290 State Street 13
c. 1870-71
John Bridgford, builder

In the late 1860s Albany builder John Bridgford oversaw the initial phases of the Capitol construction—property acquisition, excavation and foundation work. Conveniently close to the construction site, he built this pair of houses faced in reddish pink sandstone and trimmed with brownstone. He lived at 286 and sold 290 to banker Evert Evertson. In 1874 James Eaton took over from Bridgford at the Capitol, and five years later Bridgford left State Street for a new home on New Scotland Avenue. Bridgford also served on the original Washington Park Commission, formed in 1869.

292 State Street 14
c. mid-1840s

Set back from the street with a broad front porch, this mid-19th century "cottage" was one of a pair built for F. H. and John Ridgeway, partners in a plumbing business. The upstairs shingled bay window is a Queen Anne touch that was probably added in the 1880s.

294 State Street   15

c. 1846

Alterations, Marcus T. Reynolds, 1899

When Garrit Yates Lansing bought this house, which had been built in the 1840s by John Ridgeway, a plumber and "hydraulic engineer," he asked a Williams College classmate, Marcus T. Reynolds, to remodel it. The original house may have matched number 292. Reynolds moved the entrance to Dove Street and replaced the State Street stoop with a bay window embellished with a scroll pediment and tapered pilasters. Descended from Albany's earliest Dutch settlers, Lansing had elements from the seal of the Dutch West India Company incorporated in the stained glass of the bay window. The Candlelight Tea Room was located here in the 1920s.

16

298-300 State Street   16

c. 1873

Russell Sturgis

This commanding Ruskinian Gothic Revival townhouse was designed by New York City

architect Russell Sturgis (1836-1909) for Judge William L. Learned and his second wife, Katharine De Witt Learned, in 1873. The square corner tower with its polychrome Moorish arches is a focal point of this intersection. Stone string courses delineate the stories, and the shingled bays on the Dove Street facade and the corbeled brick cornices add other textures to this lively composition. For the interior work Learned hired German-born painter Emanuel Mickel (1820-88), whose Neo-Classical frescoes adorned many local public buildings of the day, including the Capitol, Tweddle Hall and Cohoes Music Hall. The gabled porch is supported by polished granite columns.

Born in Connecticut and educated at Yale, Learned moved to Albany as a young lawyer in 1844. When he commissioned Sturgis to build his new house on State Street, Learned was serving on the state Supreme Court. Learned's urbanity and patience as a trial judge made him popular with attorneys, jurors, and the general public. A late-1870s depiction of the interior of this house by Walter Launt Palmer is in the collection of the Albany Institute of History and Art. Mrs. Learned lived here until her death in 1932.

Next door, 300 State was designed by Sturgis and built at the same time, for Katharine's sister, Mary, and her husband, John T. Norton, who was Judge Learned's nephew. The only other building in Albany by Russell Sturgis is the former Mechanics' and Farmers' Bank on lower State Street, built the year after these houses.

304 State Street   17

c. 1888

One sees the hand of a Capitol stonecutter on the arched entrance to this Romanesque Revival house built for Gilbert Tucker, publisher of The Cultivator and Country Gentleman, said to be the first agricultural weekly in the country. The Tuckers lived here from 1888 to 1927. Most of the carving depicts botanical subjects, but one snarling beast decorates a boss at the left edge of the bay window.

306-308 State Street 18
1875

Encaustic tile and truncated granite columns embellish the facades of these two ornate, stone-trimmed Victorian rowhouses. Number 306 was built for the Vandenbergh family and 308 for Jacob H. Ten Eyck. Both families continued to occupy these houses for over a quarter of a century.

309 State Street 19
c. 1909
Walter H. van Guysling

Walter H. van Guysling is better known for his fanciful stuccoed structures like Broadway's Day Line Hudson River Day Line offices (now L'Auberge Restaurant), but he designed this restrained Neo-Classical facade for John S. Hoy, a plumbing supplier. The brick is laid in Flemish bond, and the doorway is flanked by Corinthian columns; there is a swag in the panel above the door.

311 State Street 20
1895

Banker Edward W. Visscher commissioned this house faced with narrow, buff bricks in 1895. The basement is vermiculated stone. Two embellished Ionic columns flank the doorway. The Visscher family lived here into the 1930s.

312 State Street 21
Late 1870s

This brownstone, with an arched doorway surrounded by vermiculated quoins, has unusual wrought iron with sweeping scrolls and flowers. Daniel H. Gregory moved here in 1884 and may have added the tile roof and gabled dormer. His widow, Julia, lived here through 1909.

315 State Street 22
1914

This dark red brick Neo-Classical house, trimmed with marble, has an unusual vaulted entranceway and a fine central second-story bay decorated with volutes. It was likely built in 1914 for lawyer Jacob Lansing Ten Eyck. He lived here during World War I with his wife, Kate Dyer Ten Eyck, and his daughter-in-law, while his son Cuyler was serving in the navy. Frederick Pruyn, vice president and secretary of the Federal Signal Company, lived here from 1918 to 1921, followed by Hiland Garfield Batcheller of Allegheny Ludlum Steel Company from 1921 to 1926, who sold it to Ronald Kinnear. Around 1959 Nelson A. Rockefeller donated the building to its current owner, the New York Republican State Committee.

24 - 21

317 State Street 23
c. 1898

A leading late 19th-century contractor, Morris Ryder built this Dutch Revival townhouse and lived here for his final twenty years. The front is constructed of narrow yellow bricks and trimmed with brownstone. The steeply pitched pantile roof, scrolled gable, and iron anchor beams were romantic links to the city's roots at a time when Albanians were lamenting the eradication of their Dutch past.

Morris Leslie Ryder (1852-1918) came to Albany from New York City in 1876 to work on the Capitol when James Eaton was superintendent of construction. Ryder joined Eaton's construction company from 1882 to 1885 and then branched off on his own. He was a pioneer in apartment house construction in Albany and built both 352 and 355 State Street, one block away. The M. L. Ryder Building Company in its later years took on the grander name of Ryder Architectural and Decorating Company.

319 State Street 24
Alterations, Marcus T. Reynolds, 1904-05

Next door to builder Morris Ryder's flamboyant Dutch Revival house, Marcus T. Reynolds designed a dignified Colonial Revival facade for a couple with impeccable Dutch antecedents, Edmund Niles Huyck and his wife, Jesse van Antwerp. At the time, Ryder and Reynolds were collaborating on a luxury apartment building at 355 State Street, and the extravagant swags of fruit by the door of this stately townhouse resemble decoration on the apartment house. With a brick facade laid in Flemish bond, the four-story house has a ground floor of smooth-faced coursed stone. In front of the second-story windows are iron balconies with a bellflower motif, and the tall front fence and gate are decorated with spears and tassels. Huyck was a felt manufacturer, and Reynolds had previously designed a country house in Rensselaerville, New York, for him.

321 State Street 25
c. 1840

This charming two-and-one-half-story house with a steep, gable roof and dormers was built for cabinetmaker John Metz. It is typical of the first frame houses on State Street that were built in the 1840s and 1850s and replaced by grander ones of brick and stone in the latter half of the century.

323-327 State Street 26
c. 1871

Set back from the street, these three brownstones have small front yards enclosed by

cast-iron railings. They were built for A. Bleecker Banks, a publisher and twice mayor of Albany (1876-78, 1884-85). Banks occupied 327, the largest one with the most ornate facade, for many years. Banks and his brother, David, were law book publishers. The flourishing firm had been founded by their father in 1804, who, when he died in 1872, had a store in New York City and a large warehouse and salesrooms in Albany at 473-475 Broadway.

28, 27

329 State Street 27
c. 1889

Twice Democratic mayor of Albany, A. Bleecker Banks commissioned this interesting Romanesque Revival double house in 1889 for his daughter, Harriet, and son-in-law, William Lawrence Green. Banks owned the brownstone row next door as well as a house on this lot, so the 1889 work may have represented alterations to the earlier structure. The irregular front facade of rusticated stone links the 1870s row on the right to the 1888-89 Goodwin house on the left. The wrought-iron work adds to the fluidity of the front facade;

there is a billowing balcony, and the distinctive latticework is transformed into a bench by the front door. The initials CB can be seen in the gable. The Greens lived here through 1909.

333 State Street 28

Alterations, Ernest Hoffman with Franklin Janes, c. 1888-89

This remarkable stone facade is one of the delights of State Street. The prospect of marriage at the age of forty-four motivated Scott Dumont Goodwin (1845-1935), a cultured, well-traveled and well-read lawyer, to transform his bachelor home. Architect Ernest Hoffman's 1888 specifications required the owner to remove the front and rear walls of the earlier house and to furnish the cut stone and bluestone for the new facade. The foliated and geometric motifs of the facade most likely are the work of Capitol stone carvers, as Goodwin was apparently a friend of Isaac Perry, architect of the Capitol. Each of the three stories is distinctive. There are slightly bowed, triple windows on the first and second floors and a row of arched windows on the third.

Goodwin's interior alterations are chronicled in letters. On September 27, 1889, he wrote that "the marble floor in the vestibule was put down today and it looks splendid. The hall will look very fine and will be completed in a few days, then I shall go on with the library and the middle parlor." Five months later he married Sarah Coffin Waite, an old family friend from Glens Falls, where he spent his summers. The Goodwins had five children who grew up here, and one remained until her death in 1972.

334-336 State Street 29

c. 1831

In the 1870s when most modest frame houses of this vintage were replaced, this pair survived and was given Italianate cornices. They are said to have been built for Andrew Brown. Episcopal Bishop Wilber E. Hogg lived at 336 in the 1980s.

341 State Street 30

c. 1844

Alterations, Albert Fuller, 1896

At first glance the handsome early 19th-century ironwork here looks quite incongruous on the stoop of a yellow brick house of the 1890s. In fact, when young Albert Fuller altered this house in 1896, he retained the Greek Revival doorway and cast-iron railing and added some fretwork and dentils on the second-story bay. The earlier house may have been erected by Peter Coburn, a builder and house painter, who lived here in the mid-1850s and later moved to Lark Street. Similar examples of this late 1830s cast iron survive in Manhattan and Troy.

343-351 State Street 31

1890

Attributed to Albert Fuller

With their elaborate entrances, contrasting colors, textures and materials, these five rowhouses are good examples of the stylistic experimentation of the 1890s. Many features are similar to Albert Fuller's Fourth Precinct Police Station on Madison Avenue built in 1891. Fuller owned 345-351 and William Gick, a contractor, owned 343, so the project was probably a speculative collaboration between builder and architect. Both Gick and his partner William Sayles were born on the Isle of Man in 1848. They became partners in Albany in 1873 and lived side by side at 283 and 285 Hudson. During the 1890s they frequently worked with Fuller. Over a period of fifty years they constructed hundreds of buildings, including many in the Pine Hills area.

Albert Fuller also owned the corner building, 353 State. He added the third story and lived here at the end of his life. Around the corner he designed 204 Lark for Franklin Townsend.

342-344 State Street 32

c. late 1870s

James Eaton (1817-91) was superintendent of construction of the Capitol when he built this pair of brick rowhouses. At the Capitol Eaton worked with granite, which he chose to trim this pair of townhouses. The polished Egyptian-influenced columns are similar to those at 298 State Street, designed by Russell Sturgis in 1873.

207 Lark Street 33
1830s
New facade, 1930s

A frame building has stood at this corner since the mid-19th century, when Henry Shields had a grocery store here. Later in the 1920s this was Frederick Hosler's ice cream store. The delicate Federal Revival-style facade with pilasters, arched door and windows, urn and fanlight in the gable are attributed to Norman R. Sturgis, architect of Saint Andrew's Church in Pine Hills and associate architect of the 1930s post office on Broadway.

352 State Street 34
1905
Morris Ryder, builder

355 State Street 35
1904-05
Marcus T. Reynolds

Facing each other across State Street, these two apartment houses were built in the same year by the same builder, Morris Ryder, who lived nearby. They signal the beginning of Albany's apartment house era.

Number 352 was built on the site of the Tweddle Malt House, the last large industrial complex in the area. Formerly called The Washington, the six-story brick building stands on a high, granite foundation. Stone carved in a geometric wave-like pattern surrounds the arched door on State Street, while bay windows extend the full height of the building on both facades. Large French windows overlooking Lark Street open onto balconies.

Marcus T. Reynolds's first plan for 355 State was a seven-story palazzo in the spirit of his earlier Van Rensselaer townhouses, at 385-389 State Street. The final design, however, was this Baroque four-story building, which became one of Albany's most fashionable addresses as many elderly residents of large State Street houses retreated in the 1920s to its comfort and convenience. The apartments were large and luxurious, on a scale of those in Manhattan at the turn of the century. Each floor had only two units, with living rooms overlooking State Street. The brick-and-stone exterior is characterized by exaggeration and excess, with bountiful clusters of fruit and lavish swags forming the consoles that support the bay windows.

Walk south on Lark Street, and turn east onto Chestnut Street.

Chestnut Street 36

Looking back to her childhood in this neighborhood in the early 1920s, Polly Peltz Schultze wrote that "Chestnut Street was where we usually played in the afternoons—Spring and Fall. Automobiles did not park at the curbs then and deliveries by horse and wagon kept on the move. So we had the block pretty much to ourselves for Prisoner's Base, Baby, etc. We all built wonderful snow forts and when there was no snow, equally wonderful dams in the gutters."

172-174 Chestnut Street 37
1899

John G. Myers was a leading Albany merchant during the last quarter of the 19th century and a neighborhood figure who lived on nearby Lancaster Street. In the late 1890s he bought two Chestnut Street breweries that stood here—Coleman Brothers and James Kennah's—and transformed this block with an impressive row of speculative housing. The houses at 172 and 174 Chestnut are distinct from the adjacent Brides Row but share the same materials and may also have been the work of Edward Ogden and Sons. Edward Ogden had also designed Myers's department store on North Pearl Street in 1884.

144-170 Chestnut Street 38
1899
Edward Ogden and Son

One of the longest speculative rows in Center

38

around the doors and along the cornice is a familiar motif of the period.

142 Chestnut Street   40
1875
Conversion to house, 1913

This one-time stable was apparently built for John G. Myers, builder of Brides Row, who lived around the corner on Lancaster. In 1913 it was converted to a residence, with a stuccoed square bay in the second story.

140 Chestnut Street   41

This half-timbered-and-stucco facade, enlivened with a series of overhanging bays on the upper stories, may well have been added to an existing structure in the early 20th century.

Welcome Chapel Missionary   42
Baptist Church
c. 1881
124 Chestnut Street

Both black and white congregations have worshiped here over the past 120 years. An 1876 map shows a "colored Baptist Church" on this site, and today Welcome Chapel is one of Center Square's several active black churches.

The church building seems to have been constructed in the early 1880s by the Second Congregational Christian Church, a white congregation, which presumably demolished the earlier building or incorporated it into the current structure. The Romanesque Revival facade with its low, crenellated tower is pressed brick with sandstone trim. The stained-glass windows were installed at the turn of the century. Eventually this congregation merged with the First Congregational Church on Quail Street. The Welcome Chapel Missionary Baptist Church purchased this building in 1958.

115 Chestnut Street   43
1908

This was the stable and later garage of Gerrit Lansing, who owned 294 State Street. His State Street house was extensively altered by Marcus Reynolds in 1899.

Square, these twelve houses are now known as Brides Row but were earlier affectionately called "Poverty Row" or just the Myers Row. They were built on the site of two malt houses for merchant John G. Myers in 1899. Intended as homes for young couples, they were constructed of yellow brick trimmed with sandstone and have second-story bay windows. Each pattern of iron railings was used for a pair of houses. Erastus Corning, mayor for an unprecedented forty-two years (1941-83), was born at 156 Chestnut Street.

163-167 Chestnut Street   39
c. 1874-76
James Eaton, builder

James Eaton owned a number of building lots in this neighborhood and developed them uring his years at the Capitol, 1874-85. These are fairly straightforward Italianate dwellings built before Eaton came fully under the influence of H. H. Richardson, whose stamp may be seen in the Romanesque Revival row that Eaton constructed at the corner of Lark and Lancaster (1888-89). The rope decoration

109-111 Chestnut Street   44
1873
John Bridgford, builder

These brick carriage houses were outbuildings to a pair of handsome sandstone houses at 290 and 286 State, built by John Bridgford for his own family and for banker Evert Evertson.

Westminster Church   45
Education Building
1928-30
85 Chestnut Street

This parish hall was built when the interior of Westminster Church on State Street was repaired after the 1928 fire. The church land had always extended through to Chestnut Street.

84-88 Chestnut Street   46
1889
Morris Ryder, builder

These three pressed-brick and rusticated brown-stones were constructed by builder Morris Ryder while he lived on Lancaster Street. There is a snake-like coil around each iron newel post. The pairs of adjacent houses were prob-ably built at the same time; they exhibit the same materials, and 90 and 92 have the same ironwork.

58-62 Chestnut Street   47
1869

64-68 Chestnut Street
1889

Florist Alfred Chatfield gradually developed this property and the Lancaster Street frontage behind it on land earlier occupied by his greenhouses.
  Head south on South Swan Street.

96 South Swan Street   48
Early 1870s

This corner house is a reminder of the days when Swan Street once had a small-scale residential character, rather than its present

monumentality. The quoins on this three-story brick house give it stature. William L. Jenison of Lodge, Gregory and Company, a Broadway woolen-goods store, moved here from Ten Broeck Street in 1875.

49

Wilborn Temple   49
1887-89
Formerly Temple Beth Emeth
SW corner of Lancaster and South Swan Streets
Adolph Fleischman with Isaac Perry

In 1885 two congregations—Anshe Emeth, a growing Reform congregation, and Beth El, a dwindling Orthodox one—merged, and this towering, rusticated stone synagogue became their new home. Thirty-five years earlier, these two groups had been bitter enemies, to the point of physical violence, on issues of reform such as using English and German hymns, singing by mixed choirs and changes in prayers. Having put their old differences aside, the congregations adopted the new name of Beth Emeth ("House of Truth"), and their new structure was a grand Richardsonian state-ment. It was designed by a member of the congregation, Adolph Fleischman; Isaac Perry, then supervising architect of the Capitol, served as consulting architect. Much of the temple's inspiration comes from H. H. Richard-son's recently completed Albany City Hall (1881-83)—the hipped roof, rusticated stone, massing around a corner tower and triple-arched doorway decorated with carvings in English and Hebrew.
  As the Jewish community moved away from downtown, the synagogue became isolated

from its congregation. In 1957 the new Temple Beth Emeth on Academy Road was dedicated, and the building was sold soon afterward to the current owner, Wilborn Temple First Church of God in Christ. Stained-glass windows were moved from this synagogue to the new one, and in 1979 the massive oak ark was salvaged and installed at B'nai Shalom Temple on Whitehall Road.

Proceed west along Lancaster Street.

126-128 Lancaster Street 50
1896
Lehman and Schmitt

With the completion of the commanding Temple Beth Emeth on the corner of Lancaster and South Swan streets in 1889, this neighborhood was an attractive location for prosperous Jewish families. Isadore Muhlfelder, a hosiery and glove dealer, and Soloman Heiser, a dry goods merchant, hired Cleveland architects, Lehman and Schmitt, to build this pair of nicely detailed houses. The ground floors are rusticated, and the upper floors are tooled stone with fluted columns between the third-story windows. The ironwork of the railings and basement windows and doors is similar to that at Morris Ryder's house at 48A Dove Street (1893) at the other end of the block. Most of the south side of lower Lancaster Street was developed around the time of the Beth Emeth synagogue.

148 Lancaster Street 51
c. 1876

The largest house on the block, this Italianate house was apparently built for Charles R. Knowles, manager of the Albany office of Western Assurance Company of Toronto. This double house is one of a series of remarkably similar structures built around 1876 on Lancaster Street. There is another five-bay-wide house at 163 Lancaster and three more that are four bays wide at the top of the next block (188, 200 and 209). The Knowles house is exceptional with its brownstone-trimmed door. Knowles developed his rear frontage on Jay Street in the late 1880s.

151-153 Lancaster Street 52
Early 1870s
James Eaton, builder

Department store owner John G. Myers and James W. Eaton lived side by side here for over twenty years. The two houses have many design elements in common, including the steeply pitched, red tile roofs, which were probably later additions.

James W. Eaton came to Albany at the age of eleven and was trained by his father as a stone mason. He began his own building business around 1840 and is said to have constructed more than five hundred public and commercial buildings and "the most elegant private residences in Albany." Many of the city's later builders, including Morris Ryder, trained under Eaton. In 1874 the Senate Finance Committee, in an effort to control construction costs at the Capitol, concluded the job ought to be "in the hands of one responsible man, who should be a practical builder of large experience." James W. Eaton was hired and efficiency picked up. While living here, Eaton built speculative houses on State, Lark and Chestnut streets, but 151 Lancaster Street remained his home until his death in 1891. About that time his neighbor John Myers moved to a new house at 155 Lancaster.

155 Lancaster Street 53
c. 1891

John G. Myers lived first at 153 Lancaster and around 1891 developed the empty lot next door with this rusticated-brownstone house. There is a tooled-stone frame around the second-story bow window and foliated carving in the gable. One wonders who the architect and builder were, perhaps Edward Ogden (1828-1900), who designed both Myers's department store and Brides Row, or builder Morris Ryder, who lived at 159 Lancaster.

48A Dove Street 54
1893-94

During the early 1890s contractor Morris Ryder lived at 159 Lancaster Street, and the

Capitol police station stood on this prominent corner. Ryder demolished the station in 1893 and built this house, where he lived from 1894 to 1896. He used the same narrow Roman yellow brick he chose for his ultimate residence, the distinctive Dutch Revival house at 317 State Street. Here Ryder built the gable end to Lancaster Street, with large second-story bowed windows and groups of arched windows on the third floor. The wrought iron-work of ribbon-like scrolls and twisted bars on the Dove Street entrance stoop was probably manufactured by James McKinney and Son. Similar ironwork is found at 126 and 128 Lancaster (1895) and 281 State (1896); Ryder was probably the contractor on those projects.

48B Dove Street   55

156 Lancaster Street
1883

Albert Fuller is known to have designed row-houses on Dove Street, and this Romanesque Revival pressed-brick group looks like his work of this period. In a neighborhood of brewer-ies, it is not surprising that 156 Lancaster was built for a maltster, Albert C. Burt. The Amsdell Brewery stood a block away at the corner of Dove and Jay. The biggest brewery structure was converted in 1910 to the Knickerbocker Apartments.

Lancaster Street   56

Except for the former Amsdell brewery stable (now the Lancaster Garage), the block between Dove and Lark streets is unified architecturally. It is essentially a street of Italianate houses developed in the 1870s with a few structures from the 1850s at the middle of both sides of the block.

163 Lancaster Street   57
1877

Like the Knowles house at 148 Lancaster, this is a large five-bay-wide, Italianate house. It was erected for George W. Lewis, a lithographer, who built the adjacent row (165-173) the year before and also owned houses around the

corner on Dove. He lived at 163 Lancaster for a few years in the early 1880s.

188 Lancaster Street   58
1876

John Coon, a mason, probably built this fine Italianate double house. Unlike the other three on the block (163, 200 and 209 Lancaster), this one has eyebrow windows in the attic story.

187 Lancaster Street   59
1872
William Sayles, builder

This house was in the Ward family for over a century. It was built for Thomas Ward, a printer at the Albany *Argus*, a leading 19th-century newspaper. The two-story Italianate house was constructed by builder William Sayles and must have been one of the first commissions in his long career. The symbols inside the circles on the cornice and elsewhere are said to be from the Isle of Man, Sayles's birthplace.

197 Lancaster Street   60
1871

The ironwork here terminates in newel posts of twisted iron rods. This house is one of several on the block said to have been built and first owned by mason Henry W. Young.

190-196 Lancaster Street   61
1870-71
W. T. Valentine, builder

W. T. Valentine was a neighborhood builder. In 1870 he constructed the first pair (194-196) of these brick Italianate rowhouses and in the following year the second pair with more elaborate doorway and window lintels.

202 Lancaster Street   62
1889
Edmund A. Walsh, builder

Richard V. De Witt, first owner of this rusti-cated brownstone house, served as a city fire commissioner, and the organic stone carving on this house is reminiscent of the City Hall, completed five years earlier. In her commentary on Albany society, debutante Huybertie Pruyn described the De Witts' arrival at a party in 1892: ''The De Witts from 202 Lancaster Street came too, tall and delicate Miss Sally, little Miss Kitty, and their good brother Mr. Richard Varick De Witt.'' Richard Varick De Witt was secretary of the Albany Insurance Company. He was a grandson of Simeon De Witt, surveyor-general of the state of New York for over fifty years and also a descendant of Richard Varick, a noted Revolutionary officer and mayor of New York.

209 Lancaster Street   63
1862-63
Alterations, 1870s

This double house was the result of an 1870s remodeling of an earlier house. The bay over the front door, the rope decoration and shell motif on the lintels are all familiar features of Lancaster Street's Italianate houses. Its owner in the 1870s, William Mitchell, was an engineer and real estate investor. In the early 20th century architect Alexander Selkirk lived here.

Trinity United Methodist Church   64
1932
NW corner of Lark and Lancaster Streets
Sundt and Wenner

In the depths of the Depression, undaunted by the destruction by fire of their two earlier churches on this site in 1901 and 1932, the Methodists started anew and succeeded in building one of the largest ecclesiastical complexes of the city. This massive Neo-Gothic and Art Deco limestone fortress is actually a collection of buildings—the immense new church, a beautifully appointed chapel and a parish hall incorporating parts of a 1926 community house, which had survived the fire. The initial plans came from the Bureau of Architecture of the Methodist Episcopal Church in Philadelphia followed by detailed designs by the Philadelphia firm of Sundt and Wenner.

The entrance is on Lancaster Street, to avoid

64

the increasing noise and congestion of Lark Street. The triangular entrance porch leads into the cavernous church, which seats over one thousand. The stained glass here and in the Kermani Chapel, endowed by Rustan K. Kermani, was made by the P. J. Reeve Company of Philadelphia. The windows on the south aisle depict scenes from church history beginning with St. Paul and ending with ''the modern student,'' one dressed in his best clothes receiving a diploma and the other in football gear. The Lark Street entrance leads to the chapel, a miniature version of the church itself; the parish hall and offices; and thirty-four church-school classrooms—all grouped around a courtyard.

204-220 Lancaster Street   65
1888-89
James Eaton, builder

These rowhouses were among the final projects of James Eaton (1817-91), who lived down Lancaster Street at 151. Working on the Capitol between 1874 and 1883, Eaton came under the influence of the great Romanesque master, H. H. Richardson. Richardson's influence is evident in the rusticated brownstone, especially when compared to Eaton's earlier buildings like the nearby Italianate pair at 163-165 Chestnut (1874-76). According to local lore, the stonework of this row was salvaged from the first Capitol, which was demolished 1883. Philip Hooker would be surprised!

65

222 Lancaster Street　　66
1890
James Eaton, builder

Number 222 Lancaster was built by Eaton in 1890 for attorney John De Witt Peltz. In 1894 Peltz married Catharine Barnard Walsh in a grand wedding at St. Peter's Episcopal Church. Bridesmaid Huybertie Pruyn was amused to see that another bridesmaid forgot to change into her pink satin slippers and trod the aisle in black oxfords, while an usher scurried around importantly with a green tag still attached to the coattail of his new Prince Albert.

The front facade of 222 Lancaster is a combination of rusticated stone, tooled stone and magnificent foliated carving over the door, at the cornice and between the windows. The Peltz house was one of the final commissions of Eaton's long career. He died in 1891.

Return to Lark Street, and then head east on Jay Street.

245 Lark Street　　67
c. 1854
Peter Coburn, builder

Set back from the street, this large brick house is reminiscent of the mid-19th century character of Lark Street. A freestanding house surrounded by gardens stood on the corner where the Eaton row is now, and attached to the Coburn house were two buildings, also set back from the street. The front garden of one of them has been taken up by a one-story store, but the old house is visible behind. Peter Coburn, who moved here in 1855, was a builder and painter. In the 1870s Ira Jagger bought the house. The Jagger Iron Company was located on Van Rensselaer Island, and Jagger may have manufactured the iron fence and balcony for his residence.

Jay Street　　68

The buildings on Jay Street between Lark and Dove tell the story of the second half of the 19th century, when the block was dominated by one of the city's major breweries.

218-226 Jay Street　　69
1888

Some thirty-five years after the rowhouses with latticework porches were built on Hudson Avenue, their rear lots were developed with this Queen Anne row. The pressed-brick facades are trimmed with rusticated sandstone, and the roofline is punctuated by gables above bowed bays.

172-198 Jay Street　　70
1867-68
John Kennedy and Son, builders

Brewery workers may well have rented accommodations in these houses owned by Charles B. Lansing, a major landlord in this neighborhood and a partner in the Albany Saw Works. Stepping down the sloping street, these fourteen simple houses with plain lintels and dentilled cornices are almost identical to those the Kennedys built for Lansing a decade before on Dove Street and Hudson Avenue.

Knickerbocker Apartments   71

c. 1850s
Formerly Amsdell Brewery
175 Jay Street
Converted to apartments, 1910-13

Brewery buildings at this location date back
to the 1850s when John White owned a large
brewery on the site of these apartments
and the Amsdell Brothers had a smaller one
next door. By the 1870s the Amsdell Brewery
and Malting Company had taken over the
entire lower half of the block between Jay and
Lancaster streets. On the eve of Prohibition
real estate agent Ulysses G. Stockwell converted the old brewery into an apartment
hotel.

59-67 Dove Street   72

late 1850s
John Kennedy and John Kennedy, Jr., builders

In the early morning hours of December 12,
1931, notorious bootlegging gangster "Legs
Diamond" was murdered in his rooming house
lodgings on the second floor of 67 Dove
Street. The murder remains a mystery to this
day. This brick row is typical of the modest row
housing constructed by builder John Kennedy
and his son John, Jr., for Charles B. Lansing on
Jay Street and Hudson Avenue in the 1850s
and 1860s, soon after the Rutten Kill ravine
was filled in 1847.

Lower Jay Street   73

A deep east-west ravine, the Rutten Kill, still
coursed through this neighborhood as it was
developed in the early 19th century. An 1813
account described Albany's several ravines
and warned that "unless the glens are filled
up, the appearance of the city must be very
inelegant and forbidding; exhibiting belts of
buildings separated by extensive, desolate and
almost impassable chasms." Between 1844
and 1847, sixty teams and as many as 250
men were employed to fill the Rutten Kill from
Hawk to Lark streets. A new "chasm"
threatened the neighborhood in the late
1960s, when early plans for the Empire State
Plaza included an arterial that would have

sliced through this area along the path of the
old Rutten Kill. In 1972 a neighborhood group,
the Center Square Association, was instrumental in halting the road work. Traffic now either
exits north on South Swan Street or doubles
back under the mammoth Plaza superstructure.

162-170 Jay Street   74

1874-75

Real estate developers Olcott and King built
this handsome Italianate row in 1874-75.
Numbers 252-256 Lark, at the head of Jay
Street, are also speculative properties built for
Olcott and King. Thomas W. Olcott was president of the Mechanics' and Farmers' Bank and
for thirty-one years president of the Albany
Rural Cemetery Association. His connection
with lawyer James King began in 1848, when
he bought the Ten Broeck Mansion from King.

161-163 Jay Street   75

1888-89

In 1888 insurance man Charles Knowles, who
lived on Lancaster Street, developed his rear
lot with this pair of Queen Anne houses.

Eighth Tabernacle Temple   76
Beth El

1873
Formerly Holland Reformed Church
151 Jay Street

Built for the Holland Reformed Church in
1873, this little brick Italianate church fits the
residential scale of its surroundings. The Italian
Christian Church (also known as Trinity Christian Church) purchased it in 1946, and in
recent years it was acquired by the current
congregation. The attached residence dates
from the 1880s.

131-135 Jay Street   77

1874
Constantine De Tiere, builder

Leopold and Constantine De Tiere were two
builders active on the lower blocks of Jay and
Hamilton streets and Madison Avenue in the

third quarter of the 19th century. This Italianate row with an elaborate cornice is typical of the De Tieres's work in the neighborhood. To the south is a gap created for the aborted arterial.

Walk south one block to Hudson Avenue.

Hudson Avenue 78

One of the principal new thoroughfares created by the massive landfill operation of the 1840s, Hudson Avenue was described in 1859 as "the most inviting avenue to the city, and comely blocks of dwellings adorn most of the streets which intersect the area of the ancient Ruttenkill." Hudson Avenue was first paved with Nicholson pavement, which proved a failure, and was later resurfaced with granite blocks. The houses on the upper block of Hudson Avenue and neighboring Jay Street were developed between 1850 and 1880 by Robert Pruyn and Charles Lansing, partners in the Albany Iron and Saw Works and later the Albany Saw Works.

Hudson Theatre 79
1872
Formerly Albany Card and Paper Company
270-276 Hudson Avenue
Converted to movie theater, 1916

Built for the Albany Card and Paper Company, this Italianate building was once part of a complex that extended through to Hamilton Street. This five-story portion was a warehouse and, according to 1892 insurance maps, was also used for card cutting, color mixing, glazing and drying. A toy manufacturer later owned the building, and from 1916 to 1932 silent movies were projected before rapt audiences sitting in a dome-covered arena, now a courtyard parking lot. In 1984 the long-vacant building was gutted for apartments.

283-285½ Hudson Avenue 80
Early 1880s

Two prominent, turn-of-the-century Albany builders, William Gick and William Sayles, became partners in 1873. They constructed hundreds of buildings, and their names were often associated with that of architect Albert Fuller. Apparently they put up these three brick houses on speculation on the site of McKeon's marble yard. In the 1890s the builders and their families lived side by side, Gick at 285 and Sayles at 283. Their office was at 266 Hudson Avenue across the street, just below the Hudson Theatre. They later moved to Pine Hills, a neighborhood they largely built.

298 Hudson Avenue 81
1848

The year after Hudson Avenue was paved following the filling-in of the old Rutten Kill ravine (1845-47), structures like this frame house and store at the corner of Dove Street were built along the new street. After the great fire of 1848 in downtown Albany, frame houses were banned.

293-329 Hudson Avenue 82
1850s
John Kennedy and Son, builder

Attorney Charles Lansing employed John Kennedy and Son to construct this long brick row during the 1850s. It backs up on another of comparable length on Jay Street, also built for Lansing in 1868; around the corner on Dove another simple row with handsome iron-work was built for Lansing by Kennedy in 1859. Lansing rarely sold his rental properties.

347-349 Hudson Avenue 83
1851

A charming surprise in this urban setting, this pair of four-bay-wide 1850s brick rowhouses has unusual two-story double porches of wooden lattice work. Such trellised porches were in the spirit of New York City architects A. J. Davis and A. J. Downing's "cottage style" popularized in *The Architecture of Country Houses* published in 1850. Similar porches, built the year after these, are found on Hall Place in Arbor Hill. Here on Hudson Avenue, 349 was built for merchant William van Gaasbeck, and its lightweight wire railings survive between the lattice bays.

83

340-356 Hudson Avenue 84
1885
Fuller and Wheeler

Fuller and Wheeler, a new and ascending architectural firm in Albany in the 1880s, designed this row of ten pressed-brick, Queen Anne townhouses. They date from 1885, the year before Fuller and Wheeler's most notable Romanesque Revival structure, the YMCA, on North Pearl Street. Robert C. Pruyn, the owner of this row, lived nearby at 38 Willett Street, overlooking the park. Number 266 Lark, on the corner, must be Fuller's work, too. It was the home of American Express agent John van Valkenburgh from 1891 through 1912.

Eastern Star Chapter House 85
1917
351 Hudson Avenue
Thomas L. Gleason

The Order of the Eastern Star is a Masonic institution made up primarily of female relatives of Master Masons but also open to Masons. Instituted in Albany in 1869, this chapter shared the Order's statement of purpose: ''to take good people and through uplifting and elevating associations of love and service, through precept and example build an Order, which is truly dedicated to Charity, Truth and Loving-Kindness.'' For sixty years, from 1917 to 1977, the Albany chapter met here. The buff-colored brick building was designed by Thomas L. Gleason. The upstairs meeting room, now a dance studio, was long used for children's dancing classes. Park Chapel stood here in the late 19th century.

Walk south along Lark Street.

273 Lark Street 86
1850

It is hard to visualize the painter of grand Baroque ceilings living in this unassuming house. By the time decorative painter Emanuel Mickel (1820-1888) moved here in 1878, he was known in the region for his masterful ''frescos'' in local private houses, churches and public spaces, including the Capitol, and also for his commissions in government buildings in Washington, D. C. Born in Darmstadt, Germany, Mickel emigrated to New York City in 1849 and first came to Albany in 1856 to paint the walls and ceilings of the Delavan House, a fashionable Broadway hotel. Three years later he painted *trompe l'oeil* scenes for the State Bank of Albany and eventually, in 1861, moved here and went into partnership with Oscar Rice.

An accomplished artist who worked quickly on dry plaster, Mickel astounded his assistants. One later remembered the effectiveness of his apparent slapdash style: ''I was putting the fine touches on a rose when Mr. Mickel said 'John you're wasting too much time on that, slap it off this way' and he gave a vigorous daub with his brush. I kept on, intent on out-doing Mr. Mickel. I finished and thought my rose was far superior to his, viewed from the scaffold, but when I got on the floor I could not tell what mine was. Mr. Mickel's? Why they looked as though they had grown there.'' Mickel lived here until his death in 1888. Over the past century, most of his contemplative cherubs, vistas through antique arcades and bounteous baskets of fruit and flowers have been lost. His best-known surviving work is at the Cohoes Music Hall. His son Charles (1847-1928) carried on the business, working with stencils as tastes changed.

275 and 277 Lark Street 87
1880-85

In 1880, furniture-maker Thomas Stephens built this house at 277 after the Washington Park Commissioners acquired his earlier quarters on upper Hamilton Street where the Moses fountain is today. A specialist in church furniture and architectural woodwork, Stephens was also a builder and constructed the first lake house in Washington Park. Here at his own house he installed an iron railing with quatrefoils and scrolls similar to that at the 1881 Brady house at 447 State Street. Number 275 Lark served as Stephens's office and shop, and in 1885 he built a larger workshop, which still stands at the rear of the two lots. During the 1880s Stephens's neighbor was Emanuel Mickel, the leading decorative painter of the period.

280-284 Lark Street 88
1869

Constructed for Ezra L. Pasco, a retired merchant, this Italianate brick row has decorative drip moldings on the basement windows and latticework in the cornice.

285 Lark Street 89
1853-54

Centered at the head of Hamilton Street, this Greek Revival brick house was built for grocer William M. Bender, whose store stood nearby on the corner of Madison Avenue. The front of this distinctive house is delineated by wide, brick pilasters. The front door is asymmetrically placed in the double center bay. The tall windows have pediment-shaped lintels, and a low-pitched pediment breaks the roof line. The Greek fretwork on the iron railing is similar to that advertised by C. W. Stillwell of Brooklyn in 1846-47. A shop is set back and attached on the south side of the house. Bender owned the land from here to Madison Avenue and in the course of the 1860s, 1870s and 1880s, he shaped the neighborhood with a series of speculative rows in a variety of architectural styles.

Bender built 281 and 283 Lark Street, the first two rental properties, at the same time as

89

his own house. In 1857 he undertook a longer speculative row on the other side of his house, at 289-297. The highly decorative Italianate houses completed in 1876 across the street at 288-300 were his third project. Finally, in 1884 Bender built a Queen Anne-style row, 299-301, with bowed bay windows and terracotta detailing. Number 299 was refaced in yellow brick in the 1890s.

Turn east on Hamilton Street.

403-407 Hamilton Street 90
1895
Thomas Stephens, builder

These three yellow brick houses have a distinctive classical elegance with swags and pilasters on the bay windows and egg-and-dart molding at the cornice. They were built by Thomas Stephens, whose home and shop were half a block away on Lark Street. Stephens, a builder, also designed architectural furniture and specialized in church furnishings.

Trolley-wire Tower 91

c. 1890

In front of 401 Hamilton Street

Beginning in the 1860s Hamilton Street was the route of horse-drawn, and later electrified, streetcars. At the top of Hamilton the line turned down Lark and then onto Madison Avenue. The 1884 *Albany Handbook* describes the Hamilton Street line: "This is the direct route to the park and persons who have not the time or strength to walk through it will get a fine idea of its beauties by riding past on this Line." This is one of Albany's two surviving towers from the 1890s, which supported the trolley's electric wires. The streetcars ceased operation in 1946.

Israel African Methodist Episcopal Church 92

1850-54

381 Hamilton Street

Attributed to the Rev. Thomas Jackson

The history of the Israel African Methodist Episcopal Church, Albany's first black church, goes back to the 1820s. In 1842 the Trustees of the Israel African Methodist Episcopal Church purchased land on the still virtually undeveloped Hamilton Street. They paid Abel French $1,800 for the site and built a church, which apparently burned soon afterward, in 1844. About ten years later, the present church was built. It is said to have been designed by the pastor, Thomas Jackson.

The church was remodeled in 1881. The stained-glass window in the balcony was dedicated that year to Adam Blake, a well-known African-American figure, who built the Kenmore Hotel on North Pearl Street in 1878 after his Congress Hotel was demolished for the new Capitol. In 1881 the Kenmore was judged "the most elegant structure on the finest street in Albany." Blake died that year and is remembered as "the man who never turned away a stranger or neighbor in need." Twice at the turn of the century, the struggling congregation nearly lost its building to the city for back water taxes, but each time they managed to redeem it. Alterations have been made over the years to the exterior. The steeple was removed and capped, and in 1952 the front facade was reclad with synthetic stone.

91 Dove Street 93

352-356 Hamilton Street

1888

Gick and Sayles, builders

Another row built by Gick and Sayles a few years after the Pruyn row on Hudson Avenue, this Queen Anne design, which includes a corner turret, may be the work of Albert Fuller.

Robinson Square 94

In the early 1970s, as the Empire State Plaza was nearing completion, concern for neighborhood preservation led to joint state-city action to establish guidelines and restrictions for the Plaza environs. The demolition of the south side of this street in 1973 precipitated this issue. The north side was renovated by the Gerrity family of Loudonville for mixed commercial and residential use.

331 Hamilton Street 95

1928

The apartment building was constructed on the site of the main factory of the Albany Card and Paper Company. One five-story, Italianate structure of the complex, now the Hudson Theatre Apartments, survives at the rear, on Hudson Avenue.

315 Hamilton Street 96

1880

Surrounded by rowhouses from the mid-19th century, this High Victorian Gothic house stands out. Built in 1880 for Charles La Dow, an agricultural machinery inventor, it is constructed of pressed brick with decorative bluestone bands and trim, a bay window and an asymmetrically placed, ornamental gable. In 1891 the La Dows moved to a considerably grander house designed by Ernest Hoffman, a stone "castle" on Thurlow Terrace overlooking the lake in Washington Park.

307 Hamilton Street   97

1869

Constantine De Tiere, builder

Constantine De Tiere and his brother, Leopold, were active builders in the Hudson-Park neighborhood during the years of intense development in the 1860s and 1870s. Constantine moved every few years throughout the neighborhood. Around the time this house was built he lived at two other locations on this block but in 1875 moved into this house (then numbered 297). Theodore Romeyn, owner of the packing box company Albany Card and Paper Company, also lived here at one time.

295-299 Hamilton Street   98

1857

Edward Courtwright, builder

This row of three houses dates from 1857; in later years Francis Sill, a prosperous coal merchant, added the mansard roof and bay window at 299. In 1876 Romeyn, the president of Albany Card and Paper Company, lived at 295 (then numbered 285).

289-293 Hamilton Street   99

1850-51

Daniel Bassett, builder

Hamilton Street developed westward from these early houses on the corner. The next block of three was built about six years later. The pioneer builder on Hamilton was Daniel Bassett, a brick maker who lived around the corner on Swan Street.

Walk south along South Swan Street. Proceed as far as Elm Street for a brief tour, if desired, and then return to Madison Avenue. Head west on Madison.

Fire Station No. 6   100

c. 1860

NW corner of South Swan and Jefferson Streets

Renovation, 1938

The yellow brick exterior of Steamer No. 6 dates from 1938, when the Works Progress Administration modernized this firehouse and several others, including numbers 3 and 7. This building probably dates from the 1860s when this hilltop station housed the city's last volunteer company. In 1867 when the fire department was reorganized, steam engines were in use at all downtown firehouses, but the old Americus Engine Company No. 13 was assigned here to cover this more sparsely populated section. In 1869 the volunteer company was disbanded, and Steamer No. 6 was assigned to this firehouse. After Steamer 6 was motorized in 1918, it was referred to as Engine 6. The north end of the main building was originally for the hose cart.

101

182-216 Elm Street   101

1871

George Martin, builder

The most impressive speculative housing of the neighborhood is this span of eighteen Italianate houses. Apparently built by George Martin on land formerly owned by coal merchant George W. Luther (whose large brick house was set back on a large lot just west of the row), these tall, three-story brick houses have high brownstone stoops, some with their original ironwork. In the late 1870s George B. Hoyt sold the houses to merchants and professionals. Some new residents were launching their careers, like architect Walter Dickson (198 Elm), who in 1886 built a substantial freestanding house at the top of State Street overlooking Washington Park; other owners retired here from larger houses on State and Lancaster streets.

220-222 Elm Street   102
1894
Feeney and Sheehan, builders

This pair of rusticated brownstones was built on George Luther's property in 1894 by well-known Albany builders Feeney and Sheehan. The wide, arched windows on the ground floor have stained-glass transoms and a block-patterned cornice.

Madison Avenue   103

Madison Avenue, a major thoroughfare west from the Hudson River, predates all the neighboring streets. It originally ran along a ridge between two gullies that have since been graded—the Rutten Kill on the north and Beaver Creek on the south. In its early days it was called Lydius Street, after the popular pastor of the First Reformed Church, the Rev. Johannes Lydius, who preached there from 1703 to 1709. When the name was altered in 1867 to commemorate President James Madison, a faction hotly resisted the change as another effort to obliterate Albany's Dutch past. Until it burned in 1937, an imposing Romanesque Revival-style Reformed Church (1881) dominated the east side of the Swan and Madison intersection, a site now transformed by the Empire State Plaza.

333-337 Madison Avenue   104
1870-75
Leopold De Tiere, builder

These large Italianate rowhouses, with lavishly decorated bays and cornices, were built by Leopold De Tiere, who lived in the middle one. The attached frame structure at 337½, built in 1871, may have been his shop. His brother, Constantine, also a builder, lived a block away on Hamilton and built a number of houses in the 1870s.

336 Madison Avenue   105
1888

For almost fifty years, from 1870 to 1918, piano maker Charles Beeny's family lived at 336 Madison. They may have altered an

earlier house to create this charming two-and-one-half-story, gabled Queen Anne "cottage" in the 1880s. The first floor is brick, and the upper stories are clad with fish-scale shingles.

345 Madison Avenue   106
1882

Floral ornaments abound on this once-grand Victorian house built for tailor Gerson Oppenheim. Trimmed with bluestone, the pressed-brick house has bay windows, a man-sard roof and a wide stairway that curves in a welcoming fashion. Edmund A. Walsh, a well-known builder who developed much of Madison Avenue facing Washington Park, probably constructed this house.

348-350 Madison Avenue   107
1847

These two-story brick houses were built for Jonathan Wing, a flour and grain merchant at 70 Quay Street. The Wing family became a major presence on the street in the latter half of the 19th century. In 1867 Albert Wing bought the largest house on the block, the old Conckling house across the street from this pair, and later the Wings subdivided the grounds.

108

353 Madison Avenue   108
1827

The oldest house in the immediate neighborhood, this late Federal-style residence was built in 1827 for U. S. District Judge Alfred

Conckling. Once surrounded by gardens and an orchard, the brick house stood alone on the ridge along which Lydius Street (renamed Madison Avenue in 1867) ran westward between the Rutten Kill and Beaver Creek. Originally, the house was two stories, and the original window lintels have simple, incised, geometric patterns.

The house became a Catholic seminary but was returned to private use in 1867, when purchased by grocer Albert Wing at 388 Broadway. In 1876 the property still extended through to Hamilton Street. After Wing moved to 281 State Street in 1882, the family subdivided the Madison Avenue frontage with two ranks of houses in the Queen Anne style—first the row on the west side (355-363) in 1885 and two years later the row on the east (349 A-E). Here the crooked iron fences surround the front yards, and the railings on the front steps have elaborately scrolled ironwork. The third story of the main house and rear addition date from around 1920, when the Wings sold the house.

354 Madison Avenue 109
c. 1830s
Alterations, 1876

Toolmaker Lewis Gomph apparently altered this 1830s house in 1876 to its present appearance with the addition of an Italianate cornice. Gomph owned a number of houses in the neighborhood. Jacob Gomph, a cabinet-maker, built 356, two doors away.

367-369 Madison Avenue 110
1887

At the time the Wings were building rowhouses down the street, Dorothea Dobler had this Romanesque pair constructed. Most of the brownstone trim has been disguised with paint. The arched lintels have a circle motif. The larger house, 367, has an arched doorway, a small stained-glass window and recessed panels of basketweave brick. The Dobler Brewery stood a few blocks away on Myrtle Avenue, east of the Hinckel Brewery.

374-376 Madison Avenue 111
c. 1848

It is hard to believe that this is the birthplace of today's Albany Medical Center. Albany Hospital, the city's first, was incorporated in 1849 and was located in this three-story brick structure for its first few years. In 1854, at the height of a cholera epidemic, the hospital moved to new quarters in the former county jail at Eagle and Howard streets.

385 Madison Avenue 112

Judging by the incised geometric pattern in the lintel over the door, this wide, brick house may date from the late 1820s, like the Conckling-Wing House at 353 Madison. The foliated carving is unusual. John Artcher owned this house in the 1870s. The storefront was added later.

386 Madison Avenue 113
1851
Henry Knight, builder

This elegant little Greek Revival brick house with two-story pilasters was built by Henry Knight, a carpenter. The Italianate cornice was probably added in the 1870s.

390 Madison Avenue 114
1868

Morgan Filkins and his brother, Welcome, made their fortune selling patented medicines. Morgan built this large, freestanding Italianate house in 1868 and added a mansard roof in 1870-71. The Albany Hospital for Incurables and the Albany Guild for the Sick Poor were located here at the turn of the century. The Filkins brothers also owned 387, across the street, one of a pair of houses with pilasters dating from the early 1850s.

395 Madison Avenue 115
1848

391-393 Madison Avenue
c. 1878
James Christie, builder

Set back on its lot, this two-story, red brick house at 395 with a wide front porch, seems to be a world of its own. Constructed in 1848, it was first owned by John Wasson. In 1874 James Christie, a builder, bought the house, which stood on the largest undeveloped lot on the block. Christie established his carpenter's shop at the rear on Garden Alley and built the two Italianate rowhouses at 391-393.

The iron fence in front of 395 is a well-preserved example of the work of William J. La Grange of Rensselaer, who retired as a railroad brakeman in 1903 and began manufacturing fences. The shield on the gate mimics those of a famous midwestern manufacturer, the Stewart Iron Works. The fence has iron pickets with fleur-de-lis finials.

402 Madison Avenue 116
1845

In the 1840s this area was on the fringes of the city, and this frame house built in 1845 conveys the earlier, nearly rural character of this now-central-city street. The house was built for a boatman, Edmund Ellis. The bracketed front porch was probably added later.

414-416 Madison Avenue 117
1863

Between 1857 and 1884 grocer and real estate developer William Bender shaped the neighborhood around this corner of Lark Street. Those buildings are all brick, but here on Madison he built this tidy frame pair in 1863.

417 Madison Avenue 118
1872-73
Formerly School 11
Ogden and Wright

Since most of their schools have been demol-ished, Ogden and Wright are unrecognized as Albany's leading school architects of the 1870s and 1880s. This brick Italianate structure, now converted to apartments, was one of their first schools and is one of the few to survive today.

Both born in England, architects Edward Ogden and Frank P. Wright formed a partner-ship in 1871. Their first project was School 15, which stood on Franklin and Herkimer streets. It appears to have been modeled on Boston's Shurtliff Grammar School and was considered Albany's first modern, scientifically planned school building. The following year they began this school on Madison Avenue, a smaller version of their landmark school in the South End. Two of Ogden and Wright's grandest school buildings were the Ruskinian-style Albany High School (1875-76) facing Academy Park, which was demolished around 1911 for the present county courthouse, and the Renaissance Revival New York State Normal School (1885-87) facing Washington Park, which burned in 1906.

419 Madison Avenue 119
c. 1891
Formerly Fourth Precinct Police Station
Fuller and Wheeler

After 340-356 Hudson Avenue (1885) and the YMCA on North Pearl Street (1886), architects Fuller and Wheeler began to move out of the Romanesque style into the more classical idiom shown in this 1891 police station. The design is symmetrical. The characteristic arched entrance is trimmed with egg-and-dart mold-ing and flanked by squat, Ionic pilasters. A terra-cotta string course with a wave pattern divides the first and second stories, and at the corners there are brick quoins.

Van Rensselaer Apartments 120
1901
SE corner of Madison and Delaware Avenues
Marcus T. Reynolds

Marcus Reynolds's Baroque style and flourishes are found here in his first apartment house, built for his physician-cousin Howard van Rensselaer. Motherless from a young age,

Reynolds was brought up by Howard's mother. Early family commissions certainly enhanced his fledgling career. In 1897 the magnificent Venetian townhouses for his Van Rensselaer cousins on State Street established his reputation in Albany. Soon afterwards, he finished this four-story corner building. Built of red stretchers and black headers in Flemish bond, the Van Rensselaer Apartments are best seen from Delaware Avenue. Over the main doorway is an elaborate cartouche with foliated carving and a balcony with a delicate railing. For many years this was a nurses' residence.

James Dwight Dana Memorial Fountain   121

1903
Madison Avenue between Lark Street and Delaware Avenue

In the Sierra Nevadas the life of James Dwight Dana is commemorated by a mountain peak, but here in Albany, we have a mere granite fountain. James Dwight Dana (1813-95) is said to have been America's first geologist and was the leading 19th-century authority in prehistoric zoology, preceding Darwin in a theory of evolution. Albany's Dana National History Society was founded in 1868 for ladies "of scientific taste and culture" and continues today as one of the oldest women's scientific groups in the country. The society raised money for this drinking fountain and chose this rustic boulder of Chester, Massachusetts, granite designed by A. A. Flint, a local cemetery memorial firm at the Albany Rural Cemetery. The society made sure that the state geologist provided "correct drawings" of the fossil forms, crinoids, trilobites and other prehistoric sea life decorating the water basin. Officers and members of the society dedicated the fountain in 1903 with the hope that children drinking here would "be led to drink of that other stream—the stream of science."

The following driving tour covers sites around Lincoln Park and along Delaware Avenue. Start at the corner of Madison and Delaware.

122

Central Fire Alarm Station   122

1917
Now Louise Corning Senior Citizens Center
25 Delaware Avenue
Morris Ryder, builder

In 1894 the city's central fire alarm telegraph office in the downtown municipal building was damaged in a fire at the neighboring Albany Theater. From that time, the fire department sought an isolated and fire-proof location to house this equipment, which consisted of storage batteries that provided electrical current along with the machinery for the telegraph alarm system. The familiar red fire alarm street boxes were all connected with the alarm station.

This fanciful Dutch Revival structure was finally built in 1917 here on Delaware Avenue by Morris Ryder; nearly twenty years earlier Ryder had built his own State Street house in the Dutch Revival style. The design of the alarm station is also in the spirit of Marcus Reynolds's Dutch Revival fire station (1911) located further out on Delaware Avenue, although the proportions and wide stone bands here are quite different. The fire department moved its equipment out of the alarm station in the 1960s; in 1976 the renovated, enlarged sturcture was opened as a senoir citizens' center.

William S. Hackett Junior High School 123

1925-27
Delaware Avenue facing Lincoln Park
Marcus T. Reynolds

Through this great Palladian-inspired structure, Marcus Reynolds sought to ennoble the minds of Albany's seventh, eighth, and ninth graders above their mundane daily lives. The junior high school movement developed slowly in New York State in the first decades of the 20th century. Mayor William Hackett, who died while this building was underway, advocated the construction of a junior high ten years after similar structures were in use in cities like Rochester. Hackett Junior High (now Middle) School was Reynolds's second school in Albany, following School 4 in Pine Hills (1922, demolished 1960s). The exterior architectural grandeur continues inside in a great central hall with two skylit grand staircases.

Turn left onto Park Avenue, and drive east.

Hinckel Brewery 124

NW corner of Park Avenue and
South Swan Street
1880s

Hinckel's Sparkling Lager was produced on this site from 1855 to 1922. The five-building complex that survives today dates from an expansion in the 1880s. Prussian brewer Frederick Hinckel established the brewery in 1855 with his partner Schinnuerer. Three years later Hinckel bought out his senior partner and managed the brewery until his death in 1881. For many years it was known as the Cataract Brewery, for its location overlooking Buttermilk Falls of Beaver Creek in the days before Lincoln Park was created. The distinctive five-story malt house was constructed in 1880, the year before Hinckel died. Additional buildings constructed by his sons and other relatives included an office, an ice-making plant, and two beer storage buildings. A rare survivor of the seventeen brewery complexes once located in Albany, the Hinckel Brewery has been adapted as apartments.

123

124

Turn right onto South Swan Street. If desired, take loop drive through the eastern half of the park and return to South Swan. Drive south through the park to Morton Avenue.

Lincoln Park 125

Begun 1894

Unlike Washington Park, Lincoln Park evolved without a comprehensive plan between 1894 and the 1930s. The irregularly shaped plot is bounded by Delaware Avenue, Park Avenue, Eagle Street and Morton Avenue. Although the site of the park was described in 1888 as "wild and rugged in every respect," it was not completely undeveloped. The few existing structures ranged from a learned man's elegant study on the hill to an Irish immigrant shantytown in the hollow.

Professor James Hall (1811-98) owned most of the southwest portion of today's park. As a young man in 1835, Hall launched a model geological survey of New York State and in the course of his long career became "one of the most influential, the most hated and most admired of American scientists." The geologist and paleontologist built "a red brick retreat" here designed by Andrew Jackson Downing and Calvert Vaux around 1852. Hall's family lived nearby in an elaborate 1880s house near the corner of Morton and Delaware, now the site of the tennis courts. Hall, however, considered his office his real home. He worked in the large galleried space surrounded by his fossils and thousands of drawings and slept in an adjoining spartan bedroom. Here he trained a generation of scholars. Eventually his collections were moved to the State Museum.

The first phase of the park, known from 1894 until 1916 as Beaver Park, was an eighty-acre parcel along Delaware Avenue. Opened in July, 1900, it was hailed as the city's first open-air public playground. James Hall's ivory tower was remodelled to accommodate children's activities conducted under the supervision of Blanche Tozier of Boston as advocated by the Albany Mother's Club (later, the Women's Club). His Downing and Vaux villa still survives, as a wing of the Sunshine School.

The park was renamed Lincoln Park in 1916 after the eastern portion began to be developed following the plans of New York City landscape architect Charles Downing Lay (1877-1936). The first step involved the demolition in 1910 of the Civil War-era tenements of Martinville, which had blighted the sides of the hollow west of Hawk Street for over thirty years. Amongst their other proposals for the city's public spaces, Charles Downing Lay and architect Arnold Brunner in their *Studies for Albany* (1914) envisioned not just an ordinary park with trees and lawns but a modern sports facility, a concept quite different from Bogart

and Cuyler's Washington Park. At this time Lay was landscape architect for the New York City Department of Parks.

Lay's plans for the picturesque terrain in Albany called for a naturalistic swimming pool, a great athletic field with a quarter-mile running track, several football fields and baseball diamonds and a grand Beaux-Arts fieldhouse. Unfortunately, Lay's swimming pool, built in 1915, turned out to be dangerously close to the Beaver Creek trunk sewer, so in 1930 the current horseshoe-shaped pool was built across Hawk Street on the land Lay had designated for athletics. Much of Lay's scheme, including the field house and a pergola and children's wading pool at the southeastern corner, was never followed. The spare Colonial Revival bathhouse, designed by Albany architect Thomas L. Gleason and built by Feeney and Sheehan, was opened in 1931.

Look southeast along Morton Avenue to the school.

Empire View Condominiums 126

1878

Formerly School 25

Morton Avenue between Hawk and Swan Streets

From this Italianate school building is a splendid view over Lincoln Park to the Empire State Plaza. The school was built in 1878, long before the creation of the park. A brick structure on a bluestone foundation with a fanciful brick cornice, it may have been designed by Ogden and Wright, who were specializing in school buildings during this period (School 15 in the South End, 1871; School 11 on Madison, 1872-73; Albany High School on Academy Park, 1875-76). The building was converted to apartments in 1989.

Turn right on Morton Avenue, continue to Delaware Avenue, and head south.

Anthony Opalka prepared the text for the remainder of the tour.

Delaware Avenue 127

After the commencement of electric streetcar service along Delaware Avenue in 1903, the area between Lincoln Park and the southern city line was transformed quickly from a rural setting to a densely built-up neighborhood of single- and two-family homes, apartment buildings, and commercial and institutional buildings intended to serve the new residents.

Like other areas of Albany opened to development by electric transit in the early 20th century, the most common residential building type here is the two-family house, usually constructed of wood, with identical apartment units, or flats, stacked one on top of the other. These buildings feature architectural embellishments common in the period, such as a mixture of clapboard and wood shingle siding, stucco, Palladian windows, bay windows, multi-paned window sash, and prominent front porches.

128

Hook and Ladder No. 4   128

1910
NE corner of Delaware Avenue
and Marshall Street
Marcus T. Reynolds

In 1909 the Albany Common Council authorized a search for land on which to build a firehouse in this area. This site was chosen,

and in 1910 architect Marcus T. Reynolds was selected to design the new building. By this time, Reynolds had already achieved prominence as architect of the United Traction Company headquarters (1899), the City Savings Institution (1902), and the Albany Trust Company (1904); later he would design one of Albany's most notable buildings, the headquarters of the Delaware and Hudson Railroad Company, now the State University of New York Central Administration Headquarters.

In an era characterized by the revival of architectural styles for both residential and institutional buildings, Reynolds chose one which had significant association with the early history of Albany, the Dutch Revival. The firehouse, which opened in 1912 to serve the newly-established Hook and Ladder Company No. 4, is constructed of red brick stretchers and a mixture of red and blue brick headers, laid in English cross bond, a pattern of alternating courses of the two sizes of brick. The building features steeply pitched, stepped gables, tracery, iron beam anchors and other picturesque elements. Notable also are the city emblems from different historical periods; the beaver recalls Albany's original function as a fur-trading post established by the Dutch West India Company in 1624.

Saint James Church   129

1927-29
389 Delaware Avenue
McGinnis and Walsh

Directly across the street is the monumental Saint James Church, the second building of this Roman Catholic parish, founded in 1911. Constructed between 1927 and 1929, the granite, Indiana limestone and Tennessee marble Gothic Revival structure was designed by the Boston architectural firm of McGinnis and Walsh.

Turn right onto Saint James Place. Proceed to Hackett Boulevard and turn left. Drive to next traffic signal, and turn right on Academy Road.

130

Albany Academy   130
1932
Academy Road
Marcus T. Reynolds

Founded as a boys' school in 1813, Albany Academy moved to its present site in 1932, having outgrown its building designed by Philip Hooker and located across from the Capitol in Academy Park. Marcus T. Reynolds, a former Academy student and an ardent admirer of Hooker, designed the new building. Executed in brick laid in Flemish bond above a marble basement and with matching stone trim, his structure acknowledges Hooker's old Academy in its arrangement of volume and spaces. Like the older structure, the new building has a pedimented central block surmounted by a cupola and flanked by wings, as well as such details as swags and round-headed windows. Some of the woodwork and the weathervane were brought from the old Academy. Reynolds also drew on his own design for the Hackett Junior High School on Delaware Avenue, built in the Georgian Revival style.

Temple Beth Emeth   131
1957
100 Academy Road
Percival Goodman

The modern brick, steel and glass building north of the Albany Academy for Girls houses the congregation of Temple Beth Emeth, which moved here from Lancaster Street. Designed by Percival Goodman, a professor of architecture at Columbia University, and dedicated in 1957, the building is distinguished by the great folded roof of the sanctuary, which suggests the tent, or mishkan, which God commanded Moses to prepare for the desert tabernacle. From the interior, the clear glass above the parapet walls gives the illusion that the roof is floating. The other buildings house educational, social and administrative activities.

Continue along Academy Road, past Helderburg Avenue, and enter the campus of JCA at the first road on the right.

131

Junior College of Albany Campus   132
140 New Scotland Avenue

In 1907 the Albany Orphan Asylum, founded in 1829 to house, feed and educate Albany's orphan population, purchased land along New Scotland Avenue near the Albany Hospital, the almshouse and the penitentiary. As the Albany Home for Children, the institution constructed ten brick buildings in a simple Georgian Revival style arranged in a vaguely symmetrical fashion around a central green. In 1959, the home (today known as Parsons Child and Family Center) abandoned its residential mission and sold seven buildings to Russell Sage College of Troy, which established the Junior College of Albany and later the Sage Evening Division at this site. Sage added a classroom building, gymnasium, and a campus center. The siting of the new buildings has respected the original design.

Washington Park:
Rooms with a View

Cornelia Brooke Gilder

389 State Street

First conceived by Frederick Law Olmsted and Calvert Vaux, the country's leading landscape architects, Washington Park is a historic landscape of primary significance. The eighty-one acre park was created in the course of the 1870s and early 1880s. The curvilinear roadways and varied topography with wooded glades and open meadows are hallmarks of Olmsted's style of naturalistic landscape. The "gardenesque" formal plantings date from the 1890s, when the park was still evolving under William S. Egerton.

A group of public-spirited Albany businessmen hired Olmsted, Vaux and Company of New York City in 1869. Olmsted and Vaux proposed that Washington Park be the centerpiece of a network of Albany parks like those in Brooklyn, Buffalo, Boston and later Chicago. While the precise boundaries of Washington Park were not drawn, the firm identified the Beaver Creek valley as the site for an ornamental lake, which was later executed, and their vision of "an open, quiet and natural landscape treatment" was followed in plans drawn in 1870 by Bogart and Cuyler. John Bogart (1837-1920) was an Albany native and graduate of the Albany Academy, and his engineering firm worked under Olmsted and Vaux on Central Park in New York City and Prospect Park in Brooklyn. Bogart was chief engineer for the New York City Department of Parks from 1872 to 1877 and state engineer beginning in 1888. He worked on parks and boulevards in Baltimore and Chicago and at the grounds of the state Capitol in Nashville, Tennessee.

Much of the site of Washington Park was already open space. Since the beginning of the 19th century, a parade ground faced Willett Street, and the city's burial ground, with beautiful mature trees, extended west along State Street from the present Henry Johnson (formerly Northern) Boulevard to Englewood Place. In 1868 the remains and some stones were removed to the Albany Rural Cemetery, which had opened in 1845.

Two areas acquired for the park involved demolition of existing structures. Two short blocks of rowhouses that stood where the Moses statue and formal gardens are located were acquired in 1880. The final parcel, purchased in 1882, was the large house and landscaped grounds of John Taylor, which stood on a plateau at what is now the southwest corner of the park (tennis courts since 1889). The property at the northwest corner, owned mostly by the Barnes family and never part of the park, was developed into large lots facing Englewood Place and Thurlow Terrace.

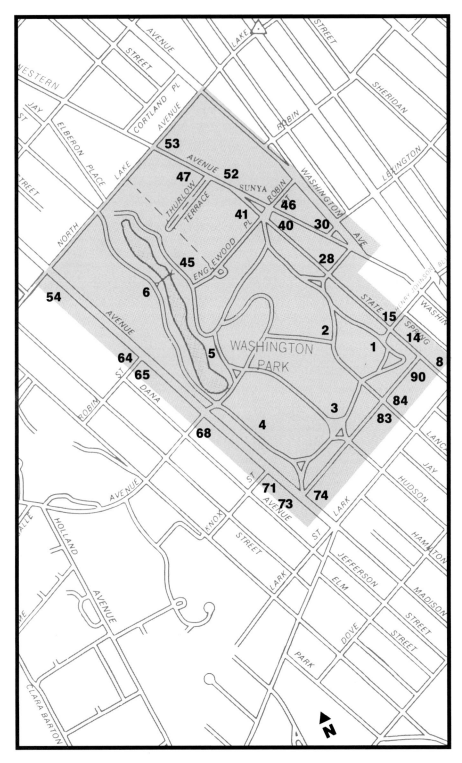

More than any other single figure, William S. Egerton shaped Washington Park. From 1870 to 1873 he worked under Bogart and Cuyler as they prepared detailed plans, saving handsome old trees, specifying new plantings, and designing a refectory and drinking fountain shelter. In 1873, when the park commissioners terminated the contract with Bogart and Cuyler, Egerton became engineer-in-chief and later superintendent, first to the Washington Park Board and in 1900 as first head of the newly created Bureau of Parks, a city agency created to replace the board of commissioners of Washington Park. During Egerton's thirty-eight-year span at the park, the plan reached maturity. Trees, flowering shrubs and formal gardens were planted, six structures were built (of which only the footbridge over the lake remains), and an array of monuments was installed.

Start at intersection of Henry Johnson Boulevard and State Street. Because of the length of the tour, driving may be preferable for some parts.

1

Soldiers and Sailors Monument 1
1912
Near State Street and Henry Johnson Boulevard
Hermon Atkins MacNeil, sculptor
Lord and Hewett, architects

Situated at the head of Henry Johnson Boulevard, this grand Civil War memorial was unveiled on October 5, 1912. Behind the large bronze figure with arms laden with palm branches is a procession of more than sixty life-size figures carved in marble in low relief. The monument is the work of Hermon Atkins MacNeil, who is best known as a medalist and the designer of the Standing Liberty quarter dollar of 1916. The tree-lined pedestrian mall

terminating at the south side of the monument follows the old route of Knox Street, which ran parallel to Willett Street. In the days before the park, a parade ground was located east of Knox Street and a burial ground to the west. A vehicular entrance to the park on Henry Johnson Boulevard was introduced a few years after the memorial was installed. In 1986, the memorial was restored for the city's tricentennial, and new paving and light fixtures were installed.

Head west on road in park, and take first left.

Armsby Memorial 2
1879
Near Lancaster Street extension into park
Erastus Dow Palmer, sculptor

Young Huybertie Pruyn loved to look out of her grandfather's carriage at "the jack-in-the box statue" soon after this monument to Dr. James H. Armsby was unveiled in 1879. Perched on a granite column, the bronze bust was the work and gift of Albany sculptor Erastus Dow Palmer. The first monument placed in Washington Park, it was cast in Paris by F. Barbedienne. Dr. Armsby was a founder of Albany Medical College, the Albany Hospital, Albany Law School, and Dudley Observatory.

Continue east to Henry Johnson Boulevard, turn right and continue to next intersection.

Robert Burns Statue 3

1888
Near Hudson Avenue and Henry
Johnson Boulevard
Charles Calverley, sculptor
George H. Boughton, bas relief panels

This bronze statue of the famed Scottish bard is one of Washington Park's earliest sculptures. The memorial is set on a granite plinth and surrounded by a circular path. It was provided for in the will of Mary McPherson, a Scottish resident of Albany, and is the work of two of Albany's native sons—Charles Calverley, the sculptor of the figure, and George H. Boughton, a landscape painter, who designed the panels around the base and who was said to be "famous among London artists." The bas-relief panels depict four of Burns's best-known poems. The Saint Andrew's Society funded the conservation of the statue in 1978.

Continue along Henry Johnson Boulevard, take next right, and head west.

Moses Smiting the Rock 4

1893
King Memorial Fountain
Near New Scotland and Madison Avenues
J. Massey Rhind, sculptor

An early work of Scottish sculptor J. Massey

Rhind, this allegorical fountain proved to be a turning point in his career in America. John Q. A. Ward, the dean of American sculptors, recognized Rhind's talent soon after he arrived in America in 1889. Ward recommended Rhind for the competition for this fountain, in which he was pitted against such giants as Daniel Chester French. The monumental bronze Moses stands, staff in hand, on a large rock formation that depicts Mount Horeb, where he smote the desert rock for water. The smaller figures personify the stages of life—infancy, youth, adulthood, and old age. A memorial to banker Rufus H. King (1794-1867), third president of the New York State Bank, the fountain stands amidst formal gardens laid out by William S. Egerton. (Rhind's grand personifications of the branches of learning at Alexander Hall at Princeton University also date from 1893.) The statue of Philip Schuyler (1925) in front of the Albany City Hall is one of Rhind's more sedate later works.

Continue heading west to the lake.

Washington Park Lake House 5

1929
Near New Scotland and Madison Avenues
J. Russell White

"Festooned in jeweled lights of vari-colors, the lake house cast myriad reflections of soft illumination in the water"—this was the fantasy depicted by a journalist on the night of October 14, 1929, as the new Washington

Park Lake House opened just days before the harsh reality of the stock market crash. This flamboyant Spanish Revival structure replaced an earlier frame one in the Stick style that had been designed by Frederick Brown and constructed in 1876 by Thomas Stephens. Albany architect J. Russell White designed the new lake house in buff-colored brick decorated with polychrome terra cotta. It was built by Anthony Marinello. The two towers have iron balconies; above the stage looms a twenty-foot-high arched recess of Guastavino tile. The interiors are elaborately detailed, with pink terrazzo floors, green terrazzo baseboards, pilasters, and wrought-iron chandeliers.

Footbridge 6

Over Washington Park Lake
1875
T. J. Sullivan, fabricator

The only original structure remaining in the park, this footbridge was installed in 1875, two years after the picturesque lake was created in the path of the Beaver Creek. Fabricated by T. J. Sullivan, a local brass and iron founder, the bridge was lighted at either end by elaborate gas lamps, which were electrified in 1881. The wooden planks date from a renovation in the 1960s. Paddle boats ply the lake in the summer and skaters, in the winter.

Retrace the route, to corner of State and Willett streets.

State Street Facing the Park

The three blocks of State Street facing Washington Park are an architectural exhibit of styles from the early 1880s through the 1900s. Here are houses by nationally known architects Henry Hobson Richardson and Stanford White, as well as by leading local architects—Albert Fuller; the Ogdens, father and son; Marcus T. Reynolds; and Walter Dickson. Only a few houses pre-date 1880, when the park was nearing completion.

The State Street part of the tour is a walking tour. Start at the corner of Willett and State streets, and head west.

6

First Presbyterian Church 7

1882-84
SE corner of Willett and State Streets
J. Cleveland Cady

The First Presbyterian Church was begun in 1882, a watershed year for architecture in Albany. With Henry Hobson Richardson working in Albany at the Capitol, on the City Hall, and on the Sard house on State Street, the Romanesque Revival style was sweeping the city. Washington Park was virtually finished, and properties facing this great "breathing place" for the city were at a premium. The Presbyterians bought this prominent corner lot and hired New York City architect J. Cleveland Cady, who was known not only for his churches but also for his many buildings at Yale University and Williams College. Cady chose Richardson's builder, Orlando Whitney Norcross, and his trademark Longmeadow sandstone for the building.

A Presbyterian, Cady designed churches in the spirit of the English "dissenting chapel" rather than in the Catholic and Anglican tradition of cruciform plans. In 1897 critic Montgomery Schuyler praised "the dignity and churchliness" of Cady's convenient, theater-like plans. Here in Albany, as in his other Presbyterian churches in Morristown, New Jersey, and Greenwich, Connecticut, Cady integrated the social needs of the church with the sanctuary. The adjacent assembly room was originally separated by sliding wood-and-glass doors that were opened for large services, making the two spaces one.

A solid wall with stained-glass windows was built between the two rooms in the early 1930s.

The church is known for its stained-glass windows. The two walls of windows in the sanctuary, each with five arched panels and three medallions, form an interesting juxtaposition of the work of the competing New York City studios of Louis Comfort Tiffany and Frederick Symetz Lamb. The Tiffany window, installed in December, 1915, forms a continuous scene of an exquisite lake landscape. The Lamb windows, installed a month later, are more traditional, with scenes of the life of Christ in the panels. When lighted at night, the windows can be seen from State and Willett streets.

In the assembly room, there are three more Tiffany windows on the south wall. In the center arch is a magnificent Adirondack view of Lake Luzerne (1914), the first work by Tiffany installed in the building. It memorializes a young missionary, Alice McElroy Kingsbury, who died the year before in Turkey. Twelve years later her mother, Mrs. James McElroy, gave a second Tiffany window depicting the local scientific 19th-century figure Joseph Henry teaching his Albany Academy students about the principles of electromagnetic induction. The third Tiffany window, of Christ blessing the children, was given by Dr. Albert Vander Veer in 1928 in memory of his wife and their three children who died in childhood.

8

363-369½ State Street   8
1893-94
Edmund A. Walsh, builder

This rusticated brownstone row was built by Edmund A. Walsh, a well-known Albany builder who, with his brother John, erected a number of speculative Italianate rows on Madison Avenue overlooking the park in the 1870s. This row resembles a row built by James Eaton at the corner of Lancaster and Lark but has stonecarving in alternating designs, and the underside of the wooden bay windows are carved.

9

371 State Street   9
c. 1906
Worthington Palmer

Commissions by relatives have started many an architect's career. Worthington Palmer (1878-1940) was listed as a mere draughtsman in the city directory when he designed this exquisite Colonial Revival house for his elderly step-grandmother, Martha E. Palmer, the widow of Amos P. Palmer. The finished house was published in *American Architect and Building News*, launching the talented young designer. Around 1920, Palmer used many of these elements—Flemish-bond brick, marble trim and stoop and other Colonial Revival decorative details—on a grander scale at 54 Willett Street. In the course of his career, Palmer worked occasionally for Marcus T. Reynolds.

385-389 State Street 10
1897
Marcus T. Reynolds

Here again a young architect's career was advanced by a commission for his family. Marcus T. Reynolds, just twenty-eight years old and fresh from one and one-half years in Europe, designed a Venetian palazzo, which is actually three houses, for his cousins William Bayard and Dr. Howard van Rensselaer. With this, his first major work, Reynolds set a high standard of design, which he maintained for the next forty years, much to the city's benefit. His hallmarks are seen here—exuberant detailing, imaginative design that draws on historical motifs, and the clever new use of materials in place of ancient construction methods (in this case, terra cotta used for alternating bands of fish scale and vermiculation). The flaming-basket motif in the frieze is taken from the crest of the Van Rensselaer coat of arms.

The three houses were probably intended to accommodate the brothers, Howard and William, and their mother, Laura, side by side, but soon after completion, 387 was sold to felt manufacturer F. C. Huyck and 389 to banker Samuel S. Bullions. William Bayard van Rensselaer and his wife, Louisa, who lived at 385, brought with them some decorative details salvaged from the old Van Rensselaer Manor House, which the family had disassembled four years earlier. Under Marcus Reynolds's supervision, it was partially reconstructed at Williams College as the Sigma Phi fraternity house.

391 State Street 11
1890
Fuller and Wheeler

Published in Albert Fuller's *Artistic Homes* in 1891, this brick and brownstone house was built for Edward McKinney of the Albany Architectural Iron Works. Interestingly, carved stone, rather than ironwork, is the decorative highlight of this house. Flanking the generously proportioned doorway are two pilasters carved with cherubic heads, griffins, and garlands. Fuller's characteristic third-story arched windows have Corinthian columns with twisted shafts. The hinges, doorknob, and escutcheon plates (similar to those on his father's house at 150 Washington Avenue) are testimony to McKinney's lifework with iron.

393 State Street 12
1888

This two-color rusticated brownstone house typifies the influence of H. H. Richardson's Sard house, two doors away, on domestic architecture in Albany in the 1880s. Alice Morgan Wright (1881-1975), sculptor and suffragette, spent most of her long life here in the house built for her father, Henry R. Wright. After her education at Smith College and the Art Students League of New York, Wright went abroad. During her years based in Paris from 1909 to 1914, she became active in the women's suffrage movement. For two months in 1912, she was jailed in London's Holloway Prison with suffrage leader Emmeline Pankhurst as punishment for window smashing. Back in New York City in 1921, Wright helped found New York's League of Women Voters. Some of her sculpture during these years shows an early understanding of cubism, but she never restricted herself to one particular style. In 1923 she exhibited at the National Sculpture Society and won the National Arts Club prize. Wright returned to her parents' house in Albany and set up a studio on the top floor. The *Fist* and *Medea*, two plaster works of the 1920s with feminist themes, are at the Albany Institute of History and Art, where she had her first solo exhibition in the 1930s. Wright's increasing social and humanitarian causes, including a concern for the humane treatment of animals, gradually overshadowed her sculpture. She shared her State Street house with sometimes as many as fifty cats.

395 State Street   13
1890

The stepped gable of this Dutch Revival house is a notable feature of the State Street roofscape. Constructed of Roman yellow brick on a high brownstone basement, it is similar in materials and spirit to Morris Ryder's house at 317 State (1898). Most of the windows have stained-glass transoms, and the original, sinuous Art Nouveau number plate is to the left of the door.

The house was built for Edward P. Durant, a dry goods commission merchant. Durant died two years after the house was built, but his widow, Jennie, and son Clark remained here through 1900. T. Howard Lewis of New York Mutual Life Insurance lived here from 1901 until 1909, when he moved to Boston. Mrs. Emma B. Thacher, widow of John Boyd Thacher, mayor in 1886, 1887, and 1896-97, resided here from 1912 to 1925.

14

397 State Street   14
1882-85
Henry Hobson Richardson
Annex, 1925

The Sard house was Richardson's final project in Albany and his only residential commission in the city. Richardson's architectural activity in Albany began in 1875, when he and Leopold Eidlitz of New York City took joint responsibility for continued work on the Capitol. In 1880-81, Richardson designed the new City Hall after the old one burned. Just as it was nearing completion and Washington Park was being finished, this house was constructed for stove manufacturer Grange Sard, Jr. It had a profound effect on Albany domestic architecture over the next decade, sweeping away the Italianate styles of the 1870s. Modern Albanians wanted the rustication, Romanesque arches, swelling bays and foliated arches of the Sards' house on this double lot overlooking Washington Park.

Richardson employed some of the stonecarving crew from the Capitol to embellish the facade. Over the ogee-arched doorway are two carved heads, said to be likenesses of the Sards, and beneath them a coiled snake. The arch springs from the mouth of a griffin. A dog-like creature is biting its tail under the bulging parapet of the porch, nicknamed "Sard's bathtub."

Real estate developer Ulysses Stockwell bought the house after Grange Sard's death in 1924. Stockwell already owned the Dana Apartments and had converted the Amsdell Brewery into the Knickerbocker Apartments. Here at 397 State Street he had another vision: he kept the Sard house intact, making a large apartment for himself on the second floor. In the rear garden he constructed a thirteen-story building with nearly one hundred efficiency apartments linked to the house through the original mahogany-paneled front hall. The solarium on the top floor of the new apartment building was originally designed as social rooms for the residents. A tiny Dutch-style dwelling atop the tower houses elevator equipment.

1 Henry Johnson Boulevard   15
1898
Fuller and Pitcher

One can easily imagine this grand and richly detailed Renaissance Revival house as the home of a portly and genial man, James McCredie, a maltster and general superintendent of the

United Traction Company. The east facade of this brick-and-sandstone house has an irregular composition. The dominant feature is the second-story Palladian window. Unlike most of Fuller's houses, the off-center front door, rather than being a major feature, matches the adjacent arched window with quoined trim. This block of State Street has three more houses designed by Fuller and Pitcher in the 1890s.

407 State Street   16
c. 1890
Ogden and Wright

The fanciful ironwork outdoes the architecture of this relatively simple brownstone facade designed by Ogden and Wright. The handrail spirals down the newel post. The stair panels are flat iron strips woven together, and on the landing large circles are filled with scrollwork. The owner, Eugene Hartt, was a partner in the grocery business of Wing Brothers and Hartt. Ogden and Wright designed two other rusticated brownstones around Washington Park at this time: 483 State in 1886-87 and 26 Willett in 1889, which has a similar arched doorway flanked by plain piers.

411 State Street   17
1900
Now Clifton and Delores Wharton Research Center, Nelson A. Rockefeller Institute of Government
William Ross Proctor

Built on grand hopes for a young married couple at the beginning of a new century, and probably the largest rowhouse ever built in Albany, this Dutch Renaissance Revival house had a tragic start. It was to be the wedding present of Singer Sewing Machine vice president and director William F. Proctor to his daughter Ada. Her brother, William Ross Proctor, was the architect, and her fiancé, Charles van Heusen, is said to have sketched the plan on a billiard table at the Fort Orange Club. But before the grand structure was finished, the Van Heusens' short-lived marriage was dissolved. In 1902, construction and utilities magnate Anthony N. Brady bought the

17

house and had the interior completed. Brady commissioned Albany artist Will H. Low to decorate the music room with four lunette wall murals of allegorical subjects with the intertwined initials of the owner.

After the deaths of Mr. and Mrs. Brady, Benjamin Whitbeck converted the house into apartments, known first as the Chateau Plaza and in 1921 as the Colony Plaza. The second-floor ballroom was a venue for children's dancing lessons in the 1920s. From 1964 to 1985, the building was owned by the Research Foundation of the State of New York, which restored it in 1981-82. It is now occupied by another branch of the state university, the Nelson A. Rockefeller Institute of Government. The former carriage house, now used for offices, stands around the corner at 13 Henry Johnson Boulevard.

415 and 423 State Street   18
c. 1900
Fuller and Pitcher

Albert Fuller's abundant creativity produced this Renaissance Revival pair for two brothers-in-law, who were partners in a pharmaceutical firm. Unified by scale, proportion and materials, each building has its own distinct design that is apparent in the doorway details, window treatments and cornices. Both houses have delicate ironwork on the front steps and are linked by an iron fence that once enclosed a garden.

William J. Walker's house (423) was completed first, prior to the birth of his fifth child, Edith Walker. Soon afterward, 415 was finished for his sister, Anna, and her husband, Charles Gibson. The houses had a shared gardener's cottage on Washington Avenue. Two generations of cousins grew up in the houses, and both William W. Gibson, son of Charles, and Janet Walker, granddaughter of William J. Walker, were trustees of the YMCA. In 1949 both houses were sold to the Y, which established its executive offices in the Walker house and a dormitory in the Gibson house.

18

Eventually the YMCA built a new building on the property facing Washington Avenue. Both houses are now owned by a not-for-profit corporation affiliated with the state university. They were recently restored and renovated by Mallin, Mendel and Associates, Architects.

425 State Street 19
1890
Fuller and Wheeler

Built a decade before the neighboring Gibson and Walker houses, this brick and stone-trimmed house was published in Albert Fuller's *Artistic Homes* in 1891. Horace Young was vice president of the Delaware and Hudson

Railroad and chairman of the Albany Trust Company. The copper-sheathed second-story bay has swags above foliated decoration. The arched front door is framed by a simple bluestone surround with Ionic pilasters and egg-and-dart molding. The nicely executed ironwork is bolted inventively to the side of the stoop.

429 State Street 20
1867
New facade, 1904

The yellow brick and cast-stone facade dates from 1904, when this Civil War-era house was remodelled, probably by contractor John M. Collins, who moved here from 953 Madison Avenue in 1905. The railing, with cast-iron posts and a variety of scrolls, also dates from this period.

433 State Street 21
1867
Remodeled, 1889

The earliest facade on the block, 433 was built the year before the graves of the old burial ground across the street were removed to Albany Rural Cemetery. An 1876 map shows four brick houses owned by Harvey Wood standing virtually alone on this section of the block. In 1889, when Charles Bissell remodeled the property, he joined two houses and added the brownstone stoop and railing. The Bissell family lived here well into the 20th century.

434-437 State Street 22
1880

Towering over the adjacent two-story brick row of the 1860s to the east, this brownstone row of 1880 heralded the new scale of fashionable State Street. The houses are paired, with wide stoops and massive cast-iron railings. The flat facades have rosettes and incised decoration on the lintels. The row appears to have been built for Albert V. Bensen, who lived for many years at 439.

439 State Street   23
1880

This pressed-brick and rusticated brownstone house, built for Albert V. Bensen of the China Tea Company, may well have been the work of Albert Fuller. It has his characteristic arched front door and double window treatments on the ground floor, and the upper stories are defined by strong belt courses. A pair of carved beavers decorates the second-story string course. The third-floor trio of arched windows is framed by a subtle Dutch gable. The Bensen family lived here for more than forty years.

441 State Street   24
1890

Built in 1890 for grocer Albert J. Wing after his family subdivided property on Madison Avenue, this house remained in the family for the next sixty years, until Cornelia Wing's death in 1949. The four-story brick house is trimmed with stone and has vermiculated courses at the basement level. The second-story bay is supported by sharply stepped brickwork. The iron railing, with its undulating bars, is similar to a pattern exhibited at the 1876 Centennial Exhibition in Philadelphia and is also found at 30 and 44 Willett Street.

443 State Street   25
1881

This rusticated brownstone was occupied by the family of lawyer David Brockway from 1883 through the end of the 19th century. The Neo-Classical projecting bay, with swags and shield, is similar to one at the rusticated 483 State by Ogden and Wright (1886-87).

449-455 State Street   26
1879

Originally these houses were a matched row, probably unpainted, with bands of stone trim like that at 449 and with bay windows and cresting over the mansard roofs. Inset blue tiles decorate the window lintels and sills. The original iron railings at 451 and 453 have a two-dimensional design, with foliated scrolls and panels pierced with quatrefoils, a motif seen at the gates of the Centennial Exhibition in 1876.

461 State Street   27
1872-73
Remodeled facade, Charles Ogden, 1917

Albany architect Charles Ogden (1867-1931) lived here during the most productive period of his life, from 1907 to 1918. His corner house, as well as the two adjacent ones, had been early structures on this part of State Street. In 1917 Ogden stuccoed his house, giving it a Spanish character reminiscent of the work of his former apprentice and partner Walter van Guysling. Two doors down, 457 was refaced in brick in 1929.

28

1 Sprague Place   28
1902-04
McKim, Mead and White

Bon vivant Stanford White complained about Albany when sent here by H. H. Richardson on an assignment at the Capitol in 1878: "Of all the miserable, wretched, second class, one horse towns this is the most miserable—not even a church fair or dance saloon to go to."

But White did return some twenty years later for this, his only Albany commission, built on the site of the Sprague Presbyterian Church. Facing Sprague Place, with swelling front bays, Ionic-columned entrance porch, and plenty of marble and terra-cotta trim, the Arnold house makes a strong visual definition for this corner. Benjamin Arnold was a lumber dealer, banker, and railroad president. He was married three times, twice to Van Rensselaer women. Arnold died in 1932, and his widow, Elizabeth van Rensselaer Arnold, lived here until her death in 1945. In recent years, the house served as the chancery for the Roman Catholic Diocese of Albany. The quartered-circle pattern of ironwork on the balconies is found on other McKim, Mead and White commissions in New York City. The former Arnold family carriage house down the street at 307 Washington Avenue, now used for offices, is also brick trimmed with marble.

Turn north one block to Western Avenue.

Western Avenue 29

The plank-covered Great Western Turnpike, which was chartered in 1799, linked Albany to western New York. In 1876-77, it was repaved in granite block as a grand approach to the new Washington Park. Water, gas and sewer lines were installed at this time, and James Kidd donated a double row of Norway maples, set at forty-foot intervals.

Engine No. 1 Firehouse 30
Junction of Washington and Western Avenues
1892
Ernest Hoffman

The multi-faceted, rusticated former Steamer No. 1 firehouse is one of Ernest Hoffman's most successful compositions in the city. Commanding this key location at the convergence of Washington and Western avenues, this polychromatic sandstone and granite Richardsonian Romanesque building was built in the final years of the horse-drawn fire equipment era.

Ernest Hoffman (1852-1908) was an architect of German descent. Son of a Lutheran pastor, young Hoffman trained in Albany

30

under Charles Nichols and began practicing on his own in 1877. Among his early works are the brick St. John's Evangelical Lutheran Church (1885) on Central Avenue near Robin Street, which was built for his father's German-speaking congregation, and the Romanesque La Dow castle (1891) on Thurlow Terrace.

Return to State Street.

469 State Street 31
1884

John R. Carnell purchased Albany Business College in 1884, and in December of that year moved into this newly completed residence. Son of a Troy tailor, Carnell was a graduate of Troy Business College. Later he taught there, became the principal and then bought the school before coming to Albany. Carnell hired Ogden and Wright to design the Albany Business College building on North Pearl Street in 1887, and his State Street house, with Romanesque arches on the ground floor and attenuated windows above, may well have been the work of Albert Fuller or Edward Ogden. After the death of Carnell's daughter, Hope, in 1953, the house was used as a dormitory for the Albany Business College. In 1977 Carnell's descendants took up residence in the house.

479 State Street — 32

1888
Alterations, Albert Fuller, 1896

Albert Fuller is known to have made alterations to this large house in 1896, and the original design may have been his, as it has many elements characteristic of his work in the 1880s. The arched entrance is trimmed with rusticated sandstone, and the three stories are defined by string courses. The highlight of the facade is the varied roofline with a corner corbelled turret and unmatched gables, each decorated with a finial. The larger gable has a Palladian window.

George A. Woolverton moved here in 1892, and after his death three years later his daughter, Adda Stedman, hired Fuller to make alterations. After she died in 1909, Peter G. Ten Eyck bought the house, and the Ten Eycks spent their winters here for the next thirty-five years. A civil engineer who later went into the insurance business, Ten Eyck had a variety of interests and accomplishments, including several patents for railway signal devices. As a two-term congressman, he advocated dredging the Hudson River and the creation of the new port of Albany. Ten Eyck was the port's first commissioner and state commissioner of agriculture.

483 State Street — 33

1886-87
Ogden and Wright

Built for a prominent Albany undertaker, Marshall Tebbutt, 483 has a rusticated stone facade and fine ironwork. The railings are a dramatic composition of scrolls and swirled iron rods that form bulbous newel posts. The handrail is a simple bar of iron that doubles back upon itself to form a base for each brass ball finial. This was the first of three rusticated brownstones designed by Ogden and Wright in the late 1880s that overlooked Washington Park (the others are 407 State and 26 Willett).

485 State Street — 34

1901
Attributed to Albert Fuller

Albert Fuller (1854-1934) was one of Albany's most prolific and versatile late 19th-century architects, and in a twenty-year period he designed or remodelled at least six houses on these three blocks of State Street facing the park alone, to say nothing of his numerous public buildings and houses in other parts of the city. At the turn of the century, the prosperous architect seems to have outgrown his rowhouse at 497 and moved to 485. Built of characteristic materials, the new design shows Fuller's increasing use of Classical Revival styles. Number 485 was built about the same time as 415-423 State and School 12, nearby at Washington Avenue and Robin Street. Late in life, Fuller moved to 353 State Street, on the corner of Lark. He also had a country house across the Hudson River, near Castleton.

487 State Street — 35

1885

This handsome rusticated facade dates from 1885 and is built of a reddish sandstone. The arches of the doorway and first-floor window have keystones in the form of a scroll. The dentilled string course between the first and second floors terminates in foliated carving, a motif continued above the carved stone second-story bay and the cornice. The house was built for Stephen Whitney.

489 State Street — 36

1905-06

This fine Colonial Revival house was built in 1905-06 for Edward Waterman, whose family lived here for many years. Opulent, carved garlands droop over the arched doorway of the otherwise simply tooled stone first floor. Above is Flemish-bond brickwork, a mansard roof, and two dormers. The stoop railing is decorated with urns and terminates with sinuous, Art Nouveau scrolls.

491 State Street 37
Enlarged, 1905

John Alden Dix lived here before and after his term as governor (1910-12). Dix appears to have been responsible for engaging architect William H. Miller (1878-1922) to enlarge this house to its present appearance, altering an earlier house of lawyer James Fenimore Cooper numbered 493. The recessed, arched doorway of this semi-attached house has fine wrought ironwork similar to that of turn-of-the-century houses in New York City and Paris apartment buildings. Governor Dix (1860-1928) grew up in Glens Falls and entered politics after a career in the stone, lumber and paper industries and in banking.

495 State Street 38
c. 1905
Charles Ogden

Prentiss Carnell, son of John R. Carnell, who grew up at 469 State Street, had this house built soon after his marriage in 1903 to Ethel Bradley. Wreaths and roses decorate the tympanums of the second-story arched windows of the classically inspired facade, which was designed by Charles Ogden. The original owner moved to Slingerlands in the 1920s and rented the townhouse until his son, Prentiss Carnell, Jr., moved here for several years in the mid-1930s.

497-499 State Street 39
1884
Attributed to Albert Fuller

Albert Fuller apparently designed this unmatched pair early in his career and moved from 271 Lark Street into 497, the smaller house, in 1885. Both houses are entered through wide arches trimmed with foliated molding—Fuller's trademark of the 1880s and early 1890s. At 497 there is a big second-story window with a terra-cotta frame, as well as acanthus leaf decoration at the cornice. Number 499 has a Classical Revival bay window with Corinthian pilasters and swags.

40

503 State Street 40
1886
Walter Dickson

Just as Albert Fuller was building his relatively modest pair next door, another architect, Walter Dickson (1838-1903), built this substantial and unique house for himself. Unlike Fuller, however, Dickson left curiously little mark on Albany, aside from this remarkable house. He was the architect of the temporary structure in Academy Park for the Army Relief Bazaar (1864) and was one of a succession of architects who worked on the former Federal Building on Broadway (1879-83). He moved to New York in 1889 to become a partner to architect Frederick Withers. In the 1890s, after Withers's untimely death, Dickson supervised the construction of several buildings on Welfare (now Roosevelt) Island, notably the Neo-Renaissance Strecker Memorial Laboratory.

In contrast to the Richardsonian houses popular in Albany in the 1880s, the Dickson house is the work of an original mind using the flatiron site to its best advantage. The thick, almost medieval walls are faced with diaper brickwork. The slightly projecting center gable has an arched opening and balcony on the second story. At the entry, there is an L-shaped bench with a masonry seat and an iron lattice back.

To drive the rest of the tour, travel west along the road in the park that runs parallel to State Street. Turn left onto Englewood Place.

Englewood Place   41

Jutting into the northwest corner of Washington Park, Englewood Place was laid out in lots in 1879 and Thurlow Terrace in 1881. Although less than half of the original houses and carriage houses survive, they are indicative of the style and scale of the original residences. Fences were not permitted; instead the lawns merge with the parkland, as advocated by the park's guiding spirit, Frederick Law Olmsted.

Robin Street was renamed Englewood Place in the late 1870s, and between 1879 and 1887 five imposing houses were constructed overlooking the park. Numbers 1, 2 and 3 were designed by local architect William M. Woollett in 1879, and 5 and 7 were designed by Robert Gibson, the architect of All Saints Cathedral. Four of the five houses on Englewood Place were published in *American Architect and Building News.*

1 Englewood Place   42
c. 1879
William M. Woollett

Number 1 Englewood Place is the sole survivor of a trio of free-standing brick villas designed by William M. Woollett (1850-80) as Washington Park was nearing completion. This building is the only example of his work known to survive in Albany. When his book of prototype plans and elevations entitled *Villas and Cottages or Homes for All* was published in 1876, Woollett was said to have "inherited the high character and professional genius" of his father, architect William L. Woollett. The Englewood Place houses, elaborate versions of the preliminary studies, must have been a direct result of this entrepreneurial publication. Woollett died of consumption at the age of thirty, just as his career was taking off with his second volume, *Old Homes Made New,* and the publication of his Englewood Place houses

in the *American Architect and Building News.*

Number 1 Englewood Place was built for Benjamin W. Wooster, whose family lived here well into the 20th century. It has lost a long porch on the north side of the house, a small second-story porch and a dormer over the front door. Otherwise, the house retains many rich details, including brick corbelling and the iron cresting on its distinctive corner belvedere.

42

2 Englewood Place   43
1937
Office of Marcus T. Reynolds

This address now refers to the carriage house which once served the middle house of the three Woollett villas on Englewood Place. The main house, constructed for Oscar Hascy, resembled 1 Englewood in materials and style. When James Taber Loree bought the property, he demolished the big house and commissioned the office of Marcus T. Reynolds to built a new structure partially on the foundations of the carriage house. Reynolds's association with the Loree family went back a generation when, in 1914, he designed the Delaware and Hudson Building at the foot of State Street for James's father, Lenore Loree, president of the railroad.

5 Englewood Place 44
c. 1887
Robert W. Gibson

English-born and trained, Robert W. Gibson launched his architectural career in Albany in the 1880s. His breakthrough commission was the Episcopal Cathedral of All Saints, which he won in 1884 in competition against the architectural giant H. H. Richardson. The cathedral was underway when he began this house for James E. Craig in the same pink Potsdam sandstone that he used on the cathedral (begun in 1884) and at the lodge (1882) and chapel (1884) at the Albany Rural Cemetery. Young Gibson's admiration of Richardson and the Romanesque style is evident at the Craig house and the cemetery buildings. John N. Huyck owned 5 Englewood in the early 20th century, and in 1923 his widow, Anna, sold it to Peter D. Kiernan, whose family owned it for nearly fifty years. The Kiernan children and grandchildren enjoyed playing in "Old Snarley," the enormous weeping beech beside the porte cochere. The only major change to the exterior is the loss of an octagonal porch with a bell-shaped roof over a one-story rear wing.

45

7 Englewood Place 45
c. 1884
Robert W. Gibson
Remodeled, Charles Simmons, Jr., 1941

Sweeping expanses of clay-tile roof punctuated by Romanesque turrets, gables, and conical towers characterize this distinctive former carriage house. The marble horse trough on the front facade is a reminder of the building's original purpose. The main house, which stood in front, was built of brick with stone trim and tile roofs and was probably the largest of the grand Englewood houses. It was designed around 1884 by architect Robert W. Gibson for George Evans, who knew Gibson through his work at All Saints Cathedral. The roof tiles were manufactured by the Celadon Tile Company of Albany, which was purchased by the midwestern Ludowici Company in the 1880s.

By February, 1889, when the finished house at 7 Englewood was published for a second time in the *American Architect and Building News*, it had been acquired by Robert C. Pruyn, who moved here from across the park on Willett Street. In 1941 newlywed Charles A. Simmons, Jr., of the Simmons Machine Tool Company bought the property from the Pruyn heirs. Like James Taber Loree at 2 Englewood, Simmons envisioned the carriage house as a residence. Before demolishing the house, he salvaged the front door and many interior details and reused them in the carriage house conversion. British landscape architect John Brookes redesigned the grounds in 1989.

Return along Englewood Place.

Adult Learning Center 46
1902
Formerly School 12
NE corner of Robin Street and Western Avenue
Fuller and Pitcher

Albert Fuller designed some five schools for the city of Albany between 1890 and 1917. This Classical Revival one dates from 1902 and was originally known as School 12. Such architectural features as Diocletian windows, pilasters, coursed brickwork and quoins Fuller employed over twenty years later at the Harmanus Bleecker Library (1924). This site was previously occupied by the Protestant Orphan School, which faced the orphanage across the street, now the site of the downtown SUNYA campus.

Head west on Western Avenue, and take first left onto Thurlow Terrace.

Thurlow Terrace 47

Once lined with elms, this boulevard was developed a decade after Englewood Place. The street was laid out through the grounds of the Civil War-era house of William Barnes, Sr., and his wife, Emily, daughter of the legendary Thurlow Weed of the *Albany Evening Journal*. In the late 1880s their son, Thurlow Weed Barnes of Boston, subdivided the family property. Beginning in 1889 with the Field house, eight ''first class'' dwellings were constructed. The houses were to be set back thirty-six feet from the street. The park commissioners were to enforce the restrictions, which allowed no commercial, industrial, or public uses for the properties.

Among the important houses since demolished was one that stood behind the brick wall on the northwest corner of Thurlow and Western and was designed by Fuller and Pitcher in 1906 for E. P. Gavit, son-in-law of Anthony N. Brady, and later owned by William Barnes, Jr. Known as ''boy wonder,'' William Jr. took over the family newspaper fresh from Harvard and ran the local Republican party for twenty years, until his defeat in 1921 by the O'Connell organization, which dominated city politics for much of the rest of the century. The State University of New York at Albany, whose campus stands at the north end of the street, purchased many Thurlow Terrace properties in the late 1950s and has since sold them.

8 Thurlow Terrace 48
1916
Lewis Colt Albro

Bab-O manufacturer Jerome Mendleson rejected the designs for a house on this Thurlow Terrace site that he had commissioned of the renowned Frank Lloyd Wright (reproduced above). Mendleson ended up instead with this more prosaic house by a less well known New York City architect, Lewis Colt Albro (1876-1924). After working as a draftsman for McKim, Mead and White, Albro went into partnership with Harrie T. Lindeberg from 1906 to 1914, and together they developed a reputation for solid, comfortable, picturesque country houses in an English cottage style

48

influenced by Edwin Lutyens. Here on Thurlow Terrace, Albro's house for Mendleson has a deceptively small look with its steeply pitched slate roof, but the grand marble doorway is almost baronial, befitting a house with a large service wing concealed to the rear. The house was published in 1922 in *The American House: Being a Collection of Illustrations and Plans of the Best Country and Suburban Homes Built in the U.S. during the Last Few Years.* For over thirty years it served as a residence for the bishops of the Roman Catholic Diocese, until it became the office of the president of SUNYA in 1957.

49

10 Thurlow Terrace 49
1891
Ernest Hoffman

Built for Charles La Dow, who invented a ''self sharpening plow'' and held nearly a hundred other patents for agricultural machinery, this granite "castle" was designed by Ernest Hoffman. The original polychromatic effect has been obscured over the years, but originally the string courses separating the stories, the keystones in window arches and other trim were a lighter color. Hoffman's Steamer No. 1 firehouse (1892), located nearby at the junction of Western and Washington avenues, has more pronounced polychromy with darker sandstone trim.

La Dow moved here from Hamilton Street. Soon afterwards, a son was asphyxiated in his bedroom, apparently due to a faulty gas fixture. On Christmas Day, 1904, La Dow dropped dead while waiting for a streetcar on Central Avenue. His widow, Alice, was left in reduced circumstances, and the property, including the adjacent lot to the north, fell into the hands of Empire State Surety. Mary Hunt bought the house in 1910, and it remained in the Hunt family through 1946, when Cora Hunt "the alleged widow" of Mary Hunt's incompetent son, claimed the property.

9 Thurlow Terrace 50
1889-90

With its double porches overlooking the lake in Washington Park, this was apparently the first house to be built on Thurlow Terrace. Soon after its completion, Mrs. John W. Field, its original owner, departed for Paris. The next occupants were William Gorham Rice and his bride, Harriet Pruyn. Harriet was accustomed to the busy social pace of Elk Street and, according to her sister Huybertie, found this location "very far out and lonely." Once her own new house was under construction on Washington Avenue (now part of the Albany Institute), Harriet wrote lyrically in her diary about her final months in 1893-94 on Thurlow with her newborn son: "We live here very quietly—I not being well, and so not strong. We saw our glorious red sunsets all winter in the knowledge at its being the last we would be able to enjoy them in so full and perfect a way—even from our own library. It was a snowy winter—one great storm when we were three days shut in, and I think of those months

as more completely alone with my husband and child and nature than any before. . ."

7 Thurlow Terrace 51
1948

This one-and-one-half story suburban-style cottage fits neatly on its small lot, which was originally part of Robert Pruyn's property on Englewood Place. It was built for Katherine Morris, sold soon afterward to Frederick Tillinghast of Menands, and like others on Thurlow bought by SUNYA in 1957.

At the top of Thurlow Terrace is the SUNYA campus. Turn left and proceed west on Western Avenue toward South Lake Avenue.

52

State University of New York 52
at Albany Downtown Campus
135 Western Avenue
Draper, Hawley and Husted Halls: George L. Heins with Albert R. Ross, consulting architect, 1907-09
Page, Richardson and Milne Halls: Sullivan Jones and William Haugaard, state architects, 1927-29

A planned Georgian Revival college campus, these structures were built to house the New York State College for Teachers and located on the site of the Albany Orphan Asylum, which had been built in 1832, enlarged by William L. Woollett in 1852 and demolished in 1907. In contrast to their earlier monolithic quarters on Willett Street, which burned in 1906, this campus represents a new approach to collegiate architecture in which various departments were housed in separate structures. The campus includes two academic complexes, built twenty years apart, which face Western Avenue.

Draper Hall is the centerpiece of the 1907-09 group. It is named for the first state commissioner of education, Andrew Sloan Draper, who oversaw the construction of these buildings and had an office here while his other big project, the state Education Building (1909-11), was underway. The Corinthian capitals and other decorative details on Draper Hall foreshadow the state Education Building's great terracotta-clad Corinthian capitals.

A curved colonnade links Husted Hall on the west side and Hawley on the east side of Draper. Once an auditorium and now the Graduate Library for Public Affairs and Policy, Hawley Hall has a series of stained-glass windows given by graduating classes between 1911 and 1924. Depicting natural and allegorical subjects, the windows are probably the work of the Chapman Stained Glass Studio, an Albany workshop established in 1898, which supervised their restoration in the 1980s. The library walls are covered with canvas panels painted by William Brantley van Ingen (1858-1955), who was employed by the Work Progress Administration from 1937 to 1938 to produce these historical scenes soon after the room was converted to a library. "My constant thought. . .was to make something students would be interested in and like," he wrote later. Inspired by verdure tapestries in which trees are the unifying feature, Van Ingen painted grand scenes from local history ranging from the arrival of the *Half Moon* in 1609 to "Clinton's Ditch" and finally a Civilian Conservation Corps camp of 1933.

Sullivan Jones and William Haugaard, the team of state architects who built the Alfred E. Smith Building, designed and supervised the construction of the second academic complex between 1927 and 1929. Page Hall, which houses a new and larger auditorium and gymnasium, is the central structure with its crowning cupola and Georgian urns, cartouche, and swags. Milne Hall, to the west of Page Hall, originally housed the Milne High School, where student teachers gained practical classroom experience. David C. Lithgow painted murals in the upstairs library.

Philip Schuyler Elementary School 53
1912-13
Formerly Albany High School
NE corner of North Lake and Western Avenues

This vast classical structure of buff-colored tapestry brick and stone was built originally as a high school after the earlier high school facing Academy Park (Ogden and Wright, 1874-76) became overcrowded. This "magnificent million dollar" structure opened in 1913.

Head south on South Lake Avenue, and turn left on Madison Avenue. Buildings on South Lake are described in Tour 7, entries 1 through 21.

710 Madison Avenue 54
c. 1873

In the early 1870s, when this Italianate house and its mate, 706 Madison, were built, they overlooked the grounds of John Taylor's great Greek Revival house of 1820, Richmond Hill. In 1882 the Washington Park Commissioners acquired the Taylor property, demolished the house, and graded the land for tennis courts.

Number 710 Madison was probably built for Henry Kelly, county treasurer and an officer of Troy Laundry Machinery Company, around 1873, when he moved here. The main portion of the square brick house with its hipped roof is little changed since Kelly's day. The rear wing must have been added soon afterward. Kelly moved to South Lake Avenue in the early 1880s. During the early 20th century, 710 was the home of John A. Sleicher, a publisher and leading Republican party figure.

698 Madison Avenue 55
1895

This late Romanesque Revival house was built for Willis Winne. The exaggerated cresting and finials are reminiscent of architect Ernest Hoffman's La Dow "castle" (1891) on Thurlow Terrace. The large corner tower has a bell-shaped roof, and the turret on the right has a conical one. In the early 20th century stove manufacturer William van Wormer moved here from Thurlow Terrace and lived here until his death in 1914.

694 Madison Avenue   56
c. 1869

One of the earliest houses constructed on the block, this two-story, frame Italianate house, set back on its lot, was probably built for printer Samuel Morris, who moved here in 1869. Later it was owned by the Schweiker family from 1911 through the 1930s. John William Schweiker, Jr., of the J. L. Lochner fruit business, and Frederick A Schweiker, foreman on the New York Central Railroad, both lived here.

688C Madison Avenue   57
1897
Edward Ogden and Son

A later work of Edward Ogden, this buff brick house was built for Frank McNamee, manager of Equitable Life Assurance Society. It was purchased by the Good Samaritan Lutheran Home in the 1950s.

688B Madison Avenue   58
Late 1880s

Built for jeweller James Mix, this house is a display of fancy brickwork and terra-cotta detailing. Terra-cotta string courses, window decorations, and panels are everywhere. On the east facade a large rectangular panel depicts a bowl full of sunflowers. The roofline is enriched with chimneys, gables, and a tower. Mix's associate, Fred Hoagland, boarded with him in the 1890s, and later the Hoaglands acquired the house and lived here through the mid-1920s. Since then it has been a home for the elderly. Founded by the League of Lutheran Women of Albany and the Vicinity, the home was originally intended only for ladies. In 1933, the first resident moved in and twenty years later the home expanded to the former McNamee House (now 688C). Renamed the Good Samaritan Lutheran Home, it recently began admitting men and purchased the former Sayles house (688A).

688A Madison Avenue   59
c. 1896
William Sayles, builder

William Sayles, a prominent builder at the turn of the century and city assessor, moved here from Hudson Avenue just as the nearby Pine Hills boom was beginning. This Classical Revival frame house with its wide front porch decorated with a shell motif, stained-glass transoms and Palladian window in the gable was a showcase of the Gick and Sayles style. Arthur Sayles took over his father's business and continued to live here into the late 1940s. The Lutheran Home purchased the house in 1981 and changed the street number from 684.

662 Madison Avenue   60
1901

Nathan Hatch, owner of a shoddy mill between Hamilton Street and Hudson Avenue above Washington Park, built this spacious Classical Revival house in 1901 on the site of an earlier house that burned. Built of Flemish-bond brick (a treatment followed soon afterward in the neighboring pair at 666-668), the house has a hip roof and a balustraded widow's walk.

654 Madison Avenue   61
c. 1896
Attributed to Franklin Janes

If this is the work of architect Franklin Janes, this unique brick and stone house was one of his last projects in Albany before moving to Puerto Rico in 1899 and later to New York City. Janes's buildings were always original and lavishly detailed: the most spectacular example is the Moorish-style School 1 on Bassett Street in the South End (1889). Here at the Rickard House, the first floor is a reddish sandstone with piers supporting the overhanging second story of buff-colored brick. Although the overall design appears symmetrical, the front door is off-center next to the porte cochere, and there is a tiny, surprisingly asymmetrical gable punctuating the tile roof. The wide cornice depicts mythical faces, animals, and horticultural subjects.

The house was built for Michael Rickard,

a Horatio Alger figure of the upstate New York railroads. After his father was killed, ten-year-old Rickard, a small town youth from Herkimer County, went to work as a chain boy in the engineer construction corps. He worked his way through jobs in the ticket office and as fireman and engineer. For years he ran passenger engine number 238 from Syracuse to Utica. His nomination to the state Board of Railroad Commissioners brought him to Albany and was considered a "deserved recognition of the workingman."

Frank Guilfoyle of the Dobler Brewing Company acquired this property in 1912. In 1924 ice cream manufacturer Fredrick Hosler bought the house, which his descendants still occupy. Hosler had two ice cream stores a block apart on Lark Street. His factory stood on Spruce Street, north of Washington Avenue.

644A and B Madison Avenue 62
c. 1902
Alexander Selkirk
Front porch, 1930s

The Mendleson family, known as manufacturers of Bab-O cleanser, built this double house. Aaron Mendleson founded a potash and soap manufacturing company in 1856. Late in life he hired Alexander Selkirk to design this house with a wide entrance arch for his family of four sons—Norman, Jerome, Leon and Ira. Aaron died in 1904, but the family continued to occupy the two houses. In 1917, Jerome built a new house on Thurlow Terrace, and Ira moved further up Madison Avenue to 1006. Leon Mendleson lived at 644A through the 1920s, and in the 1930s the new owner, Theodore Simpson of the Mayfair Company, added the Colonial Revival porch.

634 Madison Avenue 63
c. 1884
Edmund A. Walsh, builder

Edmund A. Walsh was a leading Albany builder whose many speculative rowhouses of the 1870s and the early 1900s overlook Washington Park on three blocks of Madison Avenue east of Robin. This turreted brick house was built for ostrich feather merchant

Charles Fletcher. In 1915 Frances Thanhauser inherited the house from her brother, William Lowenthal, and lived here for many years.

Albany Medical Center Annex 64
1907
Formerly Academy of the Holy Names
628 Madison Avenue
Charles Ogden
Chapel, Charles Ogden, 1914-15

This massive, granite-faced Collegiate Gothic school building was constructed in two stages beginning in 1907. Throughout the later 19th and early 20th centuries the Ogdens—father Edward and his son Charles—designed a series of buildings for the Catholic Diocese of Albany including two convents on Central Avenue in the early 1890s and two churches in the South End—Saint John's (1903-08) and Saint Anthony's (1908-15). This building was the biggest and final Roman Catholic commission of Charles Ogden's career.

The Academy of the Holy Names, a girls' school, was founded in 1884, and an 1892 map shows a "French convent" located here. Ogden may have incorporated the earlier building in the new design. Inside, the upper walls of the front hall are decorated with a frieze of religious and allegorical figures said to be the work of early teachers and students. The final phase was completed in 1915 with the construction of the chapel, which now serves as a multipurpose meeting room. In 1983 Albany Medical Center renovated the academic structure for its administrative offices and restored some of the public spaces.

64

Madison Avenue rowhouses   65

Madison Avenue from Robin to Willett Streets

Compared to other streets facing the park, these three blocks of Madison have more speculative housing, and the distinctive single house is relatively rare. Many of the rowhouses were constructed by Edmund A. Walsh (1854-1904), a local builder, during two distinct building phases in the 1870s and in the early 1900s.

Walsh grew up in the neighborhood, a son of gardener Maurice Walsh, who lived on Knox Street. Maurice Walsh was probably associated with T. Davidson's Albany Nursery, which was described in Civil War-era directories as located on Madison Avenue opposite the parade ground and advertised an array of fruit and ornamental trees, raspberries, and bedding plants.

Edmund Walsh and his brother John began their construction business in 1874 while still boarding with their father at the corner of Knox and Morris streets. An 1876 map shows their shop on Yates Street (now Dana Avenue). In their first four years they constructed at least three substantial rows on Madison facing the new park—600-606, 496-506, and the row including 494, a choice corner house where their widowed mother overlooked the family holdings. At this time the Walsh brothers built 131-135 Knox Street and a substantial brownstone at 64 Willett. Their partnership ended in 1881, and Edmund continued in the building trade employing between twenty-five and fifty-five workers. By the late 1890s he was reported to have built about one hundred houses and a number of institutional and commercial structures. In 1902, two years before he died, he constructed a row of townhouse flats at 580-594 Madison Avenue. These paired, buff-colored brick structures stand on land held previously by the Washington Park Commissioners as a potential link to future parkland on the then-publicly owned grounds of the Industrial School and the Albany Alms House (now partly occupied by the Albany Medical Center). Walsh may have been involved in the development of other lots along Madison between New Scotland and Knox. A number of buff brick rowhouses and freestanding houses were built there in 1903—numbers 510-524, 536-540, and 542-552.

620 Madison Avenue   66

c. 1885

This fine Queen Anne house, built apparently for Martin van Buren Bull, has much in common with Albert Fuller's work of the mid-1880s. The entrance is on Robin Street through a wide arch under a balcony. The polygonal tower with fish-scale tiles defines the corner. Bull came to Albany from Washington County in 1866. As manager of the Albany branch of the Phoenix Mutual Life Insurance Company and, with the help of his sons who became co-partners in 1881, he supervised hundreds of sub-agencies throughout New York, Vermont and New Hampshire. The Bulls moved here from 1 Ten Broeck Place in 1885. Bull's business associate, Henry H. Kohn, acquired the house in 1913. A handsome iron fence of twisted posts and pickets runs along Robin Street, enclosing the garden. The fanciful structure next door, at 618, shares common building materials and details and was probably built about the same time.

566-578 Madison Avenue   67

1877-78

Attributed to Frederick Brown and Clarence Cutler

In the 1860s Charles Nichols and Frederick Brown became known for their church architecture, having designed five churches in Albany and several in New England. By the 1870s, they worked independently but occasionally together. Here at Parkview Terrace Brown evidently collaborated with Clarence Cutler. Frederick Brown owned 578 briefly, although he never lived here. The row originally overlooked another of Brown's works, the first Washington Park Lake House, a wooden Stick-style structure built in 1876 and demolished in 1929 for the present one.

68

546-552 Madison Avenue 68
1903

These four houses are arranged in alternating pairs. Numbers 552 and 548 are trimmed with a limestone that blends in with the buff brick facade, but the arched doors and rusticated basements of 546 and 550 are trimmed with a pink sandstone that makes a more lively composition.

528 Madison Avenue 69

Hardware dealer Gilbert H. Ackerman lived here from 1879 through 1897. He may have been responsible for this interesting brownstone facade with alternating courses of narrow rusticated stone and wider tooled stone. The iron railing has a thick, twisted newel post.

508 Madison Avenue 70
c. 1905

"We begin where others end. . .our system is entirely different from all others. . .a trial will convince you"—so boasted collection agent Anthony Neubaur, who lived in this restrained Classical Revival house from 1905 through 1917. Built of Flemish-bond brick with stone trim, the house is entered at street level. The second-story center window is framed with scrolls and has a stained-glass transom.

494 Madison Avenue 71
c. 1876
Walsh Brothers, builders

The house on this desirable corner was built by Edmund and John Walsh for their mother after their father, Maurice, died. The cast-iron window and doorway lintels of the three-story Italianate house match those advertised in 1875 by James McKinney, an Albany iron founder. Lions' heads add more embellishment, and a bay window overlooks Knox Street. The Walsh family had lived on Knox Street for many years, and Maurice Walsh, a gardener, was probably associated with T. Davidson's Albany Nursery located here.

490 Madison Avenue 72
1875
Walsh Brothers, builders

The Walsh brothers built this three-story brick house for businessman Franklin D. Tower, who lived here until his death in 1912. In the gable and beside the window lintels are flowered terra-cotta panels. The iron railing terminates with urn-shaped newels; practical iron boot-scrapers are attached to both newel posts.

472 Madison Avenue 73
Early 1870s

In the early 1890s the Albany Hardware and Iron Company, based on State Street, had a smaller shop in this Italianate building with a cast-iron storefront. The company dates back to 1790. Around 1920 Fuller and Pitcher designed a large warehouse for the company, which still stands on the riverfront at Broadway and Arch Street.

Turn left onto Willett Street at the end of Washington Park, and proceed north along Willett.

Willett Street 74

Bounding the east side of the park, Willett Street, like State, was one of Albany's most prestigious addresses at the turn of the century. Even before the days of Washington Park, the street faced a smaller flat greensward, the parade ground, which stretched from State to Madison. The present houses and apartment buildings date from the 1880s to 1920s, and most replaced earlier buildings.

There is some controversy over the derivation of the street's name. Early maps show it spelled Willet, the name of a member of the snipe family, so it may have originally been one of the flock of parallel streets named after birds—Dove, Lark, Swan, etc. Around 1890 a second *t* crept into its name and so did the theory that the street was named for Revolutionary hero Marinus Willett. Willett is commemorated on a boulder near the Madison Avenue entrance to Washington Park for his role in the siege of Fort Stanwix.

The Willett   75
84-92 Willett Street
1909

This five-story brick apartment building stands on the site of an imposing Renaissance Revival teachers' college, the New York State Normal School (Edward Ogden, 1885), which was gutted in a fire in 1906. The State Normal School was the precursor of today's SUNYA. After the fire, this Colonial Revival apartment building was built in Flemish-bond brick trimmed with stone. Once known as the Wareham, it was designed as three separate buildings, each with its own heating system and arched entrances guarded by three doormen. The center entrance is pedimented and flanked by Corinthian columns. Three-story, stone-faced bays overlook Washington Park.

78 and 80 Willett Street   76
1878

This pair of freestanding Queen Anne-style brick houses was built for Isaac Waldman and Joseph Mann of Mann, Waldman and Company, a dry goods company. The houses have carved brownstone ornaments, tooled belt courses and interesting gables. The transoms show the stylish street numbers. The interrelated Waldman, Mann, and Oppenheim families lived here for many years. The houses shared a carriage house at the rear.

Philip Schuyler Apartments   77
1927
76 Willett Street
John P. Sewell, contractor

The Philip Schuyler apartment house was the ultimate in well-appointed Albany apartment buildings when it was constructed in the late 1920s by John P. Sewell, a leading Albany contractor who owned and managed the U-shaped building, where he also had an apartment. Cedar closets and maids' rooms were provided for in the original plans, and residents could dine in the private tea room on the ground floor.

78

66-68 Willett Street   78
1927
Walter Pember

Albany architect Walter Pember designed this fanciful Spanish-style pair for Harry and Elizabeth Horton on the site of a livery stable and a bicycle shop. They were the last big houses constructed on Willett Street and had up-to-date amenities including garages. Built to last by E. J. Bear, the houses have reinforced concrete walls and floors and are faced with cast stone from Emerson and Norris Company of Brighton. But there are also hand-crafted materials—the window guards and hardware by James McKinney and Son's ironworks, the motif over the front entrance at 66 by A. M. Zottoli and Brother, and Spanish roofing tiles admired by the Hortons during their travels.

The Hortons lived in 66 and her brother and sister-in-law, Cornell and Louise Hawley, in 68.

64 Willett Street 79
1878
Walsh Brothers, builders

This substantial brownstone house was built for clothier Morris Hein and was owned by the William Turner Mayer family for some thirty-five years in the early 20th century. Its two-story bay forms almost a tower, crowned by a weathervane. The wrought-iron newels take the form of fan-shaped finials, and the railing consists of large scrolls terminating in pierced ornaments. John and Edmund Walsh, who built this house, constructed most of the Italianate rows on Madison Avenue facing the park during the course of the 1870s.

80

54 Willett Street 80
1876
Alterations, Worthington Palmer, c. 1920

Worthington Palmer's exquisite Georgian facade for Cadillac dealer Westcott Burlingame can be compared with the smaller but equally fine house he designed a decade earlier for Martha Palmer at 371 State Street. Both facades have Flemish-bond brickwork lavishly trimmed with marble. At 54 Willett, the marble steps rise in a sweeping curve. The ironwork, designed by Palmer, was fabricated by James McKinney and Son of Albany, which featured it in their advertisements in the 1920s. The doorway has an elliptical fanlight and sidelights and is similar to the design for the Vanderpoel house in Kinderhook, New York (1819). Burlingame's monogram appears in the iron shield over the gate.

The original 1876 house that Palmer remodeled had been built for Anthony N. Brady, who lived here until moving over to the opulent house at 411 State Street around 1902. Brady gave 54 Willett to his daughter Flora (Mrs. E. Palmer Gavit), who lived here briefly while building a house on Thurlow Terrace (1906).

44 Willett Street 81
1880
Potter and Robertson

Three years after completing 38 Willett for Robert C. Pruyn, architects Potter and Robertson undertook a second Pruyn house on Willett Street, this one for Charles Lansing Pruyn. In the original design, published in the *American Architect and Building News* in 1880, the house had only three stories, so that the top floor, with its three arched windows and stout columns with foliated carving, may have been added fairly soon afterward. Other alterations include the bowed window and the tripartite first-floor window. The main entrance was moved by a later owner to the basement level. Some of the ironwork, with its undulating pattern (seen also at 441 State Street) survives. Edgar Cotrell Leonard lived here from 1897 to 1927. His family hat and fur store on Broadway was an Albany institution. According to the 1884 *Albany Handbook*, their trade extended ''throughout the state and into the neighboring states of Massachusetts and Vermont, and in hundreds of country towns and villages the styles in hats are set by those bearing the Cotrell and Leonard stamp.''

81, 82

40-42 Willett Street 82
1877

This pair of Queen Anne-style houses forms a compatible link with the two residences at 38 and 44 Willett that were built to the designs of Potter and Robertson for the Pruyn brothers. Huybertie Pruyn described childhood antics snowshoeing in front of these houses in 1886: "On Saturday mornings we had what we called a 'Field Day' on the mall in front of the Olivers' house at 42 Willett. . .twelve of us with our ten dogs." Throughout the late 19th century Gen. Robert Shaw Oliver owned 42, and Huybertie's Uncle Neddy, Edward Bowditch, who was a partner in Rathbone and Sard stove works, lived next door at 40. Gardner Leonard purchased 42 Willett in 1906 and in the 1920s had Marcus T. Reynolds design alterations for it.

38 Willett Street 83
1877
Potter and Robertson
Alterations, Marcus T. Reynolds, 1905

From 1876 to 1880 New York City architect William Appleton Potter worked in partnership with Robert H. Robertson; the firm became known for High Victorian Gothic churches and civic and college buildings, including several at Princeton University. Here at the corner of Lancaster Street, Robert Clarence Pruyn commissioned the firm to design a house in their distinctive style. Three years later his brother, Charles Lansing Pruyn, hired the same architects for his house at 44 Willett. Both buildings

were published in the *American Architect and Building News*. Unlike 44 Willett, 38 has hardly been altered. Robert Pruyn, a leading Albany figure, was president of the National Commercial Bank for thirty-nine years and a partner in the Albany Saw Works. Potter and Robertson also designed the R. H. Pruyn Building at 70 North Pearl Street around 1880 for the Pruyns' father. In 1905, after Robert moved to Englewood Place, Marcus T. Reynolds made alterations here for Samuel Hessberg.

36 Willett Street 84
1869
Alterations, Franklin Janes, 1882

Architect Franklin Janes updated an earlier house here for owner Alonzo Adams, president of a laundry machine company. Janes, who had been in partnership with William M. Woollett until Woollett died in 1880, added oriels and bay windows in the spirit of Potter and Robertson, whose house for Robert C. Pruyn stands across the street.

34 Willett Street 85
Remodeled, c. 1927

In 1915 Frederick McDonald bought the old Le Grand Bancroft Italianate brownstone here and in 1927 had it transformed to its present appearance with a third floor and Classical Revival facade in Flemish-bond brick trimmed with sandstone. McDonald was the son of William McDonald and had grown up at 26 Willett Street. He was president of the New York State National Bank and later the State Bank of Albany and was also president of Albany Felt Company.

32 Willett Street 86
1899

This Classical Revival house of narrow buff bricks trimmed with marble was built for A. Alphonse Dayton of Connecticut Mutual Life Insurance. The arched doorway is decorated with swags and has a foliated keystone. This sophisticated townhouse replaced a frame house owned by a family of blacksmiths, Berten and Edward Lasher.

30 Willett Street   87
Late 1870s

Built of pressed brick with bluestone trim, terra-cotta rosettes and a center gable, this house may have been designed by William M. Woollett. The undulating pattern of the railing here is not unlike a British design exhibited at the Centennial Exhibition in Philadelphia in 1876; in 1880, Potter and Robertson used the same design at 44 Willett, and it is also found at 441 State Street.

88

28 Willett Street   88
1891

A surprisingly symmetrical Romanesque design in a pink sandstone, possibly from Potsdam, New York, this house was built for Edward Young, a banker who was killed in a riding accident in the park, apparently not far from his new house. The rusticated first floor has a porch with two round arches supported by columns with carved capitals. The upper stories are finished in red brick, with a centered bay window on the second floor and a balcony on the third. The house is known for its fine interior wood carving, reputed to be the work of Swedish craftsmen.

Martin Glynn, the first Catholic and only longtime Albany resident to serve as governor, lived here for many years. The son of Irish immigrants, Glynn was a man of many accomplishments. He was editor, publisher and owner of the Albany *Times Union* and served as a Democratic congressman and as state comptroller and lieutenant governor. Glynn became governor after the impeachment of Tammany Democrat William Sulzer in 1913. Glynn's brief administration saw the passage of the workmen's compensation law as well as an act abolishing state party conventions and instituting primaries. Republican Charles S. Whitman defeated him in the election of 1914.

Said to have been a skilled public speaker and conversationalist of rare charm, Glynn's final achievement was in the realm of international diplomacy. In 1921 while in London Glynn initiated fruitful meetings between British Prime Minister David Lloyd-George and Edmond De Valera, leader of the Irish Rebellion.

Two years later while visiting Albany Lloyd-George was full of praise for his American negotiator: "Governor Glynn and I, in a dingy room in London, the office of the prime minister, had most unusual conferences of momentous results. He told me frankly how the Irish people viewed the feud of centuries and what they desired in the way of liberty." Glynn then took Lloyd-George's views to the Irish leaders and "brought their hopes and aspirations, clarified" back to the prime minister. Lloyd-George lauded Glynn, saying "no man did more to bring a settlement to the Irish Question."

Glynn's widow, Mary C. Magrane Glynn, continued to live here through the 1930s.

26 Willett Street   89
1889
Ogden and Wright

This turreted, rusticated residence, situated on a large lot, is the most interesting composition of the three brownstones designed by Ogden and Wright around Washington Park at this time. The others are 407 State (c. 1890) and 483 State (1886-87). Ogden and Wright must

have looked to the Sard house for inspiration
in the treatment of stone, the arched entrance
and the off-center turret. Like 407 State, this
house has plain stone piers flanking the
doorway. The massive archway leads to the
carriage house. The house was built for
William McDonald, a gas meter manufacturer,
who lived here well into the 20th century. In
the 1920s, the family of Anthony Brady Farrell
lived here.

22 Willett Street 90
1872

This commodious Italianate house, built just
before Washington Park was begun, is probably the oldest building on the block to retain
its original facade. It was built for George I.
and Esther Amsdell. George and his brother
Theodore produced Albany cream ale, India
and Scotch ales and an ''unrivalled porter''
in their big brewery on Jay and Lancaster
streets (now the Knickerbocker Apartments)
and at another malt house on Central
Avenue. George I. Amsdell was described
as a ''broad-gauge public-spirited citizen,''
who represented the ninth ward on the Board
of Alderman.

Arbor Hill:
Ten Broeck Triangle
and Clinton Avenue

Anthony Opalka

Hall Place

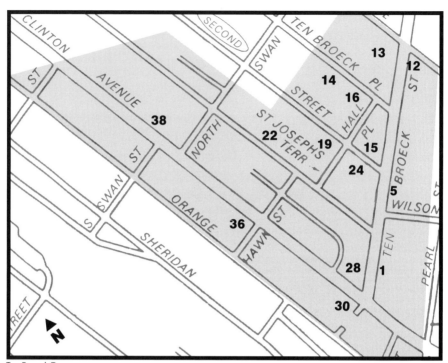

Ten Broeck Tour

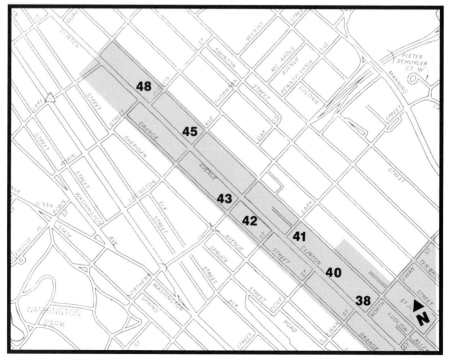

Clinton Avenue Tour

Throughout the colonial period, Albany remained a small outpost hugging the west side of the Hudson River. Its modest size, however, did not stop city leaders from planning for expansion. In 1764 the land at the crest of what is now State Street hill was laid out in a grid pattern of streets whose orientation was aligned with what is now Clinton Avenue, then the northern boundary of the city as established by the charter of 1686. North of the city in the Colonie of Rensselaerswyck, patroon Stephen van Rensselaer in the same year established a separate grid of streets and building lots that followed the same orientation. Most of the streets in the present-day neighborhood of Arbor Hill were set down at this time, although they were not yet named. At the east end of Van Rensselaer's grid was present-day Ten Broeck Street, but instead of following the grid, it ran on a diagonal parallel to Broadway, the 17th-century road that extended north from the city. Neither grid plan included any public spaces in the Clinton Avenue area.

While both grids were aligned with the city boundary, they were not otherwise related to each other when planned or even when streets were actually constructed. Consequently, to this day, north-south streets are not aligned where they cross Clinton Avenue. Furthermore, the two plans completely ignored topographical features. While some of the ravines formed by the creeks that flowed eastward into the Hudson River were filled and built upon, Sheridan Hollow, the ravine that separated Arbor Hill from the more populous portion of the city to the south, was too deep to fill completely. As a result, the Arbor Hill neighborhood has always remained somewhat isolated from the other parts of Albany to the south.

Before the Revolution, the stockade surrounding the old city was removed, and in 1794 Simeon De Witt, the city surveyor, published an official city map reiterating the gridiron plan first proposed in 1764. All street names that had been connected with English royalty on the 1764 plan were changed to the names of birds and animals; only Hawk Street retained its original name from 1764. The 1794 map also depicted an area adjacent to Clinton Avenue and just beyond the city limit as Arbor Hill, making this neighborhood the only one in the city to retain its name from this early period.

With construction of turnpikes leading from Albany in many directions during and after the 1790s, the city's population grew rapidly. Not long after the former pasture at the south end of the city was subdivided in 1791, the area adjacent to the north boundary of Albany also began to expand. In 1801 the state Legislature provided for the legal incorporation of a small area adjacent to the northern boundary called "the Colonie" (after the Colonie of Rensselaerswyck) to be taken out of the existing town of Watervliet. It was rectangular in shape and not much larger than one square mile. It included the area that Stephen van Rensselaer had laid out in 1764 and reached northward along the Hudson almost to the manor house of the Van Rensselaer family, which stood near Tivoli Street. In 1815 this town of Colonie was annexed to the city of Albany, thereby bringing the entire neighborhood now known as Arbor Hill within city limits. (In 1895 the city of Watervliet was incorporated, and what remained of the old town of Watervliet became the present-day town of Colonie.) Despite the fact that Arbor Hill had been annexed to the city, city directories persisted in including the designation Arbor Hill in the addresses of its residents up through the early 1850s, almost as if the area were not part of the city.

The Erie Canal entered the Hudson River near North Ferry Street in this newly-annexed northern ward of Albany, and soon after the canal opened, Arbor Hill became home to many persons employed in canal-related jobs, including boatmen and laborers. Albany had a small African-American population in the early 19th century, and African-American families had already taken up residence in Arbor Hill by the 1820s. They lived side-by-side with white Albanians of modest means and were engaged in similar occupations, such as gardeners, grocers and coopers.

While some development may have occurred in the Arbor Hill area during the 18th century, only the Ten Broeck Mansion still stands. In the opening years of the 19th century, many brick row buildings were erected in other parts of Albany, but only a few were built in Arbor Hill. Instead, frame dwellings and scattered commercial buildings predominated, especially along the hillside west of Ten Broeck Street. Several one-and-one-half-story buildings, such as 10 Ten Broeck Place, survive from this period.

By the late 1840s the area around Ten Broeck Street, at the east end of Arbor Hill, contained only a handful of buildings, even though it was closest to the urbanized portion of the city. Development here began only after the former burial ground for Rensselaerswyck, on the west side of Ten Broeck Street, was relocated in 1845, and the space on the west side of Ten Broeck Street between Second Street and Ten Broeck Place became Van Rensselaer Park. The park occupied the east end of this long block until the north-south street known as Hall Place was opened in 1851 and became the west boundary of the triangular park. Saint Joseph's Park was created north of Saint Joseph's Church after Saint Joseph's Park Terrace was opened in 1881.

Late in the second quarter of the 19th century, Albany became an important transshipment point for the vast quantities of lumber taken from the Adirondack Mountains, and the lumber industry gave rise to a new class of entrepreneurs in Albany.

Soon after the creation of the lumber district, which stretched north along the Erie Canal, several "lumber barons" constructed fine residences in the late Greek Revival, Italianate, Second Empire, and other styles around Ten Broeck Street, close to their businesses.

In 1850 a commentator wrote that "Arbor Hill is rapidly improving. Its elevated position renders it one of the most delightful localities in the city. A great many fine residences have been built within a few months, and now that the park is enclosed and men of taste are attracted thitherward, we shall expect it soon to become the most fashionable part of town." By the time of the Civil War, the Ten Broeck area had become an elite address.

Immediately west of Ten Broeck Street, masonry houses of a similar scale were constructed along First and Second streets, which climb the hill. Originally owned and occupied by the families of lawyers, doctors and businessmen, these buildings either replaced earlier houses or stand cheek-by-jowl with the more modest, earlier frame and brick neighbors. In some cases, the early houses were modernized; some Greek Revival houses, for instance, were updated with bracketed Italianate cornices.

Meanwhile, a different type of development had been underway on Clinton Avenue. During the 1840s, speculators constructed brick rowhouses in the Greek Revival style at the east end of the street. By 1870, the rows stretched as far west as Swan Street, where the Italianate style predominated. West of Swan Street there were only brickyards and a few scattered houses before 1870. However, Clinton Avenue developed rapidly after the city annexed a large tract of land north and west of Arbor Hill in 1870 and the Albany Railway Company constructed a horsecar line along Clinton Avenue from North Pearl Street to Lexington Avenue in 1872. Large parcels of land along Clinton Avenue were soon purchased by many of Albany's most prominent land speculators and builders, who constructed rows of houses and sold or rented them to middle-class families. One large landholder along upper Clinton Avenue was the president of the Albany Railway, Henry Crandell, who undoubtedly profited from the sale of land and the financing of new houses.

By 1890, the dense development of Clinton Avenue and adjacent streets was substantially complete. After 1900, the rapid development that had characterized Arbor Hill moved to other parts of Albany, such as Pine Hills and along Delaware Avenue. At the same time, the rowhouse ceased to be the dominant residential building type: it was supplanted by the single-family, more suburban-style house on a large lot that was preferred by the middle and upper classes and by the two-family double-decker houses with identical flats built for families of more modest means.

While some apartment and institutional buildings were constructed in Arbor Hill in the early 20th century, the changes which characterized the area after 1900 were much less physical than socio-economic. As immigrants from eastern Europe arrived in Albany in the early 20th century, many made their homes in Arbor Hill, and as African-Americans migrated northward after World War II, many settled in Arbor Hill.

In the 1960s the area north of Livingston Avenue became a massive urban renewal project, and in the 1970s and 1980s, the historic buildings in Arbor Hill attracted the interest of residents and preservationists. The Arbor Hill–Ten Broeck and Clinton Avenue historic districts were listed in the National Register of Historic Places, and both districts saw massive public and private investment in housing rehabilitation, sidewalks, trees and park improvements. The appearance of this part of Arbor Hill today is largely a result of that interest and investment.

Ten Broeck Tour

Start at the northeast corner of Ten Broeck Street and Clinton Avenue. Walk north on the east side of Ten Broeck Street.

1

11 Ten Broeck Street   1
1856

This dwelling was built in 1856 for Steven Alden, a printing contractor, who had built

number 1 in 1849 and number 9 in 1852. The four-bay width of the facade is unusual among Albany rowhouses, and the elaborately carved, pedimented entry and lintels make this house one of the finest on the street from this early period. It has notable interior painting by Emanuel Mickel.

13 Ten Broeck Street   2
1858

The large scale, full brownstone front and elegant carving at the entrance and window lintels make this house one of the grandest on the street. It was built in 1858 for William G. Thomas, a partner in the lumber firm of Hill, Thomas and Company. The floor plans and interior decorative features of residences in this neighborhood are similar to contemporary rowhouse architecture in other parts of Albany, with two major exceptions. First, several buildings have exceptional wood trim, including paneling, door and window casings, and in some instances, entire wood ceilings, due to the fact that the homes belonged to owners of lumber yards. Second, many houses, particularly on the east side of Ten Broeck Street, have on the first floor a third parlor at the rear, sometimes with an oriel window, which originally overlooked the lumber district.

15-23 Ten Broeck Street   3
1848

These seven buildings, one of the earliest rows of speculative housing on the street, were built in 1848 by James Turner of Coffee, Bruce and Turner, lumber dealers. They were sold to various individuals, including Benjamin Spelman, who occupied 15 in the 1850s and 1860s and with his two brothers owned and operated the Boston comb and fancy goods store on Broadway, which had been established in 1824. The buildings have Flemish-bond brickwork and sandstone basements, and all except 27 have simply carved, Greek Revival door surrounds. Number 17, with its cast-iron railing, sidelights and transom, and brick frieze cornice, is the least altered. Others in the row have later doors, bracketed cornices and artificial-stone fronts.

31 Ten Broeck Street   4
1848

Constructed in 1848, this building has many Greek Revival features, including pilasters and sidelights at the entry, six-over-six double-hung window sash, and eyebrow windows below the cornice. An Italianate bracketed wood cornice was added later in the 19th century. From its construction up through the 1870s, the house was owned by John Vosburgh, a mason, who may have built it for himself.

41 Ten Broeck Street   5
1845

This five-bay, three-story house was constructed in 1845 for Lawson Annesley, a dealer in looking glasses and picture frames, whose company, established in 1802, became a prominent area art store. Annesley, who lived here until 1897, also owned and developed nearby property. His residence exhibits characteristics of the most austere Greek Revival style in its use of a brick frieze cornice and flush stone lintels. Only the carved pilasters and entablature at the entrance and the dentils in the cornice embellish the facade. The building was converted to apartments in the early 20th century.

43-45 Ten Broeck Street   6
1899
William Lee Woollett

This unusual pair of two-story buildings was constructed in 1899 to the designs of Albany architect William Lee Woollett, whose father and grandfather had been architects before him. The buildings have a facade of narrow, Roman bricks above a marble basement. Among the early owners of these buildings were Herbert Bugden, who was superintendent of the Albany school district's buildings and lived at 45 in the early 1910s, and Alexander Clark, a carpenter, who lived at 43.

49 Ten Broeck Street   7
1859

One of the few brownstone-front buildings in the neighborhood, this residence was built in 1859 for George Dawson, who was connected with Weed, Parsons and Company, a well-known Albany printing and publishing firm. The Dawson family lived here for nearly forty years. The building is particularly notable for its classical portico with fluted Ionic columns. Since the building does not touch its neighbor to the south, it is possible to see how brownstone was laid vertically; this construction technique has caused the stone to delaminate over time, a common problem with brownstone.

57-59 Ten Broeck Street   8
1871

This pair of narrow, three-story Italianate rowhouses, just two bays wide, was built for tobacconists John and Alexander Greer. John Greer lived at 59 from 1872 until 1898 and maintained 57 as rental property. The buildings exhibit such typical features of the Italianate style as cast-iron window lintels and bracketed wood cornices.

67 Ten Broeck Street   9
1889

The rough-cut stone front distinguishes this building from its neighbors along Ten Broeck Street, where facades are often either brick or smooth-faced brownstone. Constructed in 1889, this was originally the home of the family of James Ackroyd, owner of a roofing and a sheet-metal company, which is still in business.

93 Ten Broeck Street   10
1871-72

This semi-attached house was built in 1871-72 for John Smyth, a postmaster, brewer, banker and broker, who lived here until 1885. The side yard made the south facade visible and allowed for windows; as a result, when viewed from the south, the building has the appearance of a freestanding Italianate brick house rather than a typical rowhouse. It has elaborate cast-iron window and door lintels decorated with lions' heads, a bracketed wood cornice, bay windows, cast-iron railings, and a remarkable wood entranceway to the side yard.

97-103 Ten Broeck Street   11
1871-73

This four-building row was built between 1871 and 1873 by Robert Aspinall, a brickmaker, mason, builder and eleventh ward alderman.

Like many other 19th-century builders and developers, Aspinall lived near the buildings he had erected, in this case, first at 32 First Street, part of another group of buildings he constructed, and later a block west. Among the early residents of this row were Estelle Grindrod; Edward Johnson, pastor of the First Reformed Church on North Pearl Street; Charles Dunn, pastor of the Third Presbyterian Church, which once stood on Clinton Square; and William Osborne, a lumber shipper. Like many later buildings in the area, these residences are decorated with sheet-metal door and window lintels and bracketed wood cornices.

105 Ten Broeck Street   12
1873

This unusual, five-sided house was constructed in 1873 for John Grindrod, a nephew and associate of Robert Aspinall, who had built the neighboring row at 97-103 Ten Broeck. Grindrod, also a mason and builder, lived here for twelve years. The iron cresting remains intact atop the slate-covered mansard roof, and bat-winged light fixtures flank the entrance. The house was once hit by a streetcar careening out of control as it came down the steep Livingston Avenue hill.

From 1885 until 1913, the house was the rectory for the Church of the Holy Innocents

12, 11

around the corner on North Pearl Street. The Church of the Holy Innocents, built by lumber baron William De Witt as a memorial to his children, dates from 1850 and was designed by prominent church architect Frank Wills. The chapel, built in 1866, was designed by Albany architects Woollett and Ogden.

Cross Ten Broeck Street at Livingston Avenue, and walk down the west side of Ten Broeck to Ten Broeck Place. Then walk west on Ten Broeck Place to the Ten Broeck Mansion.

Ten Broeck Mansion   13
1797-98
9 Ten Broeck Place

The Ten Broeck Mansion was built in 1797-98 for Abraham Ten Broeck and his wife, Elizabeth van Rensselaer. Ten Broeck was one of Albany's most prominent citizens; he had served as a brigadier general, delegate to the Continental Congress, judge, state senator and, while this house was under construction, mayor of Albany. Thomas W. Olcott acquired the property in 1848. Olcott, who was president of Mechanics' and Farmers' Bank and one of the wealthiest men in Albany, named the house Arbor Hill after its surrounding neighborhood. After holding title for ninety-nine years, the Olcott family donated the property to the Albany County Historical Association, which has operated it as a house museum since 1948. It is open for tours from March through December.

A Federal-period brick mansion with Greek Revival modifications, this is one of the finest examples of residential architecture in Albany. It differs from earlier Georgian residences, such as Schuyler Mansion and Cherry Hill, in its attenuated proportions, restrained application of ornament, and use of elliptical forms in the first-floor rear door and windows. The low-pitched roof is concealed by balustrades across the front and rear and stepped gables at the ends. There are blind balustrades under the second-story windows. The Ten Broecks' initials and the date 1798 are executed in iron on the gable ends. The interior followed a traditional 18th and early 19th-century center hall plan, but the spiral staircase is more

13

common to the Federal period. The interior detailing, in the Greek Revival style, dates from the ownership of James King (1837-42). The front and rear porches were added at that time. At the south end of the building is a wing that contains, among other spaces, bathrooms added during the Victorian era. At the rear of the property is a barn dating from the 18th century.

10 Ten Broeck Place   14

This small frame cottage is most likely half of what was originally a double house. It was probably built before 1840 and is believed to have once been the home of Joseph Hall, a gardener after whom Hall Place is named. It is one of the oldest surviving buildings in Arbor Hill and particularly important as an illustration of the neighborhood's early years, when it was filled with workers' cottages. This building has such late Federal and early Greek Revival elements as pilasters on the facade and surrounding the door and a shallow, hip roof.

Continue east on Ten Broeck Place to Hall Place, and then walk south on Hall Place.

Van Rensselaer Park 15
c. 1845

Van Rensselaer Park, located between Hall Place and Ten Broeck Street, was once the burial ground for residents of the Colonie of Rensslaerswyck. The remains were moved to Albany Rural Cemetery around 1845, and the park was created.

10 Hall Place 16
1860

This residence was constructed in 1860 for John W. Dunham, a lumber dealer. The brownstone facade has heavily carved window lintels and sills and door surround. The door and sidelights were probably added later.

2-6 Hall Place 17
1852

The five houses here were constructed on speculation in 1852. The brick facades are fairly typical of the period, with French windows on the first floors and recessed double-door entranceways. The elaborate wood porches of lattice and scrollwork, however, make the row one of the most notable in the entire city. Among the early occupants were A. B. Van Gaasbeek, a prominent carpet dealer, and Barrington Lodge, who lived at 6 Hall Place from 1873 until 1899 and founded B. Lodge and Company, an establishment still operating on North Pearl Street. Additional stories and mansard roofs were added to numbers 4, 5 and 6 later in the 19th century.
Cross Second Street to Saint Joseph's Terrace.

Saint Joseph's Terrace 18
1881

Originally known as Saint Joseph's Park Terrace, this street was opened in 1881, although no buildings were constructed until 1892. They overlook the apse of St. Joseph's Roman Catholic Church, built in 1856.

12 Saint Joseph's Terrace 19
1892

This Queen Anne-style building of pressed brick was constructed in 1892 as the parish house for Saint Joseph's Church, a function it retained until the mid-1970s, when it became Mercy House, a social services branch of the church. The windows on the upper stories have multi-paned sash, and there are gables over the entrance and at the roofline.

5 Saint Joseph's Terrace 20
1895

Built in 1895 and once the home of Mrs. Bryan Mulderry, a baker, this is one of the best examples in this part of Albany of the Richardsonian Romanesque style applied to a small-scale residence. Punctuating the rusticated stone facade are an arched first-story window and an oriel window at the second-story, a common feature in residential buildings of this style.

3 Saint Joseph's Terrace 21
1914

Constructed in 1914, this is the only one-story building in the Ten Broeck section of the historic district. With its use of pan tiles on the pent roof and leaded windows, it vaguely recalls Mission and Arts and Crafts architecture.
Walk west along First Street.

65-71 First Street 22
Late 1880s

This group of houses was built in the last half of the 1880s on the site of a mansion that had been the residence of Matthew Stoneman, a ship chandler. Stoneman's family retained ownership of the houses and rented them out until the 1930s. Unlike most others in the area, these houses sit on a terrace above the street with fenced front yards. Each has a porch with bracketed columns, and those at 65 and 67 have handsome, pedimented arches. Numbers 69 and 71 have corbelled brick cornices.
Walk east on First Street.

22

23

decorative treatments. The interiors have typical rowhouse plans with double parlors on the first floors but are notable for their use of decorative filagree-plaster cornices, which incorporate grapevines, foliage and other complex patterns. Robert Aspinall, the contractor who built 97-103 Ten Broeck Street and made his home at 32 First Street, built 30-38 in 1854-58. Numbers 26-28 First Street were built in 1856-57 by contractor William Turner, who resided at 28 for a short time and later sold it to Douglas White, a lumber merchant.

Numbers 2-4 First Street were built in 1862 by James Eaton, who also constructed the brownstone-front buildings at 20-22 Ten Broeck Street. Eaton, one of Albany's most prolific builders during the mid-19th century, sold these buildings to George Wilson, a clothier and tailor, who made his home at 2 and later at 4.

2-38 First Street   23
1854-62

The nearly unbroken expanse of mainly three-bay-wide, three-story-high brick rowhouses stepping down the sloping terrain makes this one of the most aesthetically pleasing mid-19th century townscapes in Albany. Constructed between 1854 and 1862, these seventeen houses are similar in scale, materials and

Saint Joseph's Roman   24
Catholic Church
1856-60
NW corner of First and Ten Broeck Streets
Patrick Keeley
Tower, M. L. and H. G. Emery, c. 1910

The monumental Saint Joseph's Roman Catholic Church was completed in 1856 to the designs of Patrick Keeley, one of the foremost architects of Catholic churches in the United States and the architect of Albany's Cathedral of the Immaculate Conception (1848-52). St. Joseph's was the third Catholic parish established in Albany, and in 1843 the cornerstone was laid for the parish's original building at North Pearl Street and Livingston Avenue. As the parish grew, the need for a larger church became apparent. The walls of this Gothic Revival building are bluestone, and the trim was originally buff stone from the Caen quarries of France. The trim, however, was replaced in 1866 with Indiana limestone because of deterioration of the original material. The steeple, designed by Albany architects M. L. and H. G. Emery, was added around 1910. The interior is embellished with a hammerbeam roof structure with angels' heads and a polychrome ceiling. Because the

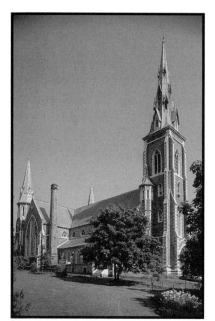

24

congregation was dwindling, the Albany Diocese decided to close St. Joseph's in the early 1980s. In an unusual arrangement, the building was sold to an individual; he maintains the structure, and masses are still offered weekly by a diocesan priest.

Walk south along Ten Broeck Street to Clinton Avenue.

20-22 Ten Broeck Street   25
1861
James Eaton, builder

This pair was built by James Eaton in 1861. The cornices match those around the corner at 2 and 4 First Street, but these fronts are faced with brownstone. From the late 1870s until 1917, number 20 was the home of Martin V. B. Wagoner, a brick manufacturer involved in residential development along Clinton Avenue and later president of the Empire Clay Mining Company. Number 22 was the home of Alexander Greer, a tobacconist, during the 1860s and 1870s.

18 Ten Broeck Street   26

Constructed in 1877, this brownstone front rowhouse was for many years the home of Samuel Gross of Craft, Wilson and Gross, clothing merchants. George Wilson, a partner in the firm, lived nearby at 4 First Street. This Gothic-influenced residence features an oriel window and Tudor arches above the door and the third-story windows.

14 Ten Broeck Street   27
c. 1850

This building was constructed around 1850 for Dr. David Martin, a graduate of Fairfield Medical College. Martin died shortly after 1850, but his widow continued to occupy the house until the early 1880s. Between 1885 and the 1940s, this was the home of the family of Daniel Whittle, of Whittle Brothers florists. The Whittles were most likely responsible for renovating the facade by adding sandstone trim and round-arched openings, reflecting the Romanesque Revival style popular in the 1880s.

28

Sweet Pilgrim Baptist Church   28
1876
NW corner of Ten Broeck Street and Clinton Avenue
John McCabe, builder

This church forms a grand anchor to the Ten Broeck Historic District. Constructed in 1876 as the Tabernacle Baptist Church by John

McCabe, an Albany mason and contractor, the building became the home of the Albany Temple Baptist Church in 1927 following a merger with Calvary Baptist Church, which had burned. Sweet Pilgrim Baptist, an African-American congregation formed about forty years ago, purchased the building in the late 1960s and has begun a restoration program that has included cleaning of limestone and brick facades, as well as roof repairs. The corner steeple was removed in the 1930s.

The historic interior is largely intact. The second-story sanctuary has a Greek-cross plan, with the altar in the west arm of the cross and a balcony opposite, at the rear. The walls of the side arms of the cross hold colossal stained-glass windows. The vaulted ceiling is supported by faceted, slender wood columns, and the ceiling is covered with corrugated metal trimmed with sheet-metal mouldings that simulate plaster. The design of the pews, altar, pipe organ and other woodwork suggest the influence of the Eastlake style. The architect of the building is not known.

Clinton Avenue Tour

This driving tour starts the northwest corner of Clinton Avenue and North Pearl Street and passes mostly speculative rowhouses, ranging from 1840s Greek Revival to 1890s Romanesque Revival. The tour extends for more than a mile along Clinton Avenue, to North Lake Avenue.

Palace Theater 29

1929-31
NW corner of North Pearl Street and Clinton Avenue
John Eberson

Dominating this busy intersection is the monumental Palace Theater, completed in 1931 and designed by John Eberson, a well-known movie palace architect. Built at a cost of $3 million, the Palace was financed by Jacob Fabian, a pioneer nationally in the motion picture industry, and was under construction at the time of the stock market crash. It was originally a movie theater with a stage for live performances. Since 1931, the Palace has housed the Albany Symphony Orchestra, and it now functions also

as a performance center for musical groups.

The arrangement of the interior is reflected in the facades. The massive, 2,800-seat auditorium is situated behind the simply decorated North Pearl Street facade, while offices are housed behind the smaller scale, two-story facade that climbs Clinton Avenue. The building is constructed of brown and buff-colored tapestry brick; the design of the terra-cotta trim is derived from Baroque architecture. The original marquee and corner entry were replaced in the 1950s. The interior retains Austrian Baroque features, with decorative plaster and ceiling murals in the lobbies.

29

42-44 Clinton Avenue 30

1876

These narrow, two-bay-wide, three-story brick rowhouses were constructed in 1876 for Daniel and Edward Boughton, dealers in hats, caps and furs. They have stone basements, embellished window lintels, and oriel windows above the recessed entries, features common to the Italianate style and typical along Clinton Avenue.

54-58 Clinton Avenue 31

1883
James Eaton, builder

James Eaton, who had constructed hundreds of buildings all over the city, built these three residences in 1883. They have pressed-brick fronts with a suggestion of rustication at the basements, two-story oriel windows and recessed narrow entrances, reflecting the more eclectic tastes of the late 19th century.

62-64 and 68 Clinton Avenue   32
c. 1845

The pair at 62-64 was constructed around 1845, perhaps by carpenter William Allen, who rented 64 and whose family lived at 62 until the 1940s. A stone course separates the brick basement from the first floor. There are simple lintels above the recessed entries, flush lintels over the windows and eyebrow windows in the half story under the gable roofs. Notable also are the Gothic-influenced iron railings. Number 68, a two-story frame structure, was constructed around the same time and rented. The shouldered and battered window and door architraves are typical features of modest Greek Revival buildings.

73-79 Clinton Avenue   33
1846

Survivors of a larger Greek Revival group constructed in 1846 on land owned by Thomas and Maria Ludlow, this is one of the earliest speculative brick rows on Clinton Avenue. The Ludlows owned several parcels along lower Clinton Avenue and gave their name to the alley that served the carriage houses behind them.

78-80 Clinton Avenue   34
1853

This pair of narrow, three-story brick residences was constructed in 1853 for Edward Visscher, whose blacksmith shop once occupied the site. Visscher and his heirs rented out the houses through the 1930s. Each has an unusual three-part window on each story, a recessed doorway and a simple cornice.

95-101 Clinton Avenue   35
1853

These four buildings were constructed in 1853. They have simple wood cornices with brackets, which signal the transition between the late Greek Revival period and the oncoming Italianate style.

35

100 Clinton Avenue   36
1861

Although now standing alone because of demolition of adjacent properties, this house is typical of the large Italianate style rowhouses constructed on Clinton Avenue around the time of the Civil War. Completed in 1861, the house has simply carved stone window lintels and foliated doorway trim.

115-119 Clinton Avenue   37
1878

These three buildings are among the more architecturally sophisticated on the street, with narrow proportions, cast-iron trim, oriel windows, and elaborate wood cornices interrupted by small, arched windows. No builder or architect has been determined.

Public School 7   38
1885-86
Clinton Avenue at head of South Swan Street
Ernest Hoffman

Public School 7 was built in 1885-86 to the
designs of Ernest Hoffman, an Albany architect who was clearly influenced by the designs
of H. H. Richardson. Built of pressed brick laid
in Flemish bond above a rusticated stone
basement, the facade has a round-arched
entrance trimmed with carved sandstone and
alternating patterns of round-arched and flat-
headed windows. The school was constructed
by Attilio Pasquini, a mason who was one of
the first Italian immigrants to make his home
in Albany and one of the most prolific local
builders in the late 19th and early 20th centuries. He was involved in real estate developments along upper Clinton Avenue about the
time he built this school.

179-189 Clinton Avenue   39
1871
Gibson Oliver, builder

These six houses were constructed in 1871 by
builder Gibson Oliver, who had purchased the
land from another builder, John Bridgford,
three years earlier. Oliver sold the buildings to
individuals immediately upon completion. In
1903, the house at 179 was purchased by
Frederick Guyer, a physician, who built the
narrow, two-story addition to the east for his
office. The facades are enlivened with prominent wood cornices, matching doorway
hoods, and typical mid-19th century cast-iron
window lintels and sills.

217 Clinton Avenue   40
Early 1860s

Constructed in the early 1860s, this frame
house is unusual for this part of town. It has a
front porch, its original entry, and French windows on the first floor.

255-315 Clinton Avenue   41
1870s

The vast majority of the buildings on the north

39

41

side of Clinton Avenue between numbers 255
and 315 were constructed in the 1870s. They
were either financed by Albany Railway president and land speculator Henry Crandell or
built for individuals who purchased the land

from him. Notable in the group are the frame buildings at 257-267, which retain their cornices and much of their other exterior trim. Number 273, a one-story frame building, was constructed as a saloon, and 277-283 were built by carpenter William Redden. Number 269 has a cast-iron storefront marked with the name of the foundry, James McKinney's iron works of Albany. The corner building at 277 housed a pharmacy for over a century, from the time of its construction in 1873 until 1978. The row of bow-fronted houses at 291-315 was financed by Crandell and built in 1877. He died during construction and willed them to friends, business associates and his housekeeper, who in turn rented them out.

278-320 Clinton Avenue 42
1870s

The entire block between Lark Street and Henry Johnson Boulevard is another example of 1870s speculative rowhouses. In 1874, William Guian, a plumber, contractor and land developer, constructed two houses and a building with a grocery store at the corner at numbers 278-282. Other developers included Henry Kelly, a financier who was active further up Clinton Avenue during the 1880s. William Ackroyd, a roofing contractor, had a sheet-metal cornice installed on his house at 306. The other houses have bracketed wood cornices and cast-iron lintels and sills. Many also retain second-story oriel windows. Number 310 was built in the late 1880s as a commercial building.

326-352 Clinton Avenue 43
1870s

West of Henry Johnson Boulevard are two groups of buildings that further illustrate the speculative nature of the street. Numbers 326-330 were constructed in the 1870s on land purchased from Henry Crandell. An intact storefront can be found at 326. The eight buildings at 338-352 were put up in 1875-76 by partners Anton Weller, a furnace dealer; John Ward, a lumber dealer; and Joel Read and Martin V. B. Wagoner, brickmakers.

362-374 Clinton Avenue 44
1872

This seven-building Italianate row was built in 1872 by Andrew Brown, a realtor, and later held by his heirs. Robert Weir, another realtor and perhaps a relative of Brown, lived at 366 Clinton and developed the row at 428-442 Clinton.

Saint Luke's Methodist Church 45
1888

The builder of this church, William Kelly, also built 425-437 Clinton as well as other nearby buildings. Erected in 1888, the three-part, asymmetrical brick facade has a tall tower marking the corner, a central gable in front of the nave, and a smaller tower. Lancet arches mark many window and door openings, and brick corbelling and stone courses articulate floor levels and buttresses. The Methodist church no longer occupies the building.

421-437 Clinton Avenue 46
1880s

Numbers 421 and 423 of this group were constructed in the early 1880s for individuals, but 425 through 437 were financed by Henry Kelly, who developed other nearby parcels. William Kelly, who may have been Henry's brother, built the row at 425-437. Kelly's row features three-story bay windows, false gables with tile inserts, and white marble trim and stoops.

46

428-442 Clinton Avenue   47
1889

Robert Weir, a real estate developer and resident of 366 Clinton Avenue, had this Richardsonian Romanesque row constructed in 1889. He sold some of the buildings immediately and retained others as rental property until after 1915. Several of the high stone stoops have basketweave wrought-iron railings. The adjacent brick buildings at 444-450 were constructed by individuals. They have arched windows and doorways, and 446 and 450 have fanciful, Colonial Revival elements under the cornice.

designs, while Pasquini undertook construction and Kinnear provided the financing.

The two sections can be easily discerned. The earlier section is constructed of common brick with stone trim, alternating flat parapet walls and false gables, and oriel windows. The name of the row appears among the terracotta ornaments atop number 11. The later portion is constructed of pressed brick with gable roofs and dormers that have alternating gable designs. First-floor bay windows alternate with second-story oriels. Some buildings have enriched cornices, and the building at the corner, known as 2 Judson, has a rusticated turret with a conical roof. The block was most likely named for John McPherson, a gardener, who had previously owned the property.

48

McPherson Terrace   48
1887-88, 1891
Clinton Avenue west of Judson Street

These sixteen buildings were constructed in two stages, most likely as a collaborative effort involving Albany architect Edward Ogden, builder Attilio Pasquini, and Peter Kinnear, owner of the Albany Billiard Ball Company, who may have financed the second phase in 1891. The relationship was personal as well as professional, as Kinnear's daughter Lizzie had married Ogden's son Charles, also an architect, in 1884. The earliest buildings, 7-15 McPherson, were constructed in 1887-88, and Edward Ogden was the first owner of what is now number 8. Pasquini, builder of School 7, was the first owner of 9 McPherson. Both men were involved in the development of the second stage of the terrace in 1891: the architectural firm of Ogden and Wright supplied the

From Tracks to Tracts:
Albany's Westward Expansion

Lorraine E. Weiss

131 South Lake Avenue

Albany's early streetcar neighborhoods and 20th-century residential developments are the focus of this four-part tour located in the area bounded by South Lake
Avenue, New Scotland Avenue, Marion Avenue, Manning Boulevard and Washington
Avenue and including several other 20th-century building sites. The first section
looks at a variety of streets developed between the 1880s and the 1930s; the second
concentrates on the original Pine Hills subdivision. The third tour surveys four distinct
builders' tracts. The fourth and final section discusses the campus of the State
University of New York at Albany built during the 1960s and an 1880s waterworks.

The tour areas were important transportation corridors but not necessarily early
population centers. The King's Highway was built in the 1660s from Albany through
the Pine Bush to Schenectady. Several turnpikes sliced through the area: the Albany-
Schenectady Turnpike of 1797, which later became Central Avenue (N.Y.S. Route 5);
the Great Western Turnpike, constructed in 1799 along what is now known as
Western Avenue and repaved as a plank road in 1849 (U. S. Route 20); and New
Scotland Avenue, a toll road also dating from the late 1790s. In 1831, the country's
first passenger train, the De Witt Clinton, operated by the Mohawk and Hudson
Railroad, departed from the "Point" at the junction of Madison and Western
avenues. Trains ran to Schenectady from there until 1844, when the tracks were
re-routed via Tivoli Hollow out to the west.

Initially, settlement south of Washington Avenue and west of Washington Park was
pushed by the growing population in the central city as much as it was pulled by
transportation and utilities improvements and the promotional activities of real estate
speculators. Up until the late 19th century the area was a mix of farmland, pastures,
orchards, streams, swampy fields, and an occasional commercial or industrial site.
Tracts remained undeveloped well into the 20th century, until farms were sold and
the streams and swamps diverted or drained.

The slow pace of this growth, along with changes in tastes between 1870 and
1960, meant that houses were built in a wide range of architectural styles that
varied even along single blocks. Throughout most of the tour areas, single- and
multi-family dwellings were intermingled, leading to a diverse socio-economic
population, and the occupations of residents are often just as interesting as the
buildings they lived in.

The construction of streetcar lines was one of the most important influences on the
development of neighborhoods west of downtown. For many residents streetcars

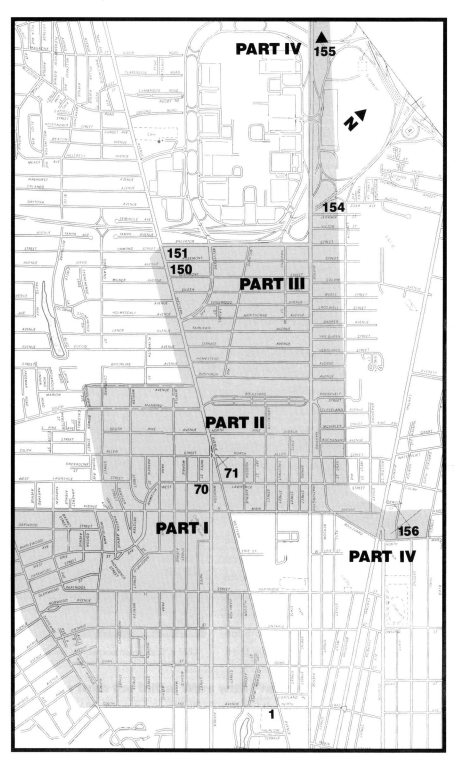

PART IV 155

PART III

151
150

PART II

71
70

PART I

156

PART IV

1

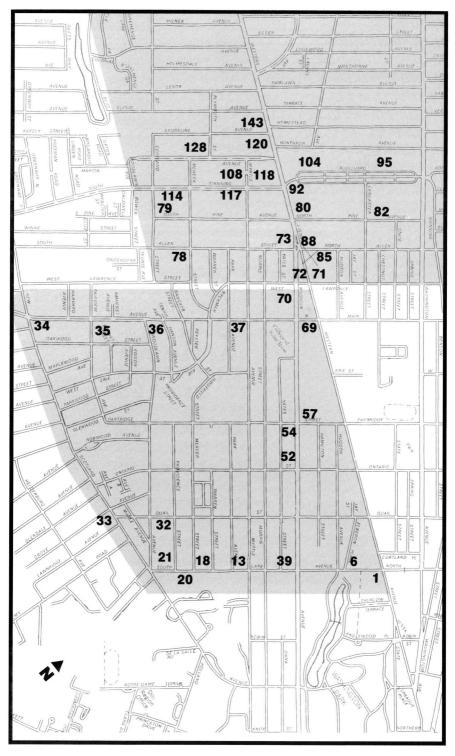

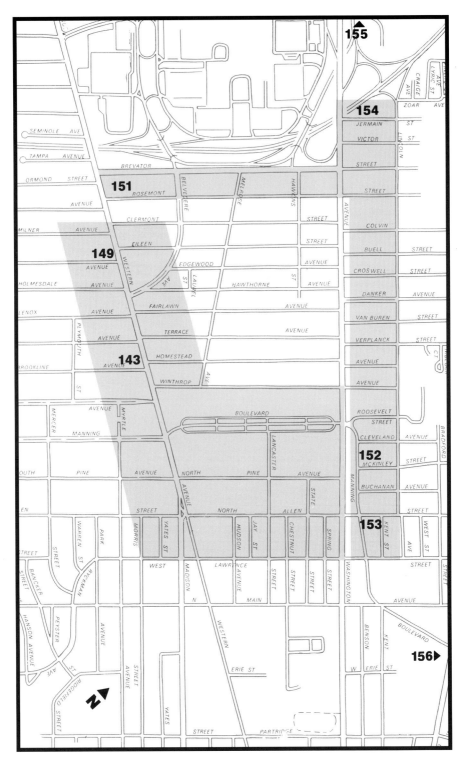

were the primary means of transportation to downtown Albany up through the 1940s. By 1875 the Albany Railway Company was running horse-drawn streetcars up Madison Avenue as far as New Scotland Avenue. The lines were electrified and extended west to Allen Street in 1890 and up to Manning Boulevard in 1906. Between 1917 and 1925, streetcars traveled out to the Albany Country Club, now the site of the SUNY campus. Bus routes were established along many of the old trolley routes by the mid-1940s.

Municipal projects, especially street improvements and the installation of utilities, also changed the early character of the area. By the 1840s, city officials were planning improvements to the water system. Bleecker Reservoir was constructed in 1850 near what is now North Manning Boulevard. It was fed by two sources, the Six-Mile Waterworks on Fuller Road and Washington Avenue Extension, which flowed through a conduit constructed along the circuitous route of the King's Highway, and Hudson River water pumped up the hill by the 1873 Quackenbush Pumping Station on Broadway. In 1877, the Prospect Hill Pumping Station was built at 14 North Manning Boulevard to serve elevated areas of Albany more effectively. It was engineered to work in tandem with the Bleecker Reservoir and was surrounded in the late 1880s by a complex of the pumping station offices and equipment houses.

Civic leaders were also concerned about the aesthetic aspects of the community. The Washington Park commissioners decided in 1874 to build a system of roads and parkways which would link sections of Albany to the newly developed Washington Park.

The route was planned to begin at Western Avenue, travel north along Manning and North Manning boulevards to Tivoli Lakes (an early reservoir west of Livingston Middle School on Henry Johnson Boulevard) and continue east to Colonie Street. Western Avenue, already in existence as a turnpike, was paved between Washington Park and Manning Boulevard. Gas and sewer lines were also laid.

In 1876 construction of the parkway began on Manning and North Manning boulevards, but two years later only a mile of the route had been completed. North Manning Boulevard was constructed along the curved path of the Six-Mile Water-works conduit. Today the street extends just slightly east of Terminal Street in the industrial park, then continues as a ''paper street'' interrupted by the undeveloped land around the remainder of Tivoli Lakes. North Manning then extends from the other side of Livingston Middle School to Henry Johnson Boulevard. Originally called the Boulevard, the street was renamed in honor of Daniel Manning, an Albany park commissioner and President Grover Cleveland's secretary of the treasury. Lined with maple trees, Manning and Western became popular carriage and sleigh routes.

These 1870s civic projects were paralleled by a growing interest in speculative housing. An 1876 city atlas delineates many subdivisions that were planned on the sites of large family farms and estates. In some instances families independently built homes on lots that they purchased. In other cases developers put up several speculative houses or constructed rental housing. A number of developers acquired large parcels of land and constructed tracts of houses that would define the character of a particular street.

One of the best known large-scale developments was the Pine Hills subdivision. Formerly part of the McIntyre and Hawkins farms, bounded by Allen Street, Cortland Street, Marion Avenue, Manning Boulevard and Washington Avenue, the land was purchased by the Albany Land Improvement and Building Company in 1888. The partners were Louis Pratt, an attorney and alderman-at-large; Gaylord Logan, his law partner; and, for a brief time, William J. Caine, Harris A. Corell, and Charles J. Peabody.

They made extensive improvements, laying out and paving Pine Avenue and Allen Street, planting trees, constructing sidewalks, and installing drains and water and sewer lines. Just as important as the physical improvements were the covenants imposed on each lot prohibiting commercial activity and the sale of liquor. The company promoted the wholesome atmosphere and desirability of their building lots in local magazines and in the 1890 city directory with such statements as:

> The most healthful and desirable residence section of the city is known as
> PINE HILLS.
> Uniform house lines, no business or manufacturing, no saloons, by covenant
> in PINE HILLS DEEDS.
> $10,000 Expended for New Sewers, $50,000 for Asphalt Pavements,
> $120,000 for New Homes at PINE HILLS.

The Albany Land Improvement and Building Company's venture failed after the financial panic of 1893. The land was then acquired by the Albany City National Bank, which foreclosed on the company's loan and eventually auctioned off lots. Although brief-lived, the company did have a lasting effect on the area through the implementation of early land-use controls and the establishment of the neighborhood's identity. The Pine Hills Neighborhood Association was formed at the turn of the century to improve municipal services and prevent developments deemed undesirable and continues to review development proposals and zoning changes today.

Several other tracts beyond the Pine Hills neighborhood bear the stamp of builders who developed large-scale projects. These include two groups of Spanish Eclectic-style houses, two long rows of townhouses, a block of bungalows, and a group of prefabricated, all-steel Lustron homes.

Lastly, the impact of Albany's educational institutions on this part of Albany cannot be overlooked. The College of Saint Rose began in the heart of the area, on

Madison and Western avenues between Ontario Street and Main Avenue, and has become a major institution over the past seventy years. The proximity of several other educational institutions on New Scotland Avenue and of the two SUNYA campuses has spawned the conversion of single-family houses to apartments in order to satisfy the demand for student accommodations.

While the central city and portions of Madison Avenue were recognized as historic districts in the 1970s and 1980s, the greater Pine Hills neighborhood has only recently gained attention as a significant historic resource. When newly settled, these areas of Albany were seemingly as distant from downtown as Saratoga Springs is today—the earliest horsecar rides took forty-five minutes to an hour to reach downtown. The streets included in these tours developed as Albany grew from a transportation hub and industrial city to a center for government and education, as businesses with local family names were replaced by regional and national chains and as the distinct communities of Troy, Schenectady and Albany merged with surrounding areas to become the Capital District. Perhaps it is difficult to see the 20th century, and even portions of our own lives, as historic; nevertheless, from Italianate to Lustron, from the horsecar to the Crosstown Arterial, these neighborhoods are an important part of Albany's growth as a city.

Part I:
Streetcar Neighborhoods and Expansion West of Washington Park

This tour covers blocks along South Lake, New Scotland, South Main, Myrtle and Madison avenues. Begin at South Lake Avenue just south of Western Avenue, and travel south toward Madison Avenue.

South Lake Avenue   1

The opening of Washington Park in 1872 sparked the growth of fashionable residential areas west of Lark Street, and in 1875 the Common Council approved the expansion of horsecar service along Madison Avenue to New Scotland Avenue. Several large estates west of the park were subdivided beginning in the late 1870s. South Lake Avenue, previously named Perry Street, remained relatively undeveloped until the 1880s. Although contemporary with blocks further south that feature single houses on large lots, houses on the west side of the street between Western and Hudson avenues were built in a decidedly urban manner. Houses on the east side of the street were built later and are more suburban in character.

Elouise Apartments   2
1927
11 South Lake Avenue

The Elouise Corporation constructed this eight-story Classical Revival building, which accommodates one hundred apartments. It was one of several large apartment buildings built in Albany during the 1920s and was renovated in 1985.

14 South Lake Avenue 3
c. 1913

A Flemish Revival gable tops this two-family house first occupied by Edmund G. Anderson, an employee of the New York Telephone Company, and by Mrs. Edward A. Keeler, a widow.

25-35 South Lake Avenue 4
1880-81

John Brown Low, one of several speculative builders on this block, is credited with building these Queen Anne townhouses. They are simply ornamented with contrasting brick and stone courses, and their steeply pitched gables are a contrast to the neighboring Romanesque Revival townhouses. Many of Low's townhouses retain original iron railings like their counterparts in the Center Square neighborhood. Number 25 was built for William Morgan, an insurance agent, who later moved to 124 South Lake Avenue. Number 27 was the Quayle family home from 1881 to 1927; it was updated with the Colonial Revival facade around 1916.

22 South Lake Avenue 5
c. 1911

Though subtle in color, brick dentils and stone quoins and lintels effectively define the facade of this house. The entablature, Ionic columns and balusters of the porch railing, along with the bracketed cornice of the gable, appear more bold due to the contrasting color of paint. Harvey M. Butts, an inspector for the New York Central Railroad, was the first owner.

37-45 South Lake Avenue 6
1888
Ernest Hoffman

Ernest Hoffman was a prominent local architect who designed several Richardsonian Romanesque buildings in Albany, including the Steamer No. 1 firehouse. These houses display characteristic contrasting stone arch surrounds at windows and doorways and carving under each bay window. Number 39 was Hoffman's own residence from 1888 until his death in 1908.

55 South Lake Avenue 7
1940

A rare Albany example of the Art Deco, this apartment house has receding bays on the north elevation that take full advantage of the lot. Contrasting bands of brick and concrete emphasize the horizontal line. Glass blocks were used at the entrance, which is sheltered by the asymmetrical curve of the porch roof.

57-87 South Lake Avenue 8
1896-97
Albert Fuller

Albert Fuller was another well-known and prolific local architect who, with various partners, worked in Albany over a fifty-year period. These rowhouses are one of several Fuller projects along South Lake Avenue. Here, an expansive line of yellow brick facades is relieved by bowed one-story porches, gables, and a slight indentation in the brickwork at the second stories. Brick is used as dentil-like detailing on the entablature and roofline. The houses were built just east of the Holroyd knitwear factory, which was constructed in 1886 between Hamilton and Hudson avenues. This mixture of land use, more common in other city neighborhoods, continued until the early 1910s, when the factory closed and the building was used as a garage by neighborhood residents.

103 and 106 South Lake Avenue 9
1880

Tax records for 1880 indicate a two-story brick house and a two-story wooden house "in progress" on these lots, which were owned by Henry Kelly, treasurer and secretary of the Troy Laundry Company and at one time treasurer of Albany County and of Albany Hospital. The townhouse at 103 suggests that Kelly anticipated that the street would develop along the urban pattern of downtown, but he built 106 in a less urban form. Curved, wraparound porches were later added to both Italianate houses.

112 South Lake Avenue   10
1890
Attributed to Charles Ogden

Charles Ogden most likely designed this two-family house for himself and his wife, Lizzie Ogden, and for her brother, David M. Kinnear. Lizzie and David were children of industrialist Peter Kinnear. Ogden was the son and the partner of well-known Albany architect Edward Ogden. The bell-shaped tower and contrasting stone of this house are found on several other houses designed by Charles, a prominent architect in his own right, who practiced from 1876 to 1931.

116 South Lake Avenue   11
1886
Attributed to Walter Dickson

William Emery, an engraver, and his son, Marshall Emery, a draftsman, were employed in the office of Albany architect Walter Dickson. They may have worked with Dickson on the design of this brick, shingle and half-timbered residence. Small, arched stained-glass windows line a staircase on the south elevation. Dickson designed several important public buildings in Albany including the former post office that is now part of SUNY Plaza on Broadway. Marshall Emery moved to Nyack, New York, in 1893 but continued to work on commissions in Albany. He and H. G. Emery are credited with the design of the Elks Building at 138 State Street. The Emery family owned this house as rental property through 1915. It was later the official city residence of Erastus Corning II and his wife, Elizabeth, during Corning's tenure as mayor. Mrs. Corning donated the house to the Roman Catholic Diocese of Albany, and it now serves as the residence of the bishop.

115 South Lake Avenue   12
c. 1889

Details such as dormers with round-headed windows and fluted pilasters, a broken pediment over the entryway and modillions along the cornice line are found on Georgian homes of the 18th century, and on late-19th and early-20th century Georgian Revival homes. This house was constructed for Linneus and Gertrude A. Burdick, who lived here for a few years before renting the property to Charles A. Cobb. Burdick was a partner of James Taylor in the printing firm of Burdick and Taylor on Broadway. Cobb worked as an inspector at the Regent's Office in the Capitol.

119 South Lake Avenue   13
1915

121 and 123 South Lake Avenue
1914

These "American Four-Square" houses were built for three siblings: Grace Barnet Muhlfelder, Esther Barnet Stern and Henry Barnet. As is evident here, the style is identified by a boxy shape, hip roofs with dormers, one-story porches and often symmetrical facades. Four-Square houses were typically embellished with details of various revival styles. These houses have Colonial Revival porches with grouped Doric columns. The family of Leo and Grace Barnet Muhlfelder lived at 119. Leo Muhlfelder was president of Heiser, Muhlfelder and Company, a wholesale dry goods firm on Broadway.

Charles M. and Esther Barnet Stern and her father, William Barnet, lived at 121, and Henry and Selma Barnet lived at 123. William and Henry Barnet operated a textile factory in Rensselaer that produced shoddy—fabric and goods made from recycled wool (in contrast to items made from "virgin wool"). Charles Stern, an attorney, later joined them in the business. In the 1930s the firm began to work with a new synthetic material, rayon, although wool continued to be the main cloth produced. The company moved out of the state in the 1970s and continues in operation in South Carolina today, ninety-five years after its founding. The Stern and Barnet households employed servants, as was common in the neighborhood. Census records for many Albany families listed household residents who were cooks, maids, nurses and butlers and identified them as immigrants from Ireland, Germany, England and Holland. William Barnet also had a chauffeur for his c. 1915

Pierce Arrow. The car had to be parked in a garage at Myrtle Avenue and Ontario Street since the house lot did not accommodate a driveway and garage.

125 South Lake Avenue   14
1911

The appearance and plan of this house closely resemble a design published in 1909 by Gustav Stickley, the progenitor of the Crafts-man style. The gambrel roof is a variation on the original design, but the shingled exterior, wraparound porch and pergola, planters and the window placement are identical. Porch pillars and window boxes are constructed of concrete, a material often recommended by Stickley. The first occupant was Arthur P. Smith of the firm Oscar Smith and Son, fuel wood dealers; by 1925 Arnold S. Hatch, secretary of the Fuld and Hatch Knitting Company was in residence. Around 1930 the Hatch family added the brick garage, which had its own gas pump and an interior sprinkler that served as a car wash.

129 South Lake Avenue   15
c. 1885
Albert Fuller

This Colonial Revival house was designed by Albert Fuller for Andrew Draper, the first state commissioner of education, who kept it as a rental property while living at 133 South Lake Avenue. Draper was instrumental in the devel-opment of the State Normal School (later SUNY) and was responsible for the construc-tion of the New York State Education Building on Washington Avenue. Draper Hall on the downtown SUNYA campus was named for him.

An iron hitching post near the curb between 129 and 131 is a reminder of the pre-auto-mobile era.

131 South Lake Avenue   16
c. 1895
Ernest Hoffman

Hoffman departed from his more usual Romanesque Revival mode when he designed

16

this Queen Anne-style house for James F. McElroy, an engineer. The style is character-ized by complex massing and generous use of ornament, achieved here with a conical-roofed tower, multiple porches, gabled dormers, a two-story bay at the side, and a variety of win-dow types, all of which enliven the rectangular main block of the house. The allover white paint schemes frequently used today on late 19th-century houses is an influence of the later Colonial Revival style. The details on this house and at 135 would most likely have been high-lighted by a multi-color paint scheme.

135 South Lake Avenue   17
c. 1895

Frederick A. Mead operated a commercial produce company with his brother, James, and by 1900 was also a second vice president at the Albany Trust Company. His house was designed with a combination of Queen Anne and Colonial Revival elements—ornate carv-ings gracing the porch gables, paired turned posts at the wraparound porch, and the recessed arch piercing the gable end at the side elevations. Mead lived here with his wife, Ellen, daughter Fredericka, and a servant. The house must have become a little more lively in 1925, when Charles B. Heisler, who was employed at the state Education Department, purchased it and brought along his family of seven.

139 South Lake Avenue 18
Now Ronald McDonald House
1891
Fuller and Wheeler

Albert Fuller designed this house with his partner, William A. Wheeler, for Judge Alden Chester. The simple Colonial Revival form with gambrel roof and modillions at the cornice line is combined with such Queen Anne details as a conical-roofed tower and turreted dormers capped with small urns. Chester was appointed a state supreme court justice in 1900. The family owned this property until 1981, when it was purchased by the Northeast Family and Children's House. Renovated and connected to 137, the James Mead house, it serves as a residence for families with seriously ill children who are patients at nearby medical facilities.

147 South Lake Avenue 19
c. 1896-1900

Only husbands are listed in the city directories of the 19th and early 20th centuries, but it is common to find property listed in a wife's or daughter's name in the Albany tax assessments of the same period. Lydia B. McCarthy was listed as the owner of this house in the 1900 tax records. Her husband, John, was the business manager at the *Press* and *Knickerbocker* newspapers. Edward H. Bridge, secretary and manager of the Eastern Tablet Company and American Paper Company, bought the property in 1915. Neo-Classical in style, the house has a two-story portico supported by Doric columns. Dormers are capped by broken segmented pediments, and scores of delicate, turned balusters form the porch railings.

Memorial Park 20
South Lake Avenue between
Myrtle Street and New Scotland Avenue

The eastern side of this block, now the site of the Capital District Psychiatric Center, was once the site of the Bender Hygienic Laboratory and the Dudley Observatory, affiliated with Union University, whose buildings were designed by Albert Fuller. The observatory was moved from Arbor Hill to a Romanesque Revival building here in 1893 and remained until 1967 when it and the laboratory, built c. 1896, were demolished. Both facilities moved to new sites. The surrounding land has long been a public park, and before being graded for construction of the CDPC, it was a popular spot for sledding.

The name of the park relates to the two World War I monuments located here. Attilo Piccirilli designed the first, which dates from 1923 and features a cloaked figure with sword and olive branch guarding a symbolic tomb. At the corner of New Scotland Avenue, a 1933 Art Deco-style monument by Albany sculptor Gertrude K. Lathrop incorporates a flagpole. Three panels display portraits of soldiers and nurses, while a fourth lists casualties.

151 South Lake Avenue 21
1911
Charles L. Cobb
Addition, Worthington Palmer, 1921

This corner house was built for W. Sherman Cobb, a gardener, to the design of a relative, Charles L. Cobb. Sherman was a son of Smith Cobb, who lived at 737 Madison and who owned several parcels of land along South Lake in the 1870s. The house was originally a Four-Square with an entrance on South Lake Avenue. In 1921 Appleton Gregory purchased the house and hired Worthington Palmer to design an addition. The Providence Street facade took on a Georgian Revival form with a slate hipped roof and a portico of fluted Ionic columns. The balcony with quartered-circle and scroll work recalls an early 19th-century ironwork motif. Palmer's garage for Gregory complements the house with its bull's-eye window and matching brickwork. Gregory was an attorney and an inventor—it was his idea to equip the thick walls of the addition with internal fans which regulate the circulation of heated air.

Turn right onto Providence Street, and proceed west.

Providence Street 22

This block of Providence Street was subdivided in 1911. The houses built over the next fourteen years provide a capsule history of the housing types and styles found throughout Pine Hills and other 20th-century blocks: revival styles used on vernacular, builder houses or on architect-designed houses; single and multi-family houses; and owner-occupied and rental houses. The occupations of inhabitants covered a wide range also—from Emil Weeber at 538, who owned the Weeber Cycle Works on Central Avenue; Charles A. Hagaman at 567, who worked at his family's Hagaman Baking Company; Dr. Harry Judge at 560, one of several physicians on the block who worked at nearby hospitals; and Edward V. Rockwood at 568, superintendent of construction at the Capitol, to salesmen, chemists and the company officers noted below. The residents formed a close-knit social group. Families gathered for block-wide birthday parties, and dozens of children who lived here during the 1920s and 1930s put on plays, competed against baseball teams from other neighborhoods and carried out Halloween antics. A 1988 reunion of residents attracted 184 people from across the United States.

534 Providence Street 23
c. 1912

This Colonial Revival Four-Square house was the home of Charles P. and Gertrude Wagoner and was also listed as an address for Charles's business, the Empire Clay Mining Company, although his office was actually on Lark Street. Gertrude Wagoner's sister, Cornelia Mills Judge, also lived on the block.

536 Providence Street 24
c. 1914

Dutch Colonial Revival houses with the gable roof oriented towards the street are less common than other types of Colonial Revival houses (the Dutch Revival houses of the 1920s and later more often have the gable end at the side). This was originally the home of Cornelia K. Mills, a widow and the mother of Gertrude Wagoner and Cornelia Judge.

541 Providence Street 25
1914
Charles H. Wood

Charles H. Wood was an engineer employed by a bridge construction firm when he and his wife, Margaret, built this home. Wood's design combined typical Colonial Revival features—six-over-one windows (this refers to the number of panes in each sash) and sidelights at the doorway—with elements more common to the Bungalow style—a broad shed dormer and porch roof fringed with extended rafters and supported by rotund Tuscan columns. Like many houses on this tour, the house was designed with a bell system to ring for a maid and has a service stairway at the back of the house, which provides access to the second floor. The Woods employed two maids who shared the attic bedroom.

25

549 Providence Street 26
1916

Horace and Mildred L. Sherwood were the first occupants of this house, which features a broad gambrel roof. Exposed rafter ends and massive columns similar to those at 541 appear at the hipped-roof, one-story porch. The Sherwood's large backyard had circular paths and was popular with young cyclists on the block.

28

555 Providence Street 27
1915
Charles A. Brigham

Charles R. Vanneman, an engineer, was the original owner of this hipped-roof, Colonial Revival house designed by Charles A. Brigham. Many of the houses of this era were designed with porches, which served as outdoor sitting rooms. French doors open out to the porch at the side of the house, and fluted Doric columns support the entablature and balustrade.

544 Providence Street 28
c. 1916

This is a "high-style" example of a Neo-Classical two-family house, distinct from the Colonial Revival style in the use of two-story columns. Fluted Ionic columns support the entablature and pediment, which has a delicate dentil molding, modillions and a fanlight. Many vernacular, front-gabled, two-family houses with double porches were built around Albany during the horsecar and trolley eras; most have simple columns and less ornament. Caroline Gorgen, a widow, and her son Phillip, a lumber broker, were the first residents. Benjamin Boss, head of the Dudley

Observatory, lived here and is credited with writing the definitive star catalog of his time. Another resident, Prof. Harold W. Thompson of SUNYA, wrote *Body, Boots, and Britches*, an early anthology of American folk songs.

559 Providence Street 29
1914

Wilbur W. Chambers, a deputy attorney general, was the owner of this side-gabled, Colonial Revival house, which has pedimented dormers, modillions lining the gables and cornices, and a one-story porch supported by fluted Doric columns. Narrow windows at the door were used in place of traditional sidelights.

564 Providence Street 30
c. 1917

This house belonged to Wilford Minor, secretary and treasurer of the Alling Rubber Company. In contrast to 559 across the street, this house was designed in a more eclectic version of Colonial Revival, with a flared hipped roof, unusual "layered" clapboard and a leaded-glass window at the second story.

570 Providence Street 31
1925
Albert Fuller and William P. Robinson

Gates Aufsesser was the treasurer of the Mohawk Brush Company in 1924 when he lived at 157 South Lake. One year later, as the new owner and president of the company, he and his wife, Bessie deBeer Aufsesser, built this house. The family business was sold to the Fuller Brush Company in the late 1960s, which continued local operations until the mid-1970s. The solid exterior of the house with its broad slate roof and tall chimney stack is softened by turned posts on the angled entry porch and half-timbering of the porch to the east. On a more practical level, the family installed a receiving cabinet at the west side of the house for home deliveries of milk. The lawn to the west served as the block's World War II Victory Garden.

577 and 579 Providence Street 32
1912

Distinct from other single family homes which have the public living areas on the first floor and bedrooms on the second floor, bungalows accommodate private and public rooms on one floor. Additional bedrooms are often placed in attic levels. Both of these bungalows were owned by Raymond and Lottie Booth, and both were presumably built as rental houses. Mr. Booth was a contractor. Like 577, number 579 probably had an open porch supported by Doric pillars. Both houses were owner occupied by the 1930s.

Turn left onto Quail Street, continue south, and turn right onto New Scotland Avenue.

New Scotland Avenue 33

New Scotland Avenue was opened in the late 1790s as a toll road. It was not, however, served by the 19th-century streetcar system despite requests from residents, and the area remained largely undeveloped, unlike other turnpike areas. An ice house and various sheds were located between South Lake and Quail Street at the turn of the century. Ice was harvested from several ponds in the western portion of Albany and sold in blocks to businesses and homes in the pre-refrigerator era. (The "ice box" was a freestanding cabinet in the kitchen cooled by ice; the invention of the mechanical freezer was decades away.)

In 1911, after trolley service was again denied by the Common Council and the United Traction Company, the Woodlawn Improvement Association established a bus route along New Scotland Avenue. Most of the commercial activity in the neighborhood is confined to the north side of the street. The houses in this part of the city are similar to those in Pine Hills and include single- and multi-family Colonial Revival and Bungalow buildings with a few other eclectic styles. By the late 1920s, the neighborhood's growth merited several new buildings: School 19, at 395 New Scotland, was designed in the Collegiate Gothic style by Albert Fuller and William Robinson and built in 1917; the church of Saint Teresa of Avila, at 435 New Scotland, was established in 1920 to serve Catholic residents cut off from Saint Vincent de Paul by swamplands to the north. In 1926 the Engine No. 11 firehouse was built across Maplewood Street. Andrew Delehanty was the architect for Saint Teresa's church and school and for the firehouse.

Continue west on New Scotland Avenue, and turn right onto South Main Avenue.

South Main Avenue 34

Many developers purchased portions of former farmland along South Main Avenue after the turn of the century. The blocks close to New Scotland Avenue were laid out with a parkway, and the area was marketed as Helderberg Heights. Many of the homes constructed in the 1920s exhibit a mixture of Colonial Revival and English-influenced styles.

Winchester Villas 35
1926
194-176 South Main Avenue

Dan H. Winchester was one of four sons who worked with their father, Charles C. Winchester, president of the J. B. Lyon Printing Company. Dan was manager of purchasing and buildings for most of his forty-six-year career with the firm, but by 1919, at the age of twenty, he was already active in real estate. These six houses were constructed by the Willig and Acker firm for him and marketed as Winchester Villas. A brochure for the houses describes amenities including concealed ironing boards, built-in bathroom fixtures including a medicine chest, electric refrigeration, breakfast nook furniture, and inlaid linoleum in the kitchen. Houses were built complete with garages and landscaping.

Continue north on South Main Avenue, and turn right onto Woodlawn Avenue. Travel east along the block to West Erie Street, make two left turns, and continue west up Hansen Avenue, ending at South Main Avenue. This area was developed as Winchester Gables.

36

Winchester Gables 36
1928-30
South Main, Woodlawn and Hansen Avenues

Dan Winchester left Colonial examples behind and chose Spanish-inspired stucco, tiles and towers for this development on South Main, Hansen and Woodlawn avenues. It was advertised as ''an exclusive development of distinctive custom-built bungalows.'' He planned a total of sixty residences and began by building three houses in 1928. A model home was furnished at 233 Hansen Avenue, and prospective owners were invited to view ''one of these fascinating bungalows of rich simplicity and pervading restfulness.'' Winchester actually built twenty-seven houses in the development and rented out seven of the homes until 1944. He then auctioned the remaining lots, and the newer brick houses were subsequently constructed.

Winchester Gables were planned to cost under $10,000 and were custom designed, unlike Winchester Villas. In addition to features described for the Villas, buyers of the Gables could choose the site, floor plan and other features to suit their needs. Owners had a choice of brick, shingle or stucco exteriors and even several stucco-finishing patterns. The buildings are L-shaped in plan, some with square or octagonal towers tucked into the ell, and the roofs are covered with pan tiles. Arched openings are found on various porches and gateways to yards and in a few of the towers. A tower on Winchester's own house at 130

South Main Avenue is embellished with a small balcony. The Spanish theme was carried out inside, with stuccoed walls and decorative iron lighting fixtures.

The sloping terrain between Woodlawn and Hansen avenues accommodates an alley where basements, garages and porches are incorporated into the rear of each house. Houses on north side of Hansen and south side of Woodlawn have attached garages.

Turn right onto South Main Avenue, and continue north to Myrtle Avenue. Turn right onto Myrtle Avenue, and continue east to South Lake Avenue.

South Main and Myrtle Avenues 37

Like South Lake Avenue, South Main Avenue was largely built up by 1915. The five-story, brick Westerly Apartments is an early apartment building at the corner of Myrtle and South Main avenues and was constructed in 1912 by Antonio De Dominicus.

At the turn of the century, streets like Morris, Myrtle and Yates were often the location of secondary buildings for houses on major streets. Greenhouses, liveries and, later, garages were built for the convenience of neighborhood residents. Garages were in use well into the 1940s.

Beginning in 1890, houses along these blocks were served by the Madison Avenue trolleys. Many of the trolley-era, two-family houses were separated only by a walkway, while others built with the car in mind allowed for a driveway to a private garage in back. After 1910, the Blanchard-Lansing Realty Company purchased property in the area and boasted in a 1913 directory ad, ''We started the boom in Pine Hills—developers of Main Avenue, West Lawrence Street, Myrtle Avenue, Morris Street, Park Avenue, Erie Street in full or part.'' The realty company marketed both vacant land and speculative houses. The lots along these streets are smaller than those along Madison and South Lake avenues, and houses are often more modest. The mixture of single- and multi-family houses was constructed in familiar Colonial Revival and Bungalow styles along with a few examples of stuccoed Arts and Crafts or Tudor houses.

Turn left on South Lake Avenue, continue north to Madison Avenue, and turn left onto Madison Avenue.

Madison Avenue 38

Madison Avenue, originally named Lydius Street, was home to many prominent industrialists and businessmen who built homes between 1880 and 1920. Two pairs of twin houses flank the beginning of the block west of South Lake Avenue: 714 and 718 at the south and 721 and 725 to the north.

714 and 718 Madison Avenue 39
c. 1883

These imposing brick mansions were built by David Skinner and Joseph Arnold about twenty years after they established a partnership to manufacture boilers, elevators, steam pumps and engines on Herkimer Street and later Broadway. Skinner had been a boilermaker in England before finding his way to Albany in 1855 as an employee of the New York Central Railroad.

Brick courses and contrasting stone window sills and trim outline the horizontal division of the stories, but the overall emphasis is a vertical one carried out by the bays, towers, steeply pitched roofs, terra-cotta panels, and the arrangement of the relatively narrow windows. Both houses originally had one-story wooden entry porches of turned spindles and carved panels. Skinner's corner house had a third-story porch of turned woodwork strategically placed for a view of Washington Park, then newly developed. The porch was later altered and enclosed. By 1930, number 714 was vacant after having served as a dormitory. Joseph Arnold's heirs remained at 718 until the early 1930s. Both houses have been converted to apartments.

39

721 and 725 Madison Avenue   40
c. 1895
Stern, Nolan and Stern

These houses were built by two brothers, Bernard and Joseph Steefel, who owned the Union Clothing Company at 80 State Street, and designed by Stern, Nolan and Stern of Chicago. Terra-cotta and brick quoins and a band of lattice-patterned brickwork reinforce the solid, boxy look. The brick course, broad windows and porches echo the horizontal line of the Prairie style. Joseph Steefel owned a barn at the back of the property, on Hamilton Street. Number 725 was purchased by the Women's Club of Albany in 1920 as their headquarters; 721 is now used for offices.

727 Madison Avenue   41
c. 1882

The vertical proportions of this Queen Anne house are emphasized by the conical tower, the bargeboard at the gable end and the tall, narrow windows marking the bays. The house was built for Donald McDonald, a retired gas meter manufacturer, whose family owned the property until 1915. Solomon H. Blatner, a partner in Blatner Brothers and Company, which dealt in "comfortables" (bed coverings similar to today's comforters), purchased the house in 1925. It was being used as student housing in 1964, when it was acquired by the present owners, the Society of Friends.

731 Madison Avenue   42
c. 1882

This Queen Anne house, with carved cornice and a peaked roof tower, was built for Peter Kinnear, who was president of the Albany Billiard Ball Company. Kinnear developed molds used to produce billiard balls from celluloid invented in 1868 by a local printer, John Wesley Hyatt. Kinnear eventually acquired the business and turned it into a successful concern, the Albany Hyatt Billiard Ball Company, which continued under family management until 1968. A civic leader as well as a prominent businessman, Kinnear was active as a real estate developer and is also credited with promoting the installation of the Burns statue in Washington Park.

737 Madison Avenue   43
1874

The Cobb family had extensive land holdings in this area and began to subdivide their property in the 1870s. Smith Cobb was a gardener, as were his sons W. Sherman Cobb, who later lived at 151 South Lake Avenue, and Perry Cobb, who inherited this property and lived here until 1920. The shape of this Italianate house is more rural in character than the more common two- and three-bay-wide Italianate townhouses in downtown Albany. Both forms, however, exhibit such details as small windows in the frieze between double brackets, ornate window hoods and bay windows. The Colonial Revival porch with paired Ionic columns is a later addition.

43

740 Madison Avenue 44

c. 1876-80

This Queen Anne-style house retains important original features such as patterned bands of decorative slate across the roof, carved woodwork under the eaves of the projecting bay, a wraparound porch of turned posts and a bit of iron cresting. This house was built for Alexander Simpson, a carpenter.

755 Madison Avenue 45

c. 1889
Attributed to Albert Fuller

Brick and masonry details highlight the vertical, Queen Anne features of this house, despite obvious neglect. The house was owned in quick succession by William McNaughton, an attorney; Isaiah Page, the head of a prominent iron foundry; and Elizabeth Tebbutt, whose family owned a funeral home. John P. Randerson, a dredging contractor, and his wife, Nannie, owned the house from 1905 to 1936. The large, frame carriage house that once served this mansion is visible at the rear of the parking lot. Like other support buildings for Madison Avenue mansions, it fronts on Hamilton Street. It is now a residence.

756 Madison Avenue 46

1881
Albert Fuller

According to an 1880 publication, Albert Fuller's design for this house, built for George W. van Slyke, a tobacconist, included a porte-cochere, several wooden porches and a conical-roofed tower at the corner. Of these, only the entry porch remains. The house retains its irregular massing, stone coursing outlining first-story windows, fish-scale shingles in the gables and checkerboard panels of patterned terra-cotta tiles along with a lively variety of windows. The William E. Drislane, Jr., family owned the house from the early 1930s to 1980. Drislane operated a grocery on North Pearl Street in a succession of buildings including a former synagogue and the former Albany Female Academy. While an extensive

46

list of products was available to retail customers, an 1890 ad for "Drislane's Big Grocery Houses" stated that the firm would "contract to supply hotels, institutions, steamboats, and large consumers, anywhere."

761 Madison Avenue 47

c. 1895-1900

The three stories of this house are emphasized by contrasting materials. The first level is faced with rough-cut stone, and the windows are capped by flat stone lintels. Splayed stone lintels are placed over windows on the brick second story, and the gable is sheathed in wooden shingles and enriched with modillions outlining the cornice and pediment. The one-story porch with grouped Ionic columns is typical of the Colonial Revival style.

Hudson Apartments 48

c. 1904
762 Madison Avenue

Morris L. Ryder, a well-known local contractor, constructed this Neo-Classical apartment house, known at one time as the Hudson Apartments. The placement of multi-family buildings among single-family homes was common in Pine Hills, as well as in other parts of the city, but is rarely allowed by today's zoning laws.

First Church of Christ Scientist   49
1929
774 Madison Avenue

First organized in Albany in 1887, the Christian Science congregation bought this site at Quail and Madison in 1898. The first chapel was built in 1902, and a building fund was begun six years later for a larger chapel. The church's history states that the building committee decided to copy the chapel at the Benevolent Association at Chestnut Hill, Massachusetts, and hired the same architect and builder, but does not name either party. In accordance with church tradition, the dedication did not take place until 1937, after all building debts had been paid. This 20th-century version of the Gothic Revival style features multi-colored brick, pointed-arch windows, stone-capped buttresses and ornate hardware at the wooden doors. The character of Madison Avenue along the two blocks west of this corner was determined by the fact that landowners platted the properties into smaller lots and built a mixture of speculative residential and commercial buildings, now joined by several institutional structures.

Madison Avenue Presbyterian   50
Church
1897
Now Crossroads Baptist Fellowship
820 Madison Avenue

Louis and Geraldine Pratt, William D. Goold, George and Theodora Hawley, and Lizzie Ogden, whose houses are included in this chapter, were among early members of the Madison Avenue Presbyterian church. Meetings began in 1886, and the congregation was officially organized in 1888. Services were held in a rented house at 821 and later in a small chapel at 816 Madison Avenue. The present building was constructed in 1897 and enlarged in 1907. The use of yellow brick and limestone produces a more subtle version of the Romanesque Revival style, with its round-arched windows and doorways, than Richardsonian Romanesque examples elsewhere in Albany.

Vincentian Institute   51
1917
SE corner of Madison Avenue at Ontario Street
Robert D. MacPherson

The Saint Vincent de Paul parish was founded in 1895 to accommodate the growing Catholic population of Albany west of Washington Park that was previously included in the parish of the Cathedral of the Immaculate Conception on Eagle Street at Madison. This parish was named in honor of the Saint Vincent de Paul Society, a men's charitable group based at the cathedral that offered Sunday School classes in homes of this neighborhood. In 1915, a donation of $100,000 and property along Madison and Yates Street from James and Margaret Brady Farrell set in motion the parish's plans for the establishment of a school. The donors were the son-in-law and daughter of multi-millionaire Anthony N. Brady. This building was constructed for the elementary school in 1917. High school classes began in 1921 and were held at 773 Madison Avenue until additions to the Institute provided more classroom space. The building also had facilities for parish activities.

The school was designed as an institutional version of the Classical Revival, with a cornice and dentil molding defining the entablature, Ionic columns at the center of the main facade and a grand cartouche and festoon at the roofline. The Institute's classes were discontinued in 1977, and the building was remodeled for senior citizens' apartments. Public School 4 stood on the playground site across Madison as a secular counterpart to the Institute: the first building, designed by Charles Ogden, burned in 1922; the second was Marcus Reynold's Federal Revival building, which was demolished in 1964 because of structural problems.

854 Madison Avenue   52
1924
Gander, Gander and Gander

This Art Deco-inspired building with marble front, stylized eagle and vertical emphasis was designed by the architects of the 1930s post office and courthouse on Broadway. It originally housed the West End Federal Savings and Loan Association.

877-885 Madison Avenue 53

Hagaman and Company, Bakers, was located in a complex of buildings that stood at this site. An ad in the 1918 city directory mentions "Sunlit, Clean, Modern Buildings" at this location and a Troy store at 32 Fourth Street. Begun in 1884 by Emma Hagaman, who convinced her father, Abram Hagaman, to sell her homemade pies downtown, the company eventually had stores located around Albany and Troy and sales routes around the region. Emma was president and secretary of the company; her brother Charles served as vice president and treasurer. The Hagamans lived two blocks west, at 971 Madison Avenue.

Saint Vincent de Paul 54
Roman Catholic Church

1904-08
900 Madison Avenue
Robert D. MacPherson
Additions, 1939, 1957, attributed to Gander, Gander and Gander

Robert D. MacPherson, who worked in the state architect's office, was responsible for the design of this limestone Classical Revival building, which replaced an earlier wooden church purchased from a Baptist congregation. Ionic columns support the broad pediment of the facade and are complemented by Ionic pilasters at the sides. The three masonry vestibules were added in 1939. An original octagonal dome at the center of the building was removed in 1957, when the sanctuary was extended to Yates Street. After a 1980 fire in the sanctuary, the church was renovated again to reduce the sanctuary space and incorporate facilities for community services. The church once owned several nearby properties that accommodated parish clergy and instructors for the Vincentian Institute and continues to own the former Hawley house and greenhouses at 994 Madison Avenue.

College of Saint Rose 55

Madison Avenue west of Partridge Street

The land from Partridge Street to West Lawrence Street was once known as

Twickenham, the country estate and summer residence of the Andrew E. Brown family. Their city house was at 2 Clinton Square, and Brown commuted to work in downtown Albany while the family enjoyed their months away from the hot, crowded city. In the 1880s, after Brown's death, the land was divided, and the house was demolished. Like the blocks to the east, this portion of Madison has larger lots and houses built by prominent industrialists and businessmen at the turn of the century. Some of these residences were the homes of German Jewish families who moved here from the South End and Center Square. An 1890 ad for the sale of 994 Madison touted the new asphalt paving and the arrangement of "all drains and water mains laid under the sidewalk." The street was described as the "main avenue for pleasure driving in the city," and trolley rides to City Hall on the Blue Line (car number 4) took only fifteen minutes.

The block did not remain strictly residential for long, however. In 1920, the new College of Saint Rose bought the house at 979 Madison for classroom space. The college was established in 1920 by the Sisters of Saint Joseph for the education of Roman Catholic women. As the student population increased from an original enrollment of twenty, so too did the college's property ownership along Madison and Western avenues and Partridge Street. New buildings were constructed in the center of the block and along Madison and Western avenues. The college has painted most of its properties a uniform white, which unites them as a complex but does not reflect the variety of deep-colored paints and stains originally used.

917 Madison Avenue 56
c.1911

919 Madison Avenue
c. 1923

The low lines of the Prairie style, popularized by Frank Lloyd Wright, are exhibited here by the hipped tile roofs, broad overhanging eaves supported by brackets, and the one-story porches across the facades. James Feeney, president of Feeney and Sheehan Building Company, was the first owner of 917 with his wife, Annie. The house at 919 was constructed for the William Drislane family, and Katherine Drislane, a daughter and treasurer of the family firm, Drislane's Olde Wine and Spirits, lived here from the 1930s to 1961.

921 Madison Avenue 57
c. 1890

Elizabeth McGraw Mills and her family occupied this Queen Anne residence until around 1910. The design incorporates a mixture of materials—rough-cut stone, clapboard and shingles. A chicken house and a barn were also on the property. The parish of Saint Vincent de Paul owned the building between 1918 and 1975, when it was purchased by the College of Saint Rose.

923 and 935 Madison Avenue 58
1890
Ogden and Wright

Designed by Ogden and Wright, this pair of houses features a mix of Queen Anne and Shingle styles, common at the turn of the century. The brick used for the first two stories of each house contrasts with the wood used in the third story conical-roofed bays, garlands and patterned shingles in the gables. Lewis E. Carr, an attorney for the Delaware and Hudson Railroad, lived at 923 with his family and servants from 1894 to 1925. Harry Burdick, a partner in Burdick and Son, a stove specialty business at Liberty and Division streets, commissioned Ogden and Wright to build 935. The family lived here from 1891 to 1908, along with a coachman and other servants. Saint Rose bought 935 in 1939 and 923 in the early 1960s.

963 Madison Avenue 59
1886

This building was the home of the William D. Goold family from 1886 to 1930. William's grandfather, James Goold, founded a carriage manufacturing firm in 1813 and built the coaches used for the 1831 run of the De Witt Clinton on the Mohawk and Hudson Railroad.

The company also provided the first horsecar used in Albany and made the transition to auto repair in the 20th century. The Goold family deeded the house to Saint Rose in 1930.

971 Madison Avenue 60
1899

This house became the second building owned by Saint Rose when it was purchased from the Hagaman family in 1921.

979 Madison Avenue 61
1886

The William Keeler home was the first building bought by the College of Saint Rose. It was built two years after William and his brother John opened Keeler's Restaurant at 56 State Street. William owned a poultry farm in North Albany and an oyster plantation in Virginia to supply his clientele and, like other successful businessmen, was very active in local politics. After the demise of the Albany Land Improvement Company, the Keeler family invested in a large parcel of land on what is now South Manning Boulevard and Marion Avenue and sold off individual lots during the 1920s and 1930s.

Saint Joseph's Hall 62
1924
985 Madison Avenue
Thomas L. Gleason

Designed by Thomas L. Gleason and completed in 1924, this was the first building constructed for the College of Saint Rose. Gleason was also the architect of the Eastern Star Temple, School 27, the Lincoln Park bathhouse, and the Cathedral Academy. Corinthian columns at the second and third stories beneath the entablature, brick lintels with stone keystones over multi-paned windows, and a broken scroll pediment over the doorway render this a Classical Revival building. An architectural drawing published in 1924 indicated that a three-part building was planned, with "room for dormitories, administrative quarters and a library," but only this wing was completed.

994 Madison Avenue 63
c. 1888

This house was built for Charles Peabody of the banking firm of Spencer Trask and Company. Peabody was one of the original partners in the Albany Land Improvement Company but moved to New Jersey in 1892 after acquiring a seat in the New York Stock Exchange. The next owners and residents were Helen Amsdell and her husband, Theodore, who had just sold his share of the Amsdell brewery on Jay Street to his brother. He began a new partnership with his son-in-law, George Hawley, at the Dobler brewery on Myrtle Avenue. Hawley was married to the Amsdell's daughter Theodora, and the couple also lived here from 1893 to 1928. Hawley donated the statue of Philip Schuyler in front of City Hall in Theodora's memory.

The towers were added to the house later, but the Palladian window and large three-part window on the west elevation are original, as is the circular porch. The Amsdells built the carriage house, which remains on Morris Street, and later purchased 992 and 998 Madison and demolished a farmhouse and a barn on those lots. George Hawley built greenhouses on Morris Street at the back of the land to the east. After the parish of Saint Vincent de Paul bought the property in 1934, quartz glass was installed to provide "therapeutic sunbathing," a popular health trend of the time. Modified in the 1950s, the buildings are still used as classrooms by the church.

1000 Madison Avenue 64
c. 1899

Carrie and Henry C. Dumary, who was president of the Helderberg Cement Company, first occupied this residence, and, after the family moved to State Street in 1910, Carrie retained ownership until 1922. Tenants included milliner Jonas Muhlfelder and his family, who lived here from 1912 to 1918, and Leonard Waldman of Waldman Brothers, who sold "ladies' furnishings." In 1922 Sal Levi, vice president of the Mohawk Brush Company, bought the house with his wife, Jeanette, who sold the property in 1951. The house served as the Pine Hills branch of the Albany Public Library from 1952 until 1991, when Saint Rose renovated it for administrative offices. Colonial Revival in style with a Queen Anne tower, the house has several stained glass windows that were widely available at the turn of the century, and large carved urns still grace the newel posts of interior staircases.

1001 Madison Avenue 65
c. 1889
Ogden and Wright

Albany architects Edward Ogden and Frank Wright designed this house for William B. and Anne Victoria Elmendorf. William was the general director of the Hudson River Day Line, which operated steamer boat service between Albany and New York City. In 1906 the Elmendorfs moved to their new house at 545 Western Avenue, and George B. and Anna LaGrange Blakeslee bought this house. Mr. Blakeslee, a prominent lumber dealer, owned several speculative lots in the Pine Hills development. Like other houses on the block, this house combines shingle and rustic masonry construction with Queen Anne towers and Colonial Revival details. It is now the Saint Rose admissions office.

66

1006 Madison Avenue 66
1911

Ira and Elizabeth Mendleson built this Arts and Crafts house, which departed from the typical

Colonial and Queen Anne styles on this block. Broad, flared eaves are supported by rafter ends and the expanse of the porch is set off by the standing-seam copper roof. A half-timber motif was used in the front gables of the stucco exterior. The Mendleson family owned the B. T. Babbitt Company, makers of Bab-O cleaning powder and other products.

1008 Madison Avenue   67
1910

Eugene and Cora Sporborg, the first owners of this house, lived here until the 1940s. Eugene Sporborg was a milliner (millinery firms sold hats, trims and notions). The tile roof is an unusual contrast to the half-timbering of the Tudor style; slate roofs are more common. Grouped pillars mounted on short piers support the roof of the spacious porch.

1010 Madison Avenue   68
c. 1909

68

This house received a full Neo-Classical treatment: a two-story portico with Ionic columns supporting a wide entablature topped with a balustrade, the entry door framed by sidelights and fanlight, and dormers with segmented, or arched, pediments. Winslow Mead, a deputy superintendent of public works at the Capitol, resided here until 1915. Jacob and Leontine Baere lived here until 1953. Like the Barnets on South Lake Avenue, Mr. Baere was a shoddy (recycled wool) manufacturer. The Whittle family had extensive greenhouses and a large wagon shed along Morris Street at this corner, where they grew "plants and ornamental shrubbery in great variety, for cut flowers, bouquets and the trade." The A. E. Whittle Company operated a store in the Tweddle Building downtown.

Saint Andrew's Episcopal Church 69
1930
NE corner of North Main and
Madison Avenues
Norman Sturgis

The first church building of this congregation was constructed by the firm Gick and Sayles at the corner of Western Avenue and North Main Avenue in 1897. There had been some disagreement over how far from the city center a new church should be located, and many preferred a site closer to Quail Street. The church had been established as a mission of the Vestry of Saint Paul in 1892 and named Saint Paul's Chapel of Saint Andrew, but by 1903 it was incorporated into the diocese as Saint Andrew's Church of the City of Albany.

The lot for the present building was purchased in 1920, and the building was constructed in 1930-31. Norman Sturgis described this Gothic Revival church as having a "simple exterior" of "granite walls, limestone trim, little carving and no meaningless decoration. Neither the arches nor the piers contain steel, but depend for their strength and endurance upon masonry alone." The 1897 building on Western Avenue served as the parish house until 1956, when it was demolished for the new parish house.

70

Madison Theater 70
1929
1032 Madison Avenue

Not known for doing things by halves, Warner Brothers opened the Madison as one of their chain of theaters on May 29, 1929, with a gala that included Al Jolson as master of ceremonies, the Vitaphone Trumpeteers, a dedication by Mayor John Boyd Thacher II, and an introductory address by Judge James T. Nolan, president of the Pine Hills Association. The line-up of films included a newsreel, a Mickey Mouse cartoon, and *The Desert Song* starring John Bowles, Carlotta King and Myrna Loy. Designed in the Art Deco style, the theater is faced with terra-cotta cast in geometric floral patterns. The Madison had competition at first from the Pine Hills Theater around the corner at 241 West Lawrence, now the site of a grocery store. In 1993 the Madison was the only single-screen cinema remaining in Albany.

Part II:
The Core of the Pine Hills Neighborhood

Begin at the junction of Western and Madison avenues at Allen Street. This tour extends along blocks of South and North Allen streets, South and North Pine avenues, Manning and South Manning boulevards, Marion Avenue and Western Avenue. Drivers may want to pull into a parking lot to read through the introduction. Touring may also be done on foot.

This neighborhood saw a great deal of traffic after the Great Western Turnpike (now Western Avenue) was opened in 1799. Two hotels were built to accommodate 19th-century travelers, the Klondike at the northeast corner of Western Avenue and Allen Street, and Carrick's Hotel on the northeast corner of Madison Avenue and West Lawrence Street. The turnpike was upgraded to a plank road in 1849 in order to combat the wear of traffic on the route.

The junction of Madison and Western avenues, known as "the Point," is prominent in Albany's history as the site of the departure for the first run of the De Witt Clinton, America's first passenger train. There was never a depot here; instead passengers arrived by horse-drawn carriages from ticket offices at the foot of Gansevoort Street and, later, downtown and transferred directly onto the train. Trains continued to run from the Point to Schenectady until 1844, but the steep grade of the route proved to be difficult. The line was rerouted from downtown through Tivoli Hollow and West Albany beginning in 1844.

The next major period of activity in the neighborhood began in 1888 when entrepreneurs Louis Pratt and Gaylord Logan and their partners formed the Albany Land Improvement and Building Company. In 1888 they bought farmland bordered by Allen Street, Cortland Street, Marion Avenue, Manning Boulevard and Washington Avenue for a residential development christened Pine Hills. As alderman-at-large, Louis Pratt strongly supported efforts to extend the street-car system westward from New Scotland Avenue. Electrification of the system in 1890 changed streetcars into trolleys, named for the device which transmitted electric power from the overhead wires. At the same time the system was extended to Allen Street. The partners had meanwhile undertaken a two-year improvement project in the subdivision. Pine Avenue and Allen Street were the first streets to be paved and laid with water and gas lines. The company advertised the subdivision extensively in the 1890 city directory and other publications and claimed that these street improvements were the best in the city.

Deeds for the fifty-by-two-hundred-foot lots prohibited commercial activity and the sale of alcohol but did not stipulate requirements for residential structures. While some commercial use of properties has been allowed since the middle of the 20th century, no neighborhood bars or liquor stores are to be found west of Allen Street. (The Klondike Hotel was located conveniently just outside the boundary, however, and was not affected by the restrictions.) In order to market the ''villa lots'' more effectively, the company sponsored the construction of about eight houses between 1888 and 1889. These early homes are scattered along Pine Avenue and Allen Streets, and most are close to Western Avenue. By 1895 there were perhaps fifty houses along these two streets.

In several cases, the Pine Hills pioneers were business associates of the land company's partners; others were speculators who had already developed property elsewhere in Albany. Still others were downtown residents attracted by the spacious lots. It is also interesting that by 1890 many lots were owned by the Barber Asphalt Paving Company. Perhaps the company was responsible for the street paving (identified as the first use of Trinidad asphalt in the city) and was paid in land by the cash-poor developers. By the late 1890s, because of the financial panic of 1893 and poor sales, the partners were unable to meet mortgage obligations and lost the majority of the lots in the subdivision through foreclosure by the Albany City National Bank. Subsequently, lots were gradually sold by the bank, often in large tracts to groups of developers. Many lots remained vacant even after 1920. A survey of the architectural styles of the houses along the streets reveals the pattern of development.

517 Western Avenue 71
1930

This brick Art Deco building served as the telephone company offices before being renovated for use as the Pine Hills Library in 1990.

Steamer No. 10 72
1891
Junction of Western and Madison Avenues and West Lawrence Street
Albert Fuller

Promotions of Pine Hills proclaimed the healthful, country atmosphere, but the construction of this firehouse in 1891 attested to the increasing density of the area. Designed by Albert Fuller in the Richardsonian Romanesque style, with characteristic rough-cut stone, contrasting trim and delicate carving, the station was closed by the city in 1988, and the building was converted into a theater. The police station, a later addition, remains in operation. A sharp eye can spot the date of the firehouse on the east gable.

Turn left onto South Allen Street, and proceed south.

South Allen Street 73

The Pine Hills Neighborhood Association was formed in 1902 and functioned much as neighborhood organizations do today. Residents screened development proposals and planned social functions. The Aurania Club stood on the site of the Elks Club at 24 South Allen Street. The property had been selected as the location of a proposed ''Hospital for Incurables'' until the association reportedly thwarted the development by purchasing the lot for the construction of the club.

The inspiration for the name of the Pine Hills subdivision is evident along several blocks of South Allen Street. The steep lawns, described as ''terraces'' in early promotions, are remnants of the hills that existed throughout the neighborhood before streets were graded by developers. The area was once part of the sandy Pine Barrens, portions of which remain undeveloped to the west in Guilderland. Of special interest is a notation in the 1889 tax records of a ''Pine Grove'' that stood between lots 88 and 112 on the west side of South Allen, where a stand of pine trees remains. Some of these houses were built during the Pine Hills development's earliest phase, although several have been altered.

44 South Allen Street   74

c. 1890

An 1898 biographical sketch of Gilbert Pearsall mentioned this residence on South Allen Street. Pearsall operated a successful photography business and owned at least two other lots along Pine and Allen. He moved to California in 1905.

88 South Allen Street   75

1890

Promotional literature for the Pine Hills subdivision included photographs of this house, built for John R. Stephenson, whose occupation was listed as ''cloaks and furs'' on North Pearl Street. The property was owned by Charles R. Steele, news editor of *The Argus*, in 1895.

112 South Allen Street   76

1890

The first owner, D. C. Rebhun, was employed with Dayton Ball and Company. The firm produced lasts, the wooden forms used by shoemakers.

122 South Allen Street   77

1889

Owner Charles Van Allen, with partner William A. Hamilton, represented several insurance companies locally.

141 South Allen Street   78

c. 1895

Charles Effler and John Farrell were business partners in a billiards hall at 562 Broadway and were neighbors on South Allen Street. The Farrells owned three lots with a frontage of about 140 feet; the Efflers owned a seventy-five-foot lot and constructed this Queen Anne style house at 141.

Turn right onto Cortland Street, turn right onto South Pine Avenue, and proceed north.

79

South Pine Avenue   79

Compared to houses along South Allen Street and to other blocks of South and North Pine avenues, the styles of houses on this block south of Mercer Street reflect the fact that the land remained undeveloped until the early 20th century. These houses are similar in character to blocks such as Lenox and Euclid to the west (the only exception is the house at 141 South Pine Avenue, which was built by 1893 and owned by Henry P. Soulier, manager of the Leland Opera House in downtown Albany). The Colonial Revival house at 150 South Pine was designed by a G. H. Anderson of Peekskill, and the current owners sculpted the lawn south of the house into a bowling green. The Arts and Crafts and Dutch Colonial Revival houses at 127 and 125 are attributed to Albany architect Walter van Guysling, who produced several Flemish Revival and Arts and Crafts buildings including the ticket office for the Hudson River Day Line Steamer, now the L'Auberge Restaurant at 351 Broadway. The house at 123 is a cottage version of the Arts and Crafts style.

The architectural styles along the rest of South and North Pine avenues and along South and North Allen streets reflect the late 19th-century transition from the English-based Queen Anne style to an early phase of the classically-influenced Colonial Revival style. Many of these homes are eclectic in their use of detail. Multiple gables, bay windows, and a variety of porches produce more complex forms than are seen on later 20th-century houses on Western Avenue and South Manning Boulevard. Houses here tend to be more vertical and often have front gables.

Many houses along South Pine were built on speculation including most of the two-family houses. Because some of the earliest houses built during the 1889-90 development by the Albany Land Improvement and Building Company were sold by 1895, they may have been built as investment properties. Nathaniel B. Spalding, an attorney with offices next to Pratt and Logan in the Tweddle Building on State Street, purchased 33 from Frances J. Nicholson; David and Althea Kirk had several female tenants at 29 who worked as teachers and stenographers; and 27 was built for William J. Caine and owned in 1895 by William Mason, a bookkeeper for a tobacco firm. Lilly Hogeboom and her husband, Frank, an attorney and a lumber merchant, built the houses at 9 and 5 and lived at number 5.

Other houses on South Pine were constructed for specific owners. These include 24, which may have been built for William Rally, whose designer applied carved wood ornamentation to this front-gabled house; 8, which has a curved bay and tower reminiscent of the Queen Anne style and was built for the Bell family; and 2, a Tudor-style house built by 1898 for the McDonald family, which owned a gas meter manufacturing plant. McDonald's house acknowledges the corner lot location with an angled porch; the front door is framed by an arched molding, and the curved wooden members of the half-timbered gables are typical of early Tudor Revival houses.

Proceed north across Western Avenue to North Pine Avenue.

6 North Pine Avenue   80
1890

Louis Pratt—attorney, alderman, and developer—was highly regarded as a brilliant young man despite the failure of the Pine Hills development. This clapboard and shingle Colonial Revival style house was his home, ornamented with wooden details in the front gable, stained-glass lights in the large window on the Western Avenue side and a bay window at the second story. Pratt later moved to Seattle, began another successful career, and was reported to have become the president of the chamber of commerce.

Only three other buildings on this block date from the earliest phase of development: 14, built for Charles H. Mills, an attorney with offices at the Tweddle Building; 21, built for Joel Eaton, an elder of the Methodist Episcopal Church; and 30, built for Mary L. Houghtaling, who rented rooms to a teacher at School 25.

63, 69, 71, and 89 North   81
Pine Avenue
1906

868, 870, 872 and 874
Lancaster Street
1906

These cast-stone houses were constructed by the Albany Material and Construction Company. Ulysses G. Stockwell, president of the company, began his career in insurance and retired in 1898 to work solely as a contractor. He was credited with the construction of 225 buildings in Albany. Stockwell was responsible for several apartment house projects including the conversion of the Amsdell brewery to the Knickerbocker Apartments and the addition of an apartment building behind the Sard House at 397 State Street. Ulysses and Florence Stockwell lived at 89 North Pine, which as a corner house has a full porch on the Lancaster side that complements Stockwell's other houses.

94-100 North Pine Avenue 82

Although the covenants placed on Pine Hills lots excluded commercial uses, educational institutions were originally allowed, and an 1892 promotional magazine described several buildings of the Albany Home School for the Deaf as being "delightfully situated" at the northwest corner of Lancaster and North Pine, now the site of several brick apartment buildings. Anna M. Black was the resident principal.

91 North Pine Avenue 83
1906

This house was also built by Ulysses G. Stockwell, who used the same rough cut stone and red mortar on his townhouse block at Manning Boulevard and Kent Street.

Turn right onto Lancaster Street, and turn right onto North Allen Street.

78 North Allen Street 84
1908

This Dutch Colonial Revival house with a front gambrel roof and oversized cornice returns was a change of pace for builder Ulysses Stockwell. The chamfered windows at the corners of the second story are an unusual feature.

School 16 85
1905
41 North Allen Street

The architect of this Classical Revival school pulled out all the stops with front gabled wings, a cornice edged with modillions, quoins around the arched doorways and at the corners, and a cartouche or crest at the center of the roofline. Morris L. Ryder was the general contractor for the original construction. Eight classrooms were added to the building in 1914.

34 North Allen Street 86
1895

This house was designed by Albany architect Charles Ogden for Peter Elliot, who owned a liquor store downtown. Ogden used his characteristic tower with arched windows at the brick base and provided a wraparound porch.

32 North Allen Street 87
c. 1895

William Gick formed a partnership with fellow Isle of Man immigrant William Sayles and became a prominent builder who worked throughout Albany. The firm owned several lots along North Pine Avenue and Manning Boulevard, and they presumably built houses in the neighborhood. This house is indicative of the "builders' vernacular" with its front gable, L-shaped porch and a bay window at the second story, embellished here with stained-glass transoms.

Continue south to Western Avenue, and pause at the corner.

527 Western Avenue 88
1897

A late example of the Queen Anne style, this house was constructed by De Witt C. Becker, of the firm David Bradt, Becker and Company. In 1915 it was the home of Francis F. Crannel, president of a lumber company. Altered for use as a two-family home and later a halfway house, the building was damaged by fire in the late 1970s. The current owner has named the property the Elliot Mansion after a grandfather who supported the daunting rehabilitation project.

Turn right onto Western Avenue, and proceed west.

1154 Madison Avenue 89
c. 1898

This home was built for Samuel C. Wooster, an obviously successful businessman. His firm, S. C. Wooster, a "Wholesale Dealer in Lake and Ocean Fish and Salt," sold "Only the Best 'Prize Medal Brand' Salt High Grade Sifted for Dairy and Table Use." The Colonial Revival proclamation made by the house is no less subtle: gambrel roof, Palladian and elliptical

89

windows, garlands, grouped Doric columns
and dentil molding at the porch form an impressive building. A stable was located at the rear.
Turn right onto Manning Boulevard.

Manning Boulevard 90

Manning Boulevard was paved, lined with
bridle paths and planted with trees during the
1876 construction of a system of ring roads
linked to Washington Park. Western Avenue,
the stretch of the 1849 plank road of the Great
Western turnpike within city bounds, was
re-paved with granite blocks as part of the
same project. The construction was carried out
as a relief program for unemployed men, and
shift assignments were made on a rotating
basis to allocate the work in a fair manner.
This portion of the city was quite rural in
character at the time of these improvements.

Manning was the western boundary of the
Albany Land Improvement and Building Company's subdivision. Just beyond the reach of
the trolley stops at Allen Street in 1890, lots on
Manning Boulevard remained undeveloped
until the early 1900s. Mayor John Boyd
Thacher was among the individuals who purchased auctioned property after foreclosure
on the development. Another prominent land-
owner was J. Howard King, an attorney and
president of the State Bank of New York and
of Albany Savings Bank. The extension of the
trolley route along Western Avenue in 1906
undoubtedly encouraged residential development of Manning Boulevard.

The parkway, the generous seventy-five-foot
set-back of the houses and the deep back
yards created the epitome of the suburban
character promoted by developers Pratt and
Logan. It should be noted, however, that the
deep lots are still narrow in comparison to
parkway developments in other cities and that
the houses were built relatively close to each
other. Manning Boulevard is lined with single-
and two-family houses built in many styles
popular during the early decades of the 20th
century. The transition from Queen Anne and
eclectic Colonial Revival styles to more acade-
mically-influenced Colonial revival styles and
Bungalow, Arts and Crafts and other more
eclectic examples is evident along this single
street.

*Begin by driving north along the service road
on the right-hand side, towards Washington
Avenue.*

1 Manning Boulevard 91
c. 1907

Known also as 579 Western Avenue, this large,
Four-Square house wraps around the corner
and has two addresses like several other nearby duplex houses constructed on corner lots.
The overhanging eaves of the low hipped roof
are supported by rafter ends.

25 Manning Boulevard 92
1907

Frank O. and Annie L. Carnes were the owners
of this Neo-Classical interpretation of the Four-
Square style. The front dormer embellished
with a broken pediment is unusual as is the
contrast of colossal Ionic columns and pilasters
with smaller columns supporting the porch.

75, 77 and 79 Manning Boulevard 93
c. 1913

These three houses are similar builders' inter-
pretations of the Colonial Revival style and
may have been constructed by the West End
Building Company, one of several firms active
in speculative development in the general
area. Varied window treatments were used

including the Palladian window at 77 and wide fanlights over French doors at the porches. The shingled second story of 75 and 77 is slightly flared at the junction of the first story.

97 Manning Boulevard   94
1910

John Kurtz, Jr., was the owner of a lumber firm and the first owner of this rustic, Craftsman-influenced house with low, horizontal lines, broad overhanging eaves, and exposed rafter ends. There is a two-story garage in rear.

The name of the Speedway Hotel, once located on the corner of Washington and Manning, alluded to weekend harness racing that took place on Washington Avenue. Western Avenue, which was paved, was traditionally reserved for more leisurely, social driving, but unpaved Washington Avenue was the place to show off in a less refined manner.

Continue along Manning to Washington Avenue. Cross Manning, and head south on the service road along the west side of Manning.

152, 148, 144 Manning Boulevard 95
c. 1940s

These small, brick apartment buildings, like others in Pine Hills, fit in with the scale of surrounding houses. Classical elements seen on earlier buildings along the block are re-used here: keystones over the windows, brick quoins, and fanlights and sidelights at the entries.

140 Manning Boulevard   96
c. 1913

The Arts and Crafts style is fully expressed in this bungalow by the half-timbering in the dormer, diamond-pane windows, cut-out balustrade, and curved eaves and rafter ends of the roof. This was the home of William F. Haywood, a ''commercial traveler,'' or salesman, for Walker and Gibson, wholesale druggists.

130 Manning Boulevard   97
c. 1918

Shrubbery fails to hide completely the charm of this Tudor-inspired cottage with its steep slate-covered roof and eyebrow window. George B. Evans was the first owner. Like his neighbor, Haywood, Evans was employed by Walker and Gibson. By 1918 he was the treasurer of Westcott Burlingame Automobiles and E. V. Stratton Motors Company on Washington Avenue.

118 Manning Boulevard   98
c. 1913

Franklin I. Knowles, a druggist on Broadway, was the first owner of this stately Colonial Revival house with an attenuated fanlight and sidelights and double end chimneys.

110 and 112 Manning Boulevard 99
1913-14

These twin houses display a pleasant mixture of stucco and clapboard construction with brick details. They were originally the homes of Mrs. J. F. Van Nouhuys and Milner D. Weaver, a grocer.

106 Manning Boulevard   100
c. 1912

This cobblestone and shingle bungalow was the home of Christian F. Weeber, who owned the C. F. Weeber Manufacturing Works, an automobile establishment located next to the bicycle firm of his brother, Emil Weeber, at 170-174 Central Avenue. The porch is sheltered by the extension of the hipped roof and provides access to both the porte-cochere and the front walkway.

102-104 Manning Boulevard   101
1909

This two-family house was built for Frederick K. Gaylord, manager of Capital Trading Company, a house furnishings business at 18 Green Street, and Charles Pye who worked with the Travelers Insurance Company. The two units have always been separately owned. Fluted Doric columns support the one-story porch.

40 Manning Boulevard   102
c. 1912

Russell, Edward and Mrs. Emma Greenman are listed as the original residents of this Arts and Crafts home, which features a central projecting block and exposed rafter ends at the flared roofline. Ornamentation is more subdued than on the houses at numbers 140 and 6 Manning.

6 Manning Boulevard   103
1911

The bay windows and broad sweep of the porch and the half-timbered porch gable provide this example of the Arts and Crafts style with a more complex form than its neighbor at 40.

104

2 Manning Boulevard   104
1908
Alexander Selkirk

Gaylord Logan, an attorney and partner in the Albany Land Improvement and Building Company, constructed a house on a four-acre lot at this corner. The house burned not long after the failure of the business venture (the 1895 tax assessments described the property as "wood ruins"). In 1908 the present house was designed by architect Alexander Selkirk, who most likely used the salvaged first floor and foundations of the Logan house. Mary G. McCabe was the owner in 1912. A bungalow with Craftsman and Colonial details, it makes full use of the corner location, now trimmed to one acre. A standing-seam copper roof

shelters the inviting wraparound porch.
Pause at the intersection of Manning Boulevard and Western Avenue.

584 Western Avenue   105
c. 1889

The cross-gabled roof and Queen Anne-style windows at the porch (smaller panes surrounding a large central pane) hint at a late 19th-century date for this house, and indeed it was one of the earliest on this portion of Western, constructed for Emma Hoy and her husband, Charles, an accountant.

586 Western Avenue   106
c. 1903

The broad front gable of this Colonial Revival house is decorated with circular raised panels on either side of the Palladian window. The generous wraparound porch is supported by Doric columns. The original owners, James C. and Margaret Minahan, also owned several lots to the west until 1940, when the land was subdivided and the two brick apartment buildings were built by the Picotte Company.
Continue across Western Avenue to South Manning Boulevard.

South Manning Boulevard   107
and Marion Avenue

A tollgate for the Great Western Turnpike was located on this once remote portion of Western Avenue. South Manning Boulevard appears on an 1889 map of Albany as Hawkins Street, named after the Hawkins farm that lay south of Western Avenue and west of Allen Street. It was renamed in the 1930s. Marion Avenue, also on the 1889 map, was named after a daughter of Daniel Pratt, one of the developers of Pine Hills. It remained the westernmost street identified on Albany city maps through 1904.

After the foreclosure of the Pine Hills development, the bank sold some of the lots along the two streets in extensive tracts to the Wards Lane Company and the Keeler family of restauranteurs. Much of the property between

South Manning and Marion was swampy, however, and was unsuitable for development before the land was graded and drainage improved in the 1930s. Until then a large pond, known at times as Keeler's or Ward's pond, was a popular spot for fishing and ice skating. It was one of several ponds in the immediate area where ice was harvested.

In contrast to the other streets in the original Pine Hills subdivision, only single-family houses were constructed along these streets. With some exceptions, revivals of historic styles remained popular, but the forms of the houses changed. Colonial Revival houses of the 1920s and later were often designed in a more historically accurate form. They no longer had the gable end facing the street, but were usually side gabled or hip roofed, three-bay or five-bay-wide structures. The symmetry of the facades was reflected on the interior, where rooms were arranged on either side of a central hallway. Houses varied in the application of historical details. Paired or tripled windows and columns are a trademark of the Colonial Revival style, not the original 18th and 19th century prototypes.

Several houses along South Manning are Tudor- or Spanish-inspired bungalows. Bungalows became popular after 1905, and are distinguished by the fact that bedrooms are placed along one side or to the rear of the first floor. Additional bedrooms are placed in attic levels. Single-family houses of other periods more often have the public living areas on the first floor and bedrooms on the second floor. This change of floor plan was carried even further by the free-flowing arrangement of rooms in post-World War II ranch-style houses. Devoid of any reference to historical style, these houses often have low-pitched roofs and bands of windows. Split-level ranch houses provided two levels of public rooms: one informal family living area on the lower level and one more public living and dining area on the main entry level. Another major change after 1920 is that the large front porches that served as outdoor sitting rooms on earlier houses were moved to more private locations at the side or rear. They were replaced by small entry porches.

Head south on South Manning Boulevard.

54 South Manning Boulevard   108
1928

The sweeping front gable and rounded door hark back to an English cottage. Abraham and Carolyn Milstein were the original owners. He was a dentist at 37 North Pearl Street and was also vice president of Union-Fern, a furniture company. They moved to Marion Avenue in 1952.

70 South Manning Boulevard   109
1930

Edward A. and Winifred J. Downes built this Spanish-inspired bungalow in 1930. Mr. Downes was secretary and treasurer of the Grace Laundering Company at 82 Arch Street.

80 South Manning Boulevard   110
1931

This Tudor house reflects both the shape and details of a medieval house with half-timbering, sheltered recessed entry, large chimney and variety of roof forms. The original owners were Florence P. and Aaron Medwin. Mr. Medwin was secretary and treasurer of two firms: the Albany Cab Company and Albany Laboratories.

106 South Manning Boulevard   111
1936
Gander, Gander and Gander

Dr. Louis DeRusso and his wife, Alice, commissioned this house from the Albany architectural firm of Gander, Gander and Gander. The three-part Palladian window and engaged quarter columns at the entry are classical details on a building whose shape is reminiscent of a Italian villa. The drain pipes function as design elements.

120 South Manning Boulevard 112
1952

The formality of this Colonial Revival is expressed by symmetrical wings, full-length shutters and panels that elongate the casement windows on the first floor and the ornate entryway surround. Frank J. and Mary E. Nigro were the first owners. He was vice president and secretary of Albany Public Markets, a business that he expanded into Albany's first "supermarkets," which featured separate bakery and self-service meat departments. Nigro founded Nigro Realty, and in 1954 he built the Westgate Shopping Center on Central Avenue.

170 and 178 South Manning Boulevard 113
c. 1934

Two versions of Tudor-inspired cottages were built for Ernest J. Daniels, a salesman, and William I. Zeitler, an optician. The house at 170 features an arched stone surround at the entry and randomly placed stone and brick details. The double front gables mimic the steep roofs of English cottages as seen at 54 South Manning Boulevard. The random use of varied stone and brick provides a more rustic character to the house at 178.

Turn around after Woodlawn Avenue, and travel up the east side of South Manning Boulevard.

119 South Manning Boulevard 114
1928

This Tudor-style house with details such as the quoins and Tudor arch of the door surround and the cornice received a more formal interpretation than the cottages previously mentioned. Harold N. Sporborg, president of the Sporborg Millinery Company on Broadway, built this house.

113

107 South Manning Boulevard 115
1927

The surrounding hedges allow a glimpse of the unusual fluted Corinthian columns on the entry porch of this Colonial Revival house, built by Frederick V. Griesman. Doric and Ionic capitals are more often used on Colonial Revival houses.

93 South Manning Boulevard 116
1927

The gambrel roof is enlarged to form the complete second story of this Colonial Revival residence built by Joseph Candido, a pharmacist. The house number is incorporated into the stained glass window of the door.

45 South Manning Boulevard 117
1931

The multi-color tile roof, a central tower that accommodates the arched doorway and the small balcony portray the Spanish style on this house built by Harry Baskin, owner of the Baskin Jewelry Company.

Turn left onto Western Avenue.

610 Western Avenue 118
c. 1930

The long, low lines of this house recall the Shingle-style houses in New England of the late 19th century. As is common, the Shingle style is paired with Colonial Revival details such as grouped windows and the entry porch with Doric columns and sidelights. This house may have been constructed by Jacob Sperber, a builder, and was owned by Robert J. Campbell in 1932.

Turn left onto Marion Avenue, and proceed south.

Marion Avenue 119

One could simply do a tour of the decorative motifs used on shutters along Marion Avenue, but there is much more to explore among the residences built here over a thirty-five-year period. The first houses were built just before the Depression; the last was constructed in 1964, the year of the Gemini 4 spacewalk. Like people who had built houses on Madison Avenue decades earlier, the families who built on Marion Avenue represented a broad spectrum of local industry and business. Several parcels on Marion remained vacant well into the 1950s as evidenced by the ranch-style houses interspersed amongst older homes. An important change in house construction noticeable along the street is the incorporation of a garage into the main block of several houses.

6 Marion Avenue 120
1932

This house was first owned by John V. and Henrietta Bucher. The witch silhouettes of the shutters are a surprising motif, but the entry porch, which combines a pedimented porch roof with curved underside, is a Colonial Revival application of details.

8 Marion Avenue 121
1929

The house built for Albert E. and Mary Jones is a more eclectic version of the Colonial Revival style, which here incorporates an eyebrow window into the low-pitched hip roof.

10 Marion Avenue 122
1937

Louis F. and Helen Weiss owned a women's clothing firm on Central Avenue. The design of their house reflects the International style with corner windows and glass blocks. Lewis Sperry, president of the Sperry Warehouse, became the second owner in 1945.

11 Marion Avenue 123
1960
Leon Einhorn

Architect Leon Einhorn designed this split-level ranch style house for his family and number of other ranch-style houses for clients on the block. These include number 3 (1960) for Samuel H. Molomot, who worked at the New York State Department of Insurance; 9 (1952) for Abraham I. and Carolyn G. Milstein, who moved from South Manning Boulevard; 13 (1955) for Milton and Cordelia Alexander, who moved here from 22 Marion; 17 (1955) for Hildred and Sidney M. Rosenstock, who was the owner of a shoddy mill; and 47 (c. 1955) for Frank S. Lyons, vice president and general manager of Roskin Brothers, appliance dealers.

15 Marion Avenue 124
1929

William C. and Mildred B. Dearstyne were the first owners of this Colonial Revival house. The broad entablature of the porch contrasts with the slender transom, sidelights and Doric columns of the entry. William Dearstyne was vice president of Albany Hardware and Iron Company.

16 Marion Avenue 125
1937

Joseph B. Hai was the vice president of Flah's, a department store which operated at several locations in the Capital District. His unusual house, like other modern examples on the block, avoids references to any traditional style. The corner window of glass blocks illuminates the stairwell.

20 Marion Avenue 126
1935

The formal symmetry of this Colonial Revival house is emphasized by details such as the double chimneys, six-over-six paned windows, and semi-circular entry porch with balustrade and urns. It was built for Henry Popp, vice president of the Fort Orange Chemical Company.

21 Marion Avenue 127
1929

William Kattrein was president and treasurer of the Watervliet Tool Company and is credited with being an early property owner on the street. One of two shingled examples on the block, his house has an open porch tucked under the second-story extension on the north and unusual eight-over-twelve double-hung windows. He owned the adjacent property at 17 Marion Avenue until 1955.

22 Marion Avenue 128
1929

Milton Alexander worked for a brush manufacturer, and, he and his wife, Cordelia, were the first owners of this house. The enclosed porches are detailed with double engaged columns and grouped small urns at the corners of the balustrade. According to contemporary advertisements, the combination of multi-paned sash over single-pane sash allowed a reference to Colonial originals while providing unobstructed vision through the bottom sash. In 1955 Gerald Converse purchased the house, and the Alexanders retired to a newly built house at 13 Marion.

129

23 Marion Avenue 129
c. 1935

Charles P. and Edith P. Drumm were the original owners of this house, a seven-bay brick interpretation of Georgian Revival, which features an unusual projecting central block under a pediment, a double line of stone coursing between stories, stone quoins at the sides and bay corners, and the lyre-shaped wooden panels at the second story window. Mr. Drumm was chairman of the board of the Albany Felt Company.

25 Marion Avenue 130
c. 1931

Benjamin Boyce, chief engineer at New York Telephone Company, lived at 702 Western Avenue while this house was being constructed. The original plan for a simple entry porch was replaced by this wide, arched recessed entry, ornamented with delicate details of the fanlight and sidelights, and the finishing touch of the leaves and shell motif in the pediment. Sydney and Betty Nathan were the owners in 1950. He worked at the Detroit Supply Company, the family firm on Central Avenue which sold auto accessories.

26 Marion Avenue 131
1929

Elmer F. De Tiere was secretary of the F. F. Crannel Lumber Company and owned several lots on the street. A second glance reveals small windows accommodated in the half-timbered elements in this Arts and Crafts home. The three-car garage is original to De Tiere's house.

32 Marion Avenue   132
1929

Fan-like details at the windows and unusual patterns along the cornice line set this Colonial Revival house apart. It was built for John H. Griffin, president and general manager of the Argus Company.

35 Marion Avenue   133
1930

This Tudor-style house combines the scale of a grand estate with the rustic appearance of a cottage. The work of a medieval craftsman is evoked through the rough cut boards of the gable over the garage, the uneven half-timbering and simulated patched brickwork at the front door, small scattered windows, the irregular slate roof and the elaborate chimney pots. It was built for William E. Walsh II, treasurer of W. E. Walsh and Sons, hatters and furriers, and his wife, Mercy.

36 Marion Avenue   134
1930

This Colonial Revival style house was constructed for Frank E. and Eleanor M. O'Brien. Frank O'Brien was treasurer of Fuller and O'Brien, Contractors Services Bureau and Insurance. The windows are detailed with brick lintels, and the dormer windows are finished with arched sash, cornice returns and pilasters. An iron fence lines the sidewalk in front of the house. Matthew Bender III and his wife, Virginia, moved here in 1937, when he was vice president of Matthew Bender and Company, publishers. He became the company's president in 1956.

37 Marion Avenue   135
1929

Multiple Ionic columns and balustrades outline the porte-cochere and shapely porch which

encircle this Four-Square house embellished in the Colonial Revival style. It was built for Rose D. Padula.

40 Marion Avenue   136
1929
Norman Sturgis

Francis C. and Frances E. Huyck hired Albany architect Norman Sturgis, who designed this house along the lines of a medieval building that would have been constructed over time. Bricks are used to mimic rafter ends at the cornice; casement windows and the quoins are further medieval touches along with the gothic arch over the entry protected by decorative iron gates. Mr. Huyck owned F. C. Huyck and Sons, Kenwood Mills, which manufactured wool products. In 1952, the house was purchased by the State University of New York and served as the chancellor's residence until the 1970s.

42 Marion Avenue   137
1932

Joseph F. and Ethel Finn's Tudor-style house differs from the version of Tudor at 35 Marion: here the multi-colored slate roof envelops the facade with its half timbering and castellation at the bay window, while the side porch is more open. Mr. Finn was supervisor of construction at James J. Finn & Son, general contractors, a firm which merged with Victor Lange's company to form the Lange-Finn Construction Company, a prominent Albany contractor.

84 Marion Avenue   138
1941
Henry Blatner

This house was designed for Oscar and Lillian Brenner, who moved here from the Spanish bungalow at 268 Hansen Avenue. Mr. Brenner was the manager of David's Women's Clothing Store and vice president of the Chamber of Commerce. This house was one of the few residences by Albany architect Henry Blatner, who designed the Albany Girls

Academy and the Colonie Country Club along with many commercial projects. He is said to have sketched the plans for the Brenners on a napkin during a meal at Keeler's restaurant.

104 Marion Avenue 139
1955

Attorney Sydney Albert was the first owner of this house. The large urn at the center of the broken pediment is a bold Colonial Revival statement.

Return to Western Avenue, turn left, and head west.

609, 611, 615, 621, and 140
625 Western Avenue
1925-28

Five Colonials in a builder's row with slight variations, these houses were likely built by Theodore Andrassy, a carpenter who owned several of these lots and lived at 621.

637 Western Avenue 141
c. 1815-20

This is not a Colonial Revival, but an original brick Federal-style farmhouse and one of the few remaining farmhouses in the neighborhood. In 1821 it was described as an abandoned "farm on an elevated, sandy tract near Albany," when it was bought by Jesse Buel, a leading journalist and agriculturalist. A second house that was part of the original property remains on Homestead Avenue, named for the farmhouses. Buel wrote extensively on agriculture and edited *The Cultivator*, a nationally known periodical. Prior to taking up farming here, he had been the publisher of newspapers in Troy, Poughkeepsie and Kingston and had established the *Albany Argus* in 1813. He followed his own advice on fertilizers, proper drainage and other farming methods to transform this property into a model farm.

Buel worked with James Wilson to establish the first fruit tree nursery in the county. And long before the invention of the tractor and word processor, he also found time to serve as a judge, hold a seat in the state Assembly, and

act as a regent of the State University. He advocated the establishment of a state agricultural school, but this was not realized until twenty-six years after his death, when the school was founded at Cornell University in 1865.

Lawns of houses to the west of Homestead Avenue retain the steep grade of the original topography of the area.

659 and 663 Western Avenue 142
1921

A change of details was used to tailor a builder's model to two individual owners. Number 659 has dormer windows, and a balustrade over the porch supported by paired Doric columns. The cornice line of 663 is broken by arched recesses over the windows; the porch roof has a central pediment and single Doric columns; and a fanlight was added to the door. Anton Gross, who ran a shoe repair business, lived at 659. His neighbor at 663 was Ernest H. Wade, secretary and treasurer of H. Horton and Company, a hotel equipment supplier.

668 Western Avenue 143
c. 1924

Ellis Ferber built this Georgian Revival house with its stern symmetry carried out by window placement and double wings. Splayed lintels extend across the triple first-story windows. Ferber was vice president at the Lurie Company, a dry goods store on South Pearl Street.

673 Western Avenue 144
c. 1923

This Dutch Colonial was first occupied by Sydney H. Coleman, general manager of the Humane Society on Howard Street. The hip roof of the porch is supported by rotund columns.

675 Western Avenue

145

c. 1932

A rare Craftsman bungalow along this portion of Western, this house features varied window types, exposed rafter ends at the eaves, and a side gabled roof which shelters the porch and is supported by brackets at the square pillars. The gabled dormer is decorated with half-timbering, small panes at the window transoms and its own balustrade.

686 and 690 Western Avenue

146

1923-25

Cobblestone and wood create the rustic appearance of these double houses, which were constructed by Edward T. DeGraff, a real estate and land developer who operated a company by the same name. DeGraff lived at 686; Howard C. Buschman resided at 690.

147

702 Western Avenue

147

1924

The entrance to this cross-gabled, U-shaped Colonial Revival cottage is through the side courtyard. A recessed porch, now enclosed, is tucked under the front gable with fluted Doric columns placed at either corner. The first owner was Albert Reynolds, a manager. Beginning in the 1950s, Bertrand and Constance Fay lived here for almost forty years. Mr. Fay was assistant receiver at the Cohoes Railway Company.

710 Western Avenue

148

c. 1931

An old farmhouse belonging to the Holmes family originally faced Western Avenue at this address but was turned to face Colonial Avenue in the late 1920s and re-numbered 3 Colonial Avenue. The current house at 710 was constructed by Donald T. Wetmore.

716 Western Avenue

149

1927

The L-shape plan of this Spanish-style house takes advantage of the corner lot; the main entrance is emphasized by the angled one-story porch. Arched recesses cap the windows and French doors. The design of the leaded-glass windows at the front door is repeated in china cabinets and living room bookcases. This was the home of Harvey Kimmey and his daughter and son-in-law, Constance and Austin F. Loucks. Austin Loucks worked for Kimmey at his plumbing specialties business, and their handiwork is evident in the backyard lily pond.

741 and 745 Western Avenue

150

1927

Textured stucco, red tile hipped roofs, iron balconies and arches outlined in brick over the first-floor windows add up to a version of the Mediterranean on these twin houses. Charles L. Palladino, a barber, was the first resident of 745. Rubin F. Kopp, who worked at the Many Lincoln clothing store on South Pearl Street, lived at 741.

Part III: Builders' Specials

The next portion of the tour includes four examples of tracts which, like the rowhouses on South Lake Avenue and Winchester Gables, were developed in a distinctive manner.

Continue west on Western Avenue to Rosemont Street, and turn right.

7-22 Rosemont Street   151

1929

Attributed to John P. Gander

While contemporary with the Spanish-influenced houses on Hansen and Woodlawn avenues, these houses were not designed with the same degree of uniformity. Of all the builders' tracts in the tour, these houses exhibit the most variety. The street was not included in the 1928 city directory, but one year later there were ten houses listed.

The owner and occupant of number 7 from 1929 to 1981 was John P. Gander, one of three brothers in the architectural firm of Gander, Gander and Gander. Their practice extended well beyond Albany to several other states. Their Albany projects included the 1930s post office on Broadway, Saint Anne's Institute on Bradford Street, and the Louis DeRusso house at 106 South Manning Boulevard. John Gander's house is set apart from the rest by its size and its details such as the carved recess over the front door and the spiraled decorations of the column at the front windows.

The other houses vary in their reference to the Spanish style. In some cases the reference is subtle with the use of stucco walls and tile roofs; in others it is more direct with a rounded chimney top, arched windows, doorways and porch openings, decorative vents, small towers at entryways, parapet roofs and arched gateways.

Continue on Rosemont to Washington Avenue, and turn right. Head east for nine blocks to Manning Boulevard, and turn left. Proceed to McKinley Street, which is one-way toward Lincoln Avenue, and turn left.

McKinley Street   152

The Leonard Realty Company constructed these bungalows beginning in 1911. Jesse Leonard was the company president. A 1949 directory ad explained that the company was involved in real estate and insurance and stated that it had developed University Heights and Holland Avenue in Albany. The firm was also associated with the Leonard Company, ''wholesalers and retailers of lumber and building supplies.'' The offices of both companies were located at 61 Maiden Lane. Given this pedigree, it is not difficult to understand the backing behind such a development as McKinley Street.

The bungalow house type became popular after 1905 and was built in a number of styles. The floor plan accommodates bedrooms on the first floor of the house. They are either arranged in a row along the side across from the row formed by the living room, dining room, and kitchen or placed at the rear of the house. Finished attic stories provide additional bedroom space. Porches are often sheltered by the extension of the main roof, which can be supported by columns, wide piers or a combination of both.

The McKinley Street houses create a unified streetscape, but there are varying individual features to be noted: the Gothic arch of the porch windows on 12, the keyhole windows on 16, and the typical open bungalow porches, which feature squat half columns positioned on low walls.

Turn right onto Lincoln Avenue, and continue east to North Allen Street (the embossed metal garage on the south side of Lincoln just after McKinley is worth a glance). Turn right onto North Allen Street. Proceed south, and turn left onto Manning Boulevard, then left onto Lawrence Street and left on Kent Street.

Stockwell Blocks   153

1909

310-352 Manning Boulevard

180-220 Kent Street

149-159 North Allen Street

Ulysses G. Stockwell began his career in insurance and retired in 1898 to work solely as a contractor. He was credited with the construction of 225 buildings in Albany, and this double block is one of several large-scale projects. Stockwell was responsible for the conversion of the Amsdell brewery to the Knickerbocker Apartments and the addition of an apartment building behind the Sard House at 397 State Street. These rowhouses were planned as though they were to be built in a dense urban neighborhood despite the fact that the surrounding neighborhood was quite different.

153

Each house has a similar plan with living room, dining room and kitchen on the first floor and two bedrooms on the second floor. Simply designed with bay windows and one-story porches, the houses were embellished with classical columns and quoins and on Manning Boulevard with leaded-glass windows on the first story. On Manning the front-gabled homes are constructed of brick and rough-cut stone with red mortar. Houses along the yellow-brick-paved block of Kent Street are of alternating red and yellow brick; spheres remain at the corners of most cornices. Many porches on both streets have been enclosed. A common alley between the streets provides access to back yards.

Stockwell also constructed the commercial block on North Allen Street between Kent and Manning and used the same rough-cut stone and red and yellow brick found on the row-houses.

Turn left onto North Allen Street, and then turn right on Washington Avenue. Continue west to Jermain Street, and turn right.

Lustron Homes 154
1949-50
1, 3, 5, 7 and 8 Jermain Street

The development of Lustron Homes, as these prefabricated steel houses were named, was a response to the post-World War II housing shortage. Carl Gunnar Strandlund, an indus-

trial engineer and general manager of Chicago Vitreous Enamel Products, had manufactured metal gas stations and other commercial buildings before working with architects Roy Blass and Morris Beckman in Wilmette, Illinois, to develop plans for modular housing. The Lustron Corporation was established in 1946 as a subsidiary of Chicago Vitreous, and specialized machinery was built to produce the porcelain-enameled steel panels and other house components at the main Columbus, Ohio, plant. Key to the enterprise were financing from the federal Reconstruction Finance Corporation and support from veterans' groups and the National Housing Administration. Components for each house were loaded onto custom-designed trucks operated by the Fruehauf Trailer Company of Detroit, which remained on site during the construction. The houses were designed to be built in 360 hours by a crew of at least three men, but construction usually took longer. Almost 2,500 houses were built before the company declared bankruptcy in 1950.

154

Wilson and Victor Sullivan were responsible for the small development of Lustrons here on Jermain Street. Wilson Sullivan was a prominent Albany realtor and developed the land along Jermain through his Waverly Realty Corporation. Victor Sullivan built many homes in the area around Jermain (Victor Street is named for him), and, as principal of the Upstate Construction Corporation, he erected these houses in 1949 and 1950. Upstate was listed as one of twelve Lustron dealers in New

York State, and Sullivan built at least eighteen houses in the area. There were originally eight Lustron houses on Jermain Street; three were moved for the construction of Route 85, the Crosstown Arterial.

Erected on a concrete slab foundation, the houses are made entirely of enameled-steel components from the wall framing and roof trusses to exterior wall panels (available in several pastel colors), roof shingles, interior walls and pocket doors. Owners could choose between a third bedroom or an open corner entry porch. Most of the porches on Jermain Street have been enclosed by later owners.

Return to Washington Avenue, turn right, and continue west past the State Office Campus to the campus of the State University of New York at Albany.

Part IV: Endpoints

The last two sites of the tours are among the most recent and the oldest of all the sites surveyed. The Prospect Hill pumping station was built just as the population began to settle west of Washington Park. The SUNYA campus was constructed on the once remote, rural site of the Albany Country Club.

State University of New York at Albany (SUNYA)   155
1962-71
Washington Avenue Extension
Edward Durell Stone

Myths and rumors abound about the design for the SUNY campus on Washington Avenue Extension—that it was a recycled design for a desert-state campus or a duplicate of a complex built in a foreign country—but the design was developed for this specific site by architect Edward Durell Stone (1902-78) of New York City. The rumors are understandable: how else to explain a largely self-contained complex that departed from the model Colonial or Collegiate Gothic campus? The tall tales were a also a reaction against the modern architecture and the changes of the former Albany Country Club site. Stone, a native of Arkansas, had indeed completed several international commissions including the U. S. Embassy in New Delhi and a number of hotels. Closer to home, he was involved with the design of the interior of the Radio City Music Hall and would go on to design the All Souls Unitarian Church in Schenectady, the Kennedy Center in Washington, D. C., and the former General Motors Building in New York City.

155

This campus was part of a statewide expansion plan guided by Gov. Nelson A. Rockefeller and by the State University Construction Fund, created by the state Legislature in 1962. The oldest school in the SUNY system, it began in 1844 as the State Normal School for the training of teachers. Renamed the New York State College for Teachers in 1909 and the State University of New York in 1948, the school retained this focus until 1961 when programs for non-teaching careers were initiated. The new campus was planned for a future student population of 20,000 and included a student center, performing arts center, a multi-storied art gallery and a major library. Today the campus accommodates 17,000 students.

Stone arranged the academic and administrative buildings along a raised platform, called the podium, which is formed by walkways and plazas and functions like the traditional college quadrangle. Four dormitory complexes located at the corners of the podium are comprised of low-rise buildings grouped around a high-rise tower. The architect made a conscious effort to separate people from vehicular traffic. Cars are restricted to parking lots and delivery vehicles use a service corridor placed below the podium level. The gymnasium, the physical plant and the infirmary are placed at the edges of the campus.

The construction modules are cast concrete and aggregate stone panels interspersed with window panels. Extended building roofs shelter walkways that form outdoor hallways and unite the podium complex. The harshness of the repeated rectangular forms and the materials used is countered by the slender stretch of the pillars supporting walkway roofs, by the curved vaults at the juncture of pillar and roof and by the strip of perforations at the exterior roof edges. Similar pillar supports are used on the interiors, and the vaults are often replaced by radiating florescent lights. Gardens and plazas included in the original plans were designed by Clarke and Rapuano of New York City. Two fountains provide contrast: a circular fountain at the entrance to the student center, and a sunken reflecting pool at the center of the podium. The tower rising

from the center of the pool is topped by speakers for the carillon and is actually the water tower for the university complex.

Students were first in residence in 1962 but had to be transported to the downtown campus for classes until the fall of 1964. Construction of the campus, Stone's largest project, continued until 1971. Some additions have been necessary: the 1978 Alumni House, an interfaith chapel, a fifth dormitory quadrangle in 1988, the recreational and convocation center built in 1992, and an extension of the student center in 1993. Also notable on the campus are the wooded areas and the large lake, remnants of the former country club grounds.

From the State University campus, head east along Washington Avenue. Turn left on Manning Boulevard, cross Central Avenue and continue to the intersection of Clinton Avenue and North Manning Boulevard.

Prospect Hill Pumping Station   156
c. 1877-88
14 North Manning Boulevard

The Prospect Hill Pumping Station complex remains as a reminder of the enormous effort required to provide city residents with water. This and other public works projects were undertaken long before work crews had the benefit of the powerful earth-moving machinery taken for granted today. Men labored by hand to construct reservoirs and lay miles of pipes. Bleecker Reservoir, now the site of Bleecker Stadium and Swinburne Park, was constructed in 1850 and was fed by two sources. The first was the conduit from the Six-Mile Waterworks on Fuller Road and Washington Avenue Extension, which was constructed along the circuitous route of the King's Highway between Schenectady and Albany. The second source was Hudson River water pumped up the hill by the 1873 Quackenbush Pumping Station on Broadway.

The Prospect Hill Pumping Station was begun in 1877 to serve elevated areas of Albany more effectively. It was designed to work in tandem with the Bleecker Reservoir and was surrounded in the late 1880s by a complex of the pumping station offices and equipment houses. This system continued in use until 1932, when Bleecker Reservoir was shut down. The earthworks for the reservoir formed a suitable base for Bleecker Stadium, a WPA project. The Prospect Hill pumps remained in operation to balance the water pressure in the area until 1966, when the buildings became the offices of Albany's Department of Public Works. Six Mile Waterworks reservoir is now a public lake.

Several buildings of the Prospect Hill complex remain today, the two most visible being the grand brick structures that were the superintendent's house and the engine house. The superintendent's house exhibits the mansard roof, iron cresting and bracketed cornices of the Second Empire style. The third story of the hipped-roofed engine house at the corner of Third Street is lined with bays of tall, slender windows topped by bull's-eye windows and framed by brick pilasters supporting a series of arched stone moldings. Paired brackets ring the corbelled brick cornice. The complex was rehabilitated for housing in the 1980s.

156

North Albany:
Factories, Foundries and the Big Dog

Duncan E. Hay

Nipper

The economy of Albany today is dominated by state government, banks, educational institutions and law firms. Although evidence of current and past industrial activity is clear in the urban landscapes of Troy, Green Island, Cohoes and Schenectady, it is less obvious on the streets of Albany. Yet during the 19th century New York's capital city did produce significant quantities of a wide range of goods that included architectural ironwork, heating and cooking stoves, iron fences, railroad car wheels, agricultural machinery, pianos, lumber and millwork, paper goods, fabrics, fire bricks, chemicals and beer.

Located at the eastern terminus of the Erie Canal and near the head of tidal navigation on the Hudson River, Albany manufacturers benefited from access to raw materials from the Northeast and Midwest. The waterways also provided access to markets that probably had a greater influence in shaping the character of Albany industry than the availability of raw materials. There was fine molding sand here, and Adirondack iron and timber from the Adirondacks and Canada were close at hand, but the ability to transport finished products inexpensively and to respond quickly to changing markets was more important. Agricultural iron works, for example, were able to ship their products by canal and railroad from Albany to farming communities throughout New England, central New York and the Midwest. The Hudson made it possible to transport heavy iron products such as stoves and architectural castings from Albany foundries to New York City and other seaboard cities at comparatively small expense.

Albany's industrial landscape was punctuated by warehouses and structures for the intermediate processing of raw materials. The city was located at a break-bulk point, where materials coming in by canal or railroad could be transferred to coastal and ocean-going ships on the Hudson. Consequently, Albany's waterfront was dominated by lumber yards, coal piers, grain elevators, salt warehouses, and other large-scale storage facilities.

Throughout much of the 19th century, downtown Albany was a center of industrial activity. Pruyn Street, Green Street, Beaver Street and Hudson Avenue were lined with foundries, machine shops, a large agricultural implement works, a shoe factory, a company that produced horse-harness hardware and another that made alphabet blocks, checkers and dominos. The area later occupied by the Delaware and Hudson Railroad office complex at the foot of State Street (now the SUNY administrative headquarters) was also full of iron works, carpenter shops, crate factories, a cigar

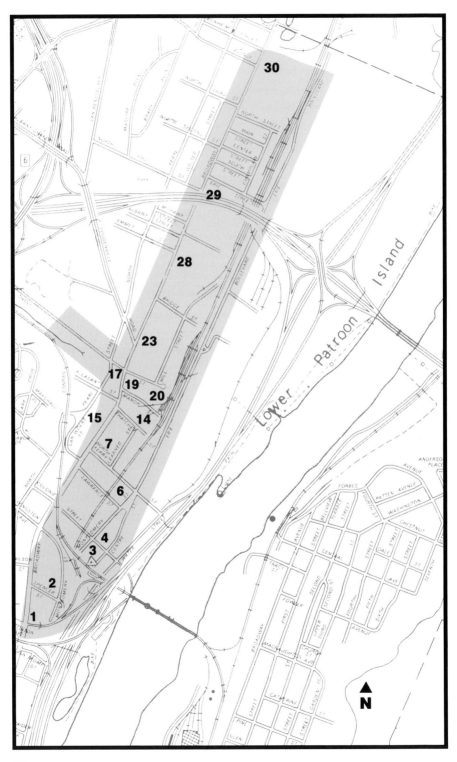

box manufacturer, and other businesses that served the dockland along the river. As in many ports, the blocks near the river were home to many of the city's wholesale grocers and provision merchants, spice mills, coffee roasters, and liquor warehouses. Here too were the tracks, yards, freight houses and docks associated with the New York Central and of the Delaware and Hudson railroads.

Very little evidence of these downtown industries survives today. Throughout the second half of the 19th century, existing manufacturers expanded, and new industries were established on the outskirts of the city where land was cheaper and where smoke, smells, noise, and other by-products of their activities would generate fewer complaints. Noxious and fire-prone chemical works located in the South End. The New York Central built its massive stockyards and repair shops on the West Albany flats. Several iron founders established operations north on Broadway and North Pearl Street and in Tivoli Hollow.

By the beginning of this century, Albany's leaders, under the influence of the City Beautiful movement, were making more conscious efforts to remove industrial activity from the center of the city or at least to hide it from view. The Delaware and Hudson Building was designed, in part, to screen Albany's working waterfront from the state Capitol and State Street commerce. The port was moved south to Westerlo Island during the 1920s, and the Albany Port District Commission erected what was then the largest grain elevator in the world and is still the most prominent structure in the South End.

There are remnants of Albany's industrial past scattered throughout the city, but the north part of Albany, from Clinton Avenue to the Menands village line, has the most coherent surviving district of industrial structures. The area includes buildings once occupied by piano factories, architectural iron works and the city's largest stove works, along with several smaller foundries, a looking-glass factory, printing plants, a gas works, a streetcar barn, a boiler shop, and a felt mill. This driving tour provides an introduction to this heritage.

Start at Quackenbush Square, located on Broadway just north of Clinton Avenue.

Quackenbush Pumping Station 1
Quackenbush Square, between
Broadway and Montgomery Street

By the third quarter of the 19th century, water
from wells, springs, streams and the Six-Mile
Waterworks was no longer adequate for
Albany's growing population. The new, high-
level Prospect Hill Reservoir, located off
Shaker Road, was connected to the existing
Bleecker Reservoir, on what is now the site of
Bleecker Stadium, in 1878. From this downtown
pumping station, water from the Hudson River
was pumped uphill to both Prospect Hill and
Bleecker reservoirs for gravity distribution
throughout the city.

1

The easternmost building of this station originally housed vertical beam steam pumping
engines, which were later replaced by three
Allis and two Holly pumps. Erected in 1873,
the building is now a garage for the city's
public works department, and the adjacent
boiler house is the Albany Urban Cultural Park
Visitor Center. The complex is constructed of
common brick with a stone water table, window
sills, and keystones. The three-story building
nearest Broadway was constructed as a residence in 1852; in 1897 it was redeveloped as
an office building for the city water department to the designs of Albany architect Edward
Ogden. Immediately south of the complex is
the Quackenbush House, which was built on
this site in the first half of the 18th century and
is one of two remaining gable-fronted Dutch
houses in Albany.

*Drive north on Broadway, turn right
on Spencer Street, and proceed east to
Montgomery Street.*

Armour Dressed Beef Company 2
c. 1890
NW corner of Montgomery and
Spencer Streets

With the development of the refrigerated railroad car at the end of the 19th century, the West
Albany stockyards, which had prospered since
the 1850s, declined as cattle were slaughtered
in the Midwest rather than in Albany. Several
dressed-beef companies, located around
Spencer Street, transferred the carcasses from
refrigerator cars and stored them in refrigerated
warehouses for distribution to markets throughout the region. The distinctive overhangs and
monorail systems for moving carcasses are
visible on the fronts of several buildings here in
what was once Albany's wholesale meat district.
Among the companies in this vicinity were Morris,
Nelson and Company, Robert Guthman and
Brothers, and Swift Chicago Meat. Most notable
is the building that housed the Armour
Dressed Beef Company of Chicago. The older,
two-story portion was constructed around
1890 of pressed brick with arched windows
and a sheet-metal cornice. The more recent
west part has more simplified detailing.

*Turn left and follow Montgomery Street to
Broadway. Turn right on Broadway and right
again under the railroad bridge onto Colonie
Street. Head east to Montgomery Street, just
across the railroad tracks.*

Central Warehouse 3
Mid-1920s
SE corner of Colonie and Montgomery Streets

This immense storage facility was built in the
mid-1920s of reinforced pillar-and-slab concrete, a construction method commonly used
for industrial buildings in the United States
after 1910. The steel-framed windows are also
typical of the period. A spur of the railroad
was built at the same elevation as the New
York Central Railroad bridge across the
Hudson, so cars could enter the warehouse
at the second-story level.

Albany Perforated Wrapping Paper Company   4

NW corner of Montgomery and
Colonie Streets

The simple brick building that occupies the
entire block along Montgomery Street between
Colonie and North Lansing streets was once
the home of Albany Perforated Wrapping
Paper Company, founded in 1878. The firm
boasted that it had originated the idea of selling paper in perforated rolls. The building has
unusual iron wall ties, which secure the wood
floor framing to the brick walls. After the turn
of the century, this building was occupied by
Albany Terminal Warehouse.

*Turn left on Montgomery Street, and head
north for two short blocks. Stop just before the
wide intersection.*

Canal Basin and Lumber District   5

Intersection of Erie Boulevard with De Witt,
Lawrence, and North Ferry Streets

The eastern end of the Erie Canal and the
southern end of the Champlain Canal terminated near the foot of Colonie Street, at the
north end of the Albany Basin. The basin was
created by the construction of docks that
stretched south along the Hudson River for
more than a mile, to Madison Avenue. The
basin and the canal attracted industry to the
north end of the city, including several iron
and stove foundries, breweries, piano manufacturing companies, and smaller establishments.

This wide intersection marks the lower end of
the Erie Canal basin and also the lower end of
what was Albany's lumber district. From here
the Erie Canal extended north underneath
what is now Erie Boulevard. A series of side
slips cut at right angles to the east side of the
canal allowed boats to deliver lumber to the
wholesale yards that gave the district its name.
Timber came from the Adirondacks via the
Black River, Erie, and Champlain canals and
from Canada via the Rideau and Champlain
canals. Albany was one of the East Coast's
principal distribution centers for cut lumber, a
place where it was received from the forests
and mills, stockpiled and then shipped to
seaboard cities. A state weighlock, where

boats were assessed tolls according to the
weight of their cargos, stood on the east side
of the basin.

Schaefer Brewery   6

Montgomery Street between Lawrence and
North Ferry Streets

This large brick building is the last remnant of
the Schaefer brewery, which closed in the early
1970s, interrupting a tradition of brewing in
Albany that dated to the mid-17th century. The
first brewery on this site was built by James
Quinn in 1845. His son took over in 1866 in
partnership with Michael N. Nolan, who later
became Albany's first Irish Catholic mayor.
The neighboring Beverwyck brewery acquired
the Quinn and Nolan brewery in 1917 and
following the repeal of Prohibition operated it
until 1951, when the complex was purchased
by the Schaefer Brewing Company. The building has streamlined entrances with aluminum
overhangs, concrete surrounds, and glass-
block windows, characteristic features of the
1950s. For a short time in the 1980s, Albany's
brewing tradition was revived by the Newman
Brewing Company, a small establishment that
was housed nearby on Learned Street.

*Turn left on North Ferry Street, and proceed
west to Broadway.*

7

Boardman and Gray Piano Factory   7

1860
883 Broadway

William G. Boardman took over a failed piano
factory in 1835 as security for a bad debt and

hired James A. Gray of New York City to manage the works. After doing business in a succession of rented quarters, Boardman and Gray built this large showroom and factory in 1860. Piano manufacturing was later carried out here by Edward McCammon's Piano Forte Manufacturing Company. The building subsequently housed the Regent Shirt Company (1908); James A. Kemp, a machinist and manufacturer of patent emery grinding and polishing machinery; and Brandow Printing (1918).

Turn right on Broadway.

Miss Albany Diner 8

1941

893 Broadway

This diner was fabricated by the Silk City Diner Company of Paterson, New Jersey, and brought to this site in 1941. Until 1965 it was called Lil's Diner after its owner, Lillian McAuliffe. When Albany author William Kennedy's novel *Ironweed* was filmed in 1986-87, the diner was refurbished and renamed the Miss Albany, a name which had been applied to other diners in the city but never to this one.

Engine No. 3 9

c. 1868

895 Broadway

New facade, 1930s

Steamer Company No. 3 was organized on September 1, 1867, a time when a paid professional fire department was being established in the city, and this building was probably built shortly thereafter. Steamer No. 3 replaced the Kearney Steamer Company, a volunteer company that had been organized to provide fire protection for the nearby lumber district. The yellow brick facade was added in the 1930s as part of a Works Progress Administration project. The building served as a firehouse until 1991, when fire protection for the entire north end of Albany was centralized in a new facility in Arbor Hill.

904 Broadway 10

This building extends through the block and is known also as 393 North Pearl Street. It was home to several brewing companies in the 19th century and may have been constructed as early as the late 1840s by Andrew Kirk, who was listed as a brewer here through the 1850s. Later occupants included the Smyth and Walker Brewery in the 1870s, the Fort Orange Brewery, and the Municipal Brewing Company.

By 1892, the building was occupied by cabinetmaker George Spalt, whose company expanded its line after the turn of the century to include store and office furniture, plate glass and mirrors. George Spalt and Sons continued operations here until after World War I, manufacturing store fixtures, soda fountains, showcases, and refrigerating machines. The North Pearl Street portion was occupied until recently by Roland Millwork and Lumber. The Broadway facade, which was probably added in the early 20th century, reflects Dutch Revival architecture with its scroll gable, buttresses, and Flemish-bond brickwork.

Marshall and Wendell Piano Forte Company 11

1872

915 Broadway

Marshall and Wendell Piano Forte Manufacturing Company built a four-story building here in 1872 and expanded it ten years later. In 1891, the piano works produced fifteen to eighteen pianos a week. At the turn of the century, various operations were housed here, including Cleveland Brothers, manufacturers of baking powder and flavoring extracts; Payn's Sons tobacco firm; and the warehouse of Matthew Bender Company, law book publishers. The facade of this large building, like that of the adjoining McKinney iron works to the north, has cast-iron lintels and sills and a prominent, bracketed cornice.

Albany Architectural Iron Works   12

1872

927 Broadway

James McKinney went into business in 1857, casting a variety of iron building, machine, and stove parts. He and his partner, Abraham Mann, occupied foundries near here in the 1850s and 1860s before building this complex for their Albany Architectural Iron Works in 1872. The four-story building on Broadway housed a machine shop on the first floor, pattern shop on the second floor, and storage above. Later it was converted to offices and a drafting and engineering space.

The McKinney firm specialized in architectural ironwork (storefronts, columns, roof crestings, and railings), and many of their products, sometimes with the foundry's name cast on them, can be found on Albany storefronts and rowhouses. Architects Ogden and Wright designed this building on Broadway, and McKinney embellished it with two other

12

types of products—row upon row of ornate cast-iron window caps and sills. At the rear, along the alley, is the foundry, an open yard, and oven used to bake cores for making hollow molds. As tastes changed in the later 19th century, the firm made architectural wrought iron, and McKinney's sons shifted the focus to structural steel fabrication during the 1920s and 1930s. In order to expand the steel yard, the firm purchased the lot up the alley on the north side of Thacher Street, once occupied by a boiler shop and earlier by the grist mill of the van Rensselaer manor, which existed until the 1890s. During World War II,

the McKinney company fabricated parts for portable barracks, Liberty ships, and Bailey bridges. The successor firm ceased operations in 1993.

Turn right onto Thacher Street and right again onto the alley behind the McKinney iron works. Drive south, turn left onto North Ferry Street, and then left onto Learned Street. Head north along Learned Street.

Rathbone, Sard and Company   13

North Ferry and Learned Streets

The blocks facing Learned Street north of North Ferry Street were occupied by Rathbone, Sard and Company, a stove manufacturer that was once Albany's largest single employer, with more than six hundred hands in the 1880s. The two-story brick building on the west side of Learned was Foundry No. 2. The small building adjacent to 34 Learned was built as a pattern shop prior to 1890. The complex on the east side of Learned Street that now houses Millwork Specialties was once a railroad car wheel foundry.

Thacher Looking Glass Factory   14

15 Thacher Street

This four-story brick building at the end of Learned Street housed George H. Thacher's looking glass factory in 1876 and later became Rathbone and Sard's Foundry No. 4. In 1896 it was rented to the newly incorporated Albany Felt Company, which made felts used by the region's booming paper industry to press excess water from raw paper stock and impart a finish to the sheets. In 1901 Albany Felt (now Albany International) purchased land just north of the city limits and constructed a new mill. This building was again used by the Thacher company, which was then making propellers and other iron products.

Turn left on Thacher Street to Broadway, turn right and then take the immediate left onto Pleasant Street. Drive west one block to North Pearl Street.

Albany Construction Company   15

c. 1890

403-409 North Pearl Street

This brick and corrugated-metal building was built around 1890 by Thomas J. Dowling and Harry E. Campbell, owners of the Albany Construction Company, which manufactured architectural ironwork. Campbell's family had operated a coal yard at this site after the Civil War. By 1908, with Harry Campbell as the sole proprietor, the firm had diversified into steel work and by 1918 was producing primarily steel windows. It closed by 1922. (The building immediately to the south, once used as a brewery, is 393 North Pearl on this end and 904 Broadway on the east end.)

Turn around, and proceed north on North Pearl Street.

CMP Industries   16

413 North Pearl Street

This four-story brick building was constructed as an office building and storehouse for the Consolidated Car Heating Company, founded in 1889 to manufacture streetcar heating systems. Prominent Albany businessman Robert C. Pruyn was president. In 1913, the firm built the reinforced concrete building in the rear at 932 Broadway.

International Harvester Company 17

1910

SE corner of North Pearl and Tivoli Streets

Stretching along the entire block of Tivoli Street between Broadway and North Pearl Street is a four-story red brick building constructed in 1910 to house a parts-distribution warehouse for the International Harvester Company. This large midwestern maker of farm equipment displaced many smaller, local manufacturers like the Dederick agricultural and machine works, which once operated nearby on Tivoli Street. The loading dock along the north side is a noteworthy reminder of the railroad siding that once ran up the middle of the street to serve the industries in Tivoli Hollow.

Turn left at Tivoli Street.

17

Tivoli Hollow   18

By the early 1890s, Tivoli Street west of North Pearl was lined with heavy manufacturing facilities, especially iron and stove works. The massive brick building on the north side of Tivoli west of North Pearl Street housed P. K. Dederick's Sons agricultural implements factory; it later became the factory of the Patent Vulcanite Roofing Company. The N. C. Clausen architectural iron works was located on the south side of the street well into the 20th century. Other companies located here included Capital City Plating Works and the Capital Co-Operative Foundry Company.

Turn around, and head east on Tivoli Street to Broadway.

Hudson Valley Paper Company   19

Early 1910s

985 Broadway

This two-story tapestry brick building was constructed in the early 1910s for the Modern Machine Tools Company. Within a few years, it housed the Simmons Machine Tool Company, which remains in operation north of Albany in the village of Menands. In 1925 this building became a storehouse for the Hudson Valley Paper Company, dealers in "paper of every description." The company later moved its entire operation here.

Drive to the east end of Tivoli Street.

Albany Terminal Warehouse Company 20
Foot of Tivoli Street

This company's first home was a building at Colonie and Montgomery streets that had earlier housed the Albany Perforated Wrapping Paper Company. As the warehouse company expanded in the 1890s, it moved to this location near the site of the Van Rensselaer Manor House. The original brick warehouse follows the line of an old railroad siding; the four-story reinforced concrete structure to the west was added later.

Return to Broadway. Turn right and proceed north.

Ackroyd Roofing 21
964 Broadway

Ackroyd Metal Fabricators is the successor firm to Ackroyd Roofing Company, which was founded by James Ackroyd in 1857. Located in these simple brick buildings at the corner of Tivoli Street since the early 20th century, Ackroyd dealt in all types of roofing materials and manufactured architectural sheet-metal work including galvanized-iron and copper cornices, skylights, and steel ceilings. Number 966 Broadway was the office building.

International Harvester Showroom 22
Late 1920s
980 Broadway

This one-story brick and concrete complex was constructed in the late 1920s as a truck showroom for the International Harvester Company. The interlocking IH logo is visible in the gables.

RTA Building 23
c. 1912
991 Broadway

This reinforced-concrete building was constructed around 1912 to house the manufacturing operations of the American Gas Meter Company. In 1958 it became the home of RTA, distributors of RCA electrical appliances. About that time a twenty-five-foot, four-ton statue of

Nipper, the symbol of the Victor Company, was erected on the roof. The statue was built by the W. L. Stansgaard Company of Chicago, shipped on railroad flat cars in five sections, and erected by James McKinney and Company using a ten-story crane. Nipper is one of Albany's most popular outdoor sculptures.

24

Adam Ross Cut Stone Company 24
1927
1001 Broadway

Adam Ross Cut Stone has produced architectural stonework since the early 20th century. The current building, which dates from 1927, replaced a series of frame buildings.

25

Argus Press 25

1913-15
1031 Broadway

This building was constructed on speculation by the Albany Commercial Company, a group of businessmen who hoped to attract more industry to Broadway. It was designed by Marcus T. Reynolds, a prominent Albany architect. Built of reinforced concrete, it is partially sheathed in red brick with a decorative pattern of yellow brick diamonds along the cornice and towers. The towers contain elevators, stairways and tanks for the fire sprinklers. The building is now home to Argus Litho, successors to the company that began publishing the *Albany Argus* newpaper in 1813.

26

Empire Welding and Boiler Repair 26

1916
1032 Broadway

This distinctive building, which was being constructed in 1916, has a gambrel roof, multi-paned sash and paneled cargo doors. It housed the Clide Auto Company, later the National Biscuit Company garage, the Albany Coca-Cola Bottling Works, and by 1950 the Albany High Grade Steel Corporation, the Albany Machine and Tool Works, and the Albany Metal Forming Works.

27

Mack Truck Showroom 27

Late 1920s
1074 Broadway

This large tapestry brick complex was constructed in the late 1920s to house Mack Truck sales and service. While the large display windows have been filled in, the building retains its massing and details, including handsome terra-cotta lettering and logos.

Niagara Mohawk Power Corporation 28

North Albany Works
Broadway opposite Emmet Street

This location has been the site of gas works for more than 120 years. The works were operated by a succession of companies, including the People's Gas Company, suppliers of coal gas for illumination (1873-86); the Municipal Gas Company of Albany, which took over the Albany Gas Light Company and People's Gas and supplied water gas for illumination, cooking and heating for Albany and Watervliet until 1925; the Mohawk-Hudson Power Corporation (1925-27); New York Power and Light Co. (1927-50); and finally Niagara Mohawk. Very few early buildings survive, because the plant has been updated frequently.

United Traction Company Car Barn 29

1890s
1201 Broadway

A complex of car barns and repair shops was

29

constructed at this location by the Watervliet
Turnpike and Railroad Company, an electric
streetcar line, in the 1890s. Above the high
brick walls of this car barn is a monitor that
illuminated the full length of the structure. The
Watervliet Turnpike and Railroad, the Albany
Railway and the Troy City Railway merged in
1899 to become the United Traction Company,
operators of electric streetcars and later buses
in Albany and Troy. This building was subsequently used as a bus garage. Two other car
barns, a power house and a repair shop were
demolished in the 1960s for Interstate 90. The
United Traction Company's routes and equipment were acquired by the Capital District
Transportation Authority in the early 1970s.

Albany International 30
1902
Formerly Albany Felt Company
1373 Broadway
Additions, 1910-89

Once Albany Felt outgrew its leased quarters
on Thacher Street, it purchased six acres strad-
dling the city line in 1901 and constructed a
three-story brick mill here in 1902. The north
wing, which houses manufacturing operations,
has simple facades; the administrative portion
at the south end has smaller windows and a
tile-roofed tower. Numerous additions were
made to the mill between 1910 and 1948. A
third floor was added to the administration
building in 1927, the fourth floor in 1948, and
the office building to the east in 1954. A lobby
was added and the stair tower and offices
reconstructed by architects Einhorn, Yaffee
and Prescott in 1989. The fencing and reservoirs ornamented with swans make this an
attractive industrial setting. Albany International is a world leader in the manufacture of
felts used in papermaking.

30

Glossary

Arcade   A series of arches supported by columns or piers; a building or part of a building with a series of arches; a roofed passageway, especially one with shops on either side.

Architrave   The lower part of a classical entablature, resting directly on the capital of a column; the molding around a window or door.

Ashlar   Hewn or squared stone, also masonry of such stone; a thin, dressed rectangle of stone for facing walls, also called ashlar veneer.

Baluster   An upright, often vase-shaped, support for a rail.

Balustrade   A series of balusters with a rail.

Band windows   A horizontal series of uniform windows that appear to have little or no separation between them.

Baptistery   A part of a church; formerly, a separate building used for baptism.

Bargeboard   A board, often ornately curved, attached to the projecting edges of a gabled roof; sometimes referred to as vergeboard.

Battlement   A parapet built with indentations for defense or decoration.

Bay   One unit of a building that consists of a series of similar units, commonly defined by the number of window and door openings per floor or by the space between columns or piers.

Belt course   A narrow horizontal band projecting from the exterior walls of a building, usually defining the interior floor levels.

Blind arch   An arch that does not contain an opening for a window or door but is set against or indented within a wall.

Bracket   A support element under eaves, shelves or other overhangs; often more decorative than functional.

Buttress   A projecting structure of masonry or wood for supporting or giving stability to a wall or building.

Cantilever   A projecting beam or part of a structure supported only at one end.

Capital   The top, decorated part of a column or pilaster crowning the shaft and supporting the entablature.

Cartouche   An ornamental panel in the form of a scroll, circle or oval, often bearing an inscription.

Casement   A window with sash hung vertically and opening inward or outward.

Castellated   Having battlements and turrets, like a medieval castle.

Cast iron   Iron, shaped in a mold, that is brittle, hard and cannot be welded; in 19th century American commercial architecture, cast-iron units were used frequently to form entire facades.

Chevron   A V-shaped decoration generally used as a continuous molding.

Chimney pot   A pipe placed on top of a chimney, usually of earthenware, that functions as a continuation of the flue and improves the draft.

Clapboard   A long, narrow board with one edge thicker than the other, overlapped to cover the outer walls of frame structures; also known as weatherboard.

Classical   Pertaining to the architecture of ancient Greece and Rome.

Clerestory   The upper part of the nave, transepts and choir of a church, containing windows; also, any similar windowed wall or construction used for light and ventilation.

Corbel   A bracket or block projecting from the face of a wall that generally supports a cornice, beam or arch.

Corinthian order   The most ornate of the classical Greek orders of architecture, characterized by a slender fluted column with a bell-shaped capital decorated with stylized acanthus leaves; variations of this order were extensively used by the Romans.

Cornice   In classical architecture, the upper, projecting section of an entablature; projecting ornamental molding along the top of a building or wall.

Coursed masonry   A wall with continuous horizontal layers of stone or brick.

Crenellation   A battlement.

Crocket   In Gothic architecture, carved projections in the shape of stylized leaves that decorate the edges of spires, gables and pinnacles.

Cupola   A dome-shaped roof on a circular base, often set on the ridge of a roof.

Doric order   The oldest and simplest of the classical Greek orders, characterized by heavy fluted columns with no base, plain saucer-shaped capitals and a bold simple cornice.

Dormer   A vertically set window on a sloping roof; the roofed structure housing such a window.

Double-hung sash window   A window with two sash, one above the other, arranged to slide vertically past each other.

Eaves   The projecting overhang at the lower edge of a roof.

Egg-and-dart molding   A decorative molding comprising alternating egg-shaped and dart-shaped motifs.

Entablature   In classical architecture, the part of a structure between the column capital and the roof or pediment, comprising the architrave, frieze and cornice.

Eyebrow dormer   A low dormer in which the arched roofline forms a reverse curve at each end, giving it the general outline of an eyebrow.

Fanlight   A semicircular or fan-shaped window with radiating members or tracery set over a door or window.

Fenestration   The arrangement of windows in a wall.

Festoon   A carved, molded or painted garland of fruit, flowers or leaves suspended between two points in a curve.

Finial   An ornament at the top of a spire, gable or pinnacle.

Flemish gable   A gable with stepped and occasionally multicurved sides, derived from 16th-century Netherland prototypes.

Fluted   Having regularly spaced vertical, parallel grooves or ''flutes,'' as on the shaft of a column, pilaster or other surface.

Foliated   Decorated with leaf ornamentation or a design comprising arcs or lobes.

Gable   A triangular wall segment at the end of a double-pitched or gabled roof.

Gambrel   A ridged roof with two slopes on each side, the lower slope having the steeper pitch.

Half-timbering   Wall construction in which the spaces between members of the timber frame are filled with brick, stone or other material.

Hipped roof   A roof with four uniformly pitched sides.

Hood molding   A large molding over a window, originally designed to direct water away from the wall; also called a drip molding.

Ionic order   An order of classical Greek architecture characterized by a capital with two opposed volutes.

Lancet   A narrow pointed arch.

Lantern   A structure built on the top of a roof with open or windowed walls.

Leaded glass   Small panes of glass held in place with lead strips; the glass may be clear or stained.

Lozenge   A diamond-shaped decorative motif.

Mansard roof   A roof that has two slopes on all four sides.

Masonry   Wall construction of materials such as stone, brick and adobe.

Medallion   An object resembling a large medal or coin.

Modillion   An ornamental bracket or console used in series under the cornice of the Corinthian order and others.

Molded brick   Brick shaped in a mold, commonly in decorative shapes.

Molding   A continuous decorative band that is either carved into or applied to a surface.

Mullion   A vertical member separating (and often supporting) windows, doors or panels set in a series.

Nave   The long, narrow main part of a church that rises higher than the flanking aisles.

Nogging   The brick or rubble material used to fill the spaces between wooden frames.

Order   Any of several specific styles of classical and Renaissance architecture characterized by the type of column used (e.g., Doric, Ionic, Corinthian, Composite, Tuscan).

Palladian window   A tripartite window opening with a large arched central light and flanking rectangular side lights.

Parapet   A low, solid, protective wall or railing along the edge of a roof or balcony.

Pavilion   A part of building projecting from the rest; an ornamental structure in a garden or park.

Pediment   A wide, low-pitched gable surmounting the facade of a building in a classical style; any similar triangular crowning element used over doors, windows and niches.

Pilaster   A shallow pier attached to a wall; often decorated to resemble a classical column.

Plinth   The base of a pedestal, column or statue; a continuous course of stones supporting a wall.

Podium   A low platform or base.

Polychromy   The use of many colors in decoration, especially in architecture and statuary.

Porte cochere   A large covered entrance porch through which vehicles can drive.

Portico   A major porch, ususally with a pedimented roof supported by classical columns.

Pressed metal   Thin sheets of metal molded into decorative designs and used to cover interior walls and ceilings.

Quoin   Units of stone or brick used to accentuate the corners of a building.

Reeded   Decoration of parallel convex moldings (the opposite of fluted).

Reredos   An ornamental screen behind an altar.

Reveal   The vertical side of a door or window opening between the frame and the wall surface.

Rinceau   A band of ornament consisting of intertwining foliage.

Rococo   The deccorative style developed from the baroque; characterized by delicacy, light colors and a general reduction in building scale.

Rosette   Stylized floral decoration.

Rustication   Masonry cut in massive blocks separated from each other by deep joints.

Sash   A frame in which the panes of a window are set.

Setback   An architectural expedient in which the upper stories of a tall building are stepped back from the lower stories; designed to permit more light to reach street level.

Shaft   The main part of a column between the base and capital.

Skeleton frame   A freestanding frame of iron or steel that supports the weight of a building and on which the floors and outer covering are hung.

Spandrel   The triangular space between the left or right exterior curve of an arch and the rectangular framework surrounding it; the space between adjacent arches and the horizontal molding or cornice above them; in skeleton frame construction, the horizontal panels below and above windows between the continuous vertical piers.

Spindle   A turned wooden element, often used in screens, stair railings and porch trim.

Stair hall   A room specifically designed to contain a staircase.

Swag   A festoon in which the object suspended resembles a piece of draped cloth.

Terra cotta   A fine-grained, brown-red, fired clay used for roof tiles and decoration; literally, cooked earth.

Tracery   The curved mullions of a stone-framed window; ornamental work of pierced patterns in or on a screen, window glass or panel.

Trefoil   A design of three lobes, similar to a cloverleaf.

Tudor arch   A low, wide, pointed arch common in the architecture of Tudor England.

Turret   A small, slender tower usually at the corner of a building, often containing a circular stair.

Vault   An arched ceiling of mansonry.

Volute   A spiral, scroll-like ornament.

Bibliography

Abriel, Warren W., ed. *The History of the Paid Fire Department: A Story of Fires and Firemen from 1867-1967.* Albany, 1967.

Albany City Directory. 1813-1993.

Albany Historic Resources Commission Files. Albany City Hall.

Albany Illustrated. Albany, c. 1893.

Albany Urban Renewal Agency Files. Albany County Hall of Records.

Bielinski, Stefan. "A Middling Sort: Artisans and Tradesmen in Colonial Albany." *New York History.* 73 (3: July, 1992).

Brown, T. Robins. "Walking Tour of Downtown Albany." Albany, 1975.

Brunner, Arnold, and Charles Downing Lay. *Studies for Albany.* New York, 1914.

Cahill, Timothy. "Hidden Heritage: Rediscovering the Lost Art of Emanuel Mickel." *Capital.* January, 1990.

Cometti, Elizabeth, ed. *The American Journals of Lt. John Enys.* Syracuse, 1976.

De Witt, Simeon. A Map of the Lower Church Pasture and A Map of the Upper Church Pasture, both c. 1791. Albany County Hall of Records.

De Witt, Simeon. *Plan of the City of Albany.* 1794.

First Church in Albany Archives. First Church in Albany.

Fuller, Albert W. *Artistic Homes in City and Country.* Boston, 1882.

Gardner, Albert Ten Eyck. *Yankee Stone Cutters.* New York, 1945.

Gehring, Charles T., trans. and ed. *Fort Orange Court Minutes, 1652-1660.* Syracuse, 1990.

Gerber, Morris, comp. *Old Albany.* 4 vols. Albany: privately printed, 1961-79.

Gilder, Cornelia Brooke, ed. *Albany Architects: The Present Looks at the Past.* Albany, 1978.

Goodwin, Scott Dumont, Papers. Albany Institute of History and Art, McKinney Library.

Groft, Tammis K. *Cast With Style.* Albany, 1981.

Hamlin, Huybertie Pruyn. *An Albany Girlhood,* ed. Alice P. Kenney. Albany, 1990.

Harris, Cyril M. *Illustrated Dictionary of Historic Architecture.* 1977. Reprint. New York, 1983.

Hazren, Edward. *Popular Technology; or, Professions and Trades.* New York, 1841.

Hinton, Louis J, letter to Charles L. Hinton, c. 1926. Capitol Papers, New York State Archives.

Historic Albany Foundation. "Two Historic Neighborhoods: A Guided Walk through Hudson-Park and Center Square." Albany, 1976.

Hooker, Philip, Exhibition. Captions for exhibition. Albany Institute of History and Art, McKinney Library.

Hooper, Rev. Joseph. *A History of Saint Peter's Church in the City of Albany.* Albany, 1900.

Hopkins, G. M. *City Atlas of Albany, New York.* Philadelphia: G. M. Hopkins, 1876.

Howell, George R., and Jonathan Tenney, eds. *Bi-Centennial History of Albany: History of the County of Albany, N. Y., from 1609 to 1886.* 3 vols. New York, 1886.

Jennings, Jan, and Herbert Gottfried. *American Vernacular Interior Architecture, 1870-1940.* 1988. Reprint. Ames, Iowa, 1993.

Johnson, E. J. *Style Follows Function, Architecture of Marcus T. Reynolds.* Albany, 1993.

Kalm, Peter. *Travels in North America.* 2 vols. 1937. Reprint. New York, 1966.

Kennedy, William. *O Albany: An Urban Tapestry.* New York, 1984.

Kestenbaum/Landscapes Joint Venture. *Historic Landscape Report: Preservation Plan and Management Proposal, Washington Park, Albany, New York.* Albany, 1989.

Louden, M. J., ed. *Catholic Albany.* Albany, 1895.

Map of Albany, Greenbush, East Albany, Bath. Albany, 1857.

McAlester, Virginia, and Lee McAlester. *A Field Guide to American Houses.* New York, 1984.

McEneny, John J. *Albany, Capital City on the Hudson, An Illustrated History.* Woodland Hills, Cal., 1981.

McNab, Peter. Ledger, 1803-14. Private collection.

Mendel, Mesick, Cohen Architects. *Ten Broeck Mansion Historic Structure Report.* Albany, 1975.

Mickel, Emanual, Exhibition. Grant proposal. Albany Institute of History and Art, McKinney Library.

Mitchell, Robert A. "Whatever Happened to Lustron Homes?" *Association for Preservation Technology Bulletin.* 23 (2: 1991) 44-53.

Munsell, Joel, ed. *Annals of Albany.* 10 vols. Albany, 1850-1859. Vols. 1-4, expanded 2nd edition, 1869-1871.

Munsell, Joel, ed. *Collections on the History of Albany from Its Discovery to the Present Time.* 4 vols. Albany, 1865-71.

National Register for Historic Places nominations for Albany historic districts. New York State Parks, Recreation and Historic Preservation, Peebles Island, New York.

Newhouse, Victoria. *Wallace K. Harrison, Architect*. New York, 1989.

Opalka, Anthony. "Orr and Cunningham: Gothic Revival Builders in Albany," *Preservation League of New York State Newsletter*. Winter, 1989.

Opitz, Glenn B., ed. *Dictionary of American Sculptors: 18th Century to the Present*. Poughkeepsie, N.Y., 1984.

Pearson, Jonathan. *Contributions for the Genealogies of the First Settlers of the Ancient County of Albany*. Baltimore, 1976.

Phelps, H. P. *The Albany Hand-Book*. Albany, 1881. 2d edition, 1884.

Phelps, Henry P., comp. *The Albany Handbook: A Stranger's Guide and Residents' Manual*. Albany, 1884.

Proceedings of the New York State Capitol Symposium. Albany, 1983.

Reynolds, Cuyler. *Albany Chronicles*. Albany, 1906.

Roberts, Anne, and Marcia Cockrell. *Historic Albany: Its Churches and Synagogues*. Albany, 1986.

Root, Edward W. *Philip Hooker: A Contribution to the Study of the Renaissance in America*. New York, 1929.

Roseberry, Cecil R. *Capitol Story*. Albany, 1964.

Roseberry, Cecil R. *Flashback: A Fresh Look at Albany's Past*, ed. Susanne Dumbleton. Albany, 1986.

Rubenstein, Lewis C., ed. "Landmarks of the Upper Hudson Valley." Notes for Society of Architectural Historians' Annual Tour, August 24-28, 1977.

Sanborn insurance maps for 1876, 1892, 1908, 1934.

Schultze, Caroline Peltz. "The Twenties in Albany." Paper given to the Junior Friday Morning Club, 1988. Albany Institute of History and Art, McKinney Library.

Sevier, Christine. *History of the Albany Cathedral of the Immaculate Conception 1852-1927*. Albany, 1927.

Sidney, J. C. *Map of the City of Albany*. New York, 1850. New York State Library.

Sinclair, Douglas. "Cottages in the City," *Historic Albany Foundation Preservation Report*. Summer, 1988.

Sinclair, Douglas. "It Came from Albany: Governor Glynn and the Irish Republic," *Historic Albany Foundation Preservation Report*. Summer, 1988.

Stickley, Gustav. *More Craftsman Homes*. 1912. Reprint. New York, 1982.

Survey of Lots and Streets in Water Vliet for S. Van Rensselaer, 1764. Albany County Hall of Records.

The Industries of the City of Albany: A Resumé of Her Past History and Progress. Albany, 1889.

Tyrrell, William G. *A Century of Spiritual Service: Church of St. Vincent de Paul*. Albany, 1985.

United Traction Company Records. Albany County Hall of Records.

Van Laer, A. J. F., trans. and ed. *Court Minutes of Albany, Rensselaerswyck, and Schenectady*. 3 vols. Albany, 1916-19.

Van Rensselaer, Mariana Griswold. *Henry Hobson Richardson and His Works*. 1888. Reprint. New York, 1969.

Van Zandt, Roland. *Chronicles of the Hudson, Three Centuries of Travelers' Accounts*. New Brunswick, 1971.

Waite, Diana S. Developmental History of Pastures Preservation District. 1971. Albany Public Library.

Waite, Diana S. *Ornamental Ironwork*. Albany, 1990.

Whiffen, Marcus. *American Architecture Since 1780, A Guide to the Styles*. Boston, 1969.

Wilson, S. *Albany City Guide*. Albany, 1844

Woollett, William M. *Villas and Cottages or Homes for All*. Albany, 1876

Wright, Alice Morgan, Exhibition. Captions for exhibition. Albany Institute of History and Art, McKinney Library.

In addition, Albany Common Council Minutes and Proceedings were sources for researching various civic buildings and parks. The entries for residences were researched mainly from city directories and *Blue Books*, city assessment rolls, New York State Parks, Recreation and Historic Preservation inventory forms, tour notes from Historic Albany Foundation, the clipping files and architectural drawing index at the McKinney Library, the Albany Significant Interiors Survey, and *American Architect and Building News*.

Index

This index lists architects, builders, owners, and occupants of buildings where known. Buildings are indexed by name, by street address and except for residences also by their building type (e.g., courthouses, libraries). Streets with buildings included in the tours are also listed.